THE 1995-96 HOCKEY ANNUAL

THE 1995-96 HOCKEY ANNUAL

MURRAY TOWNSEND

Warwick Publishing
Toronto   Los Angeles

Published by Warwick Publishing Inc.
• 24 Mercer Street, Toronto, ON. M5V 1H3
• 1424 Highland Ave., Los Angeles, CA 90027

ISBN: 1 - 895629 - 53 - 5

Front cover photograph: Dan Hamilton, Vantage Point Studios
Cover design: Kimberley Davison
Text design: Kimberley Davison

Distributed in the United States and Canada by:

Firefly Books Ltd.
250 Sparks Ave.
Willowdale, ON
M2H 2S4

Printed and bound in Canada by Best Book Manufacturers.

For my Dad

Contents

INTRODUCTION   7
WESTERN CONFERENCE
Anaheim Mighty Ducks   11
Calgary Flames   19
Chicago Blackhawks   27
Dallas Stars   35
Detroit Red Wings   43
Edmonton Oilers   51
Los Angeles Kings   59
Rocky Mountain Avalanche   67
San Jose Sharks   75
St. Louis Blues   83
Toronto Maple Leafs   91
Vancouver Canucks   99
Winnipeg Jets   107
EASTERN CONFERENCE
Boston Bruins   115
Buffalo Sabres   125
Florida Panthers   133
Hartford Whalers   141
Montreal Canadiens   149
New Jersey Devils   157
New York Islanders   165
New York Rangers   173
Ottawa Senators   181
Philadelphia Flyers   189
Pittsburgh Penguins   197
Tampa Bay Lightning   203
Washington Capitals   213
TOWNSEND'S ULTIMATE POOL PICKS   220
1995-96 COMPLETE NHL SEASON SCHEDULE   229

Introduction

Well, the news is mostly good: the National Hockey League and its players avoided killing the season. If the current fan appreciation level of Major League Baseball is any indication, forfeiting the entire season — including the championships — kills more than just *that* season. For baseball fans the World Series was sacred. They thought the owners and players felt the same way. When they realized this wasn't the case, they stayed away in droves, not only from the ballparks, but also from broadcasts and souvenir purchases. At press time attendance and viewership were still well below normal levels.

There's no reason to think the same thing — or worse — wouldn't have happened to professional hockey if the season had been scrapped.

As it turned out, the shortened 48-game season and New Jersey's storming of the Stanley Cup Championships were legitimately exciting and relatively untainted by the lockout.

What bad news there was took the form of the on-again, off-again departure of the Winnipeg Jets. At press time it was announced that the team would stay in Winnipeg for one season and then be sold. What this will do to team and fan moral in that city remains to be seen. Perhaps they'll all agree to make a party out of it and play like demons.

Additional questions of ownership uncertainty linger over the L.A.Kings, while the Stanley Cup Champion New Jersey Devils appear to be on more solid ground in their present location, after flirting with a move to Nashville late is the season.

One move did happen and the overall complexion of the league has changed dramatically since last season because of it. The Rocky Mountain Avalanche, as they are called (formerly the Quebec Nordique), will now play in the Western Conference, where they should excel in that more offensive-minded environment. The Eastern Conference remains strong and tough despite the loss. In addition, the emergence of a number of exciting young teams — the Flyers, the Oilers, the Sabres, the Mighty Ducks, the Avalanche themselves — shimmers on the horizon. League parity seems to be moving from a grudge match to a sprint. Any team can win the Stanley Cup, if they play well and hard enough — which is exactly as it should be.

This book predicts the following final overall standings (I've included their conference position in brackets):

1. St. Louis Blues (1W)
2. Detroit Red Wings (2W)
3. Rocky Mountain Avalanche (3W)
4 Philadelphia Flyers (1E)

5. New Jersey Devils.(2E)
6. Vancouver Canucks (4W)
7. Boston Bruins (3E)
8. Pittsburgh Penguins (4E)
9. Chicago Blackhawks (5W)
10. Washington Capitals (5E)
11. Calgary Flames (6W)
12. Dallas Stars (7W)
13. NY Rangers (6E)
14. Hartford Whalers (7E)
15. Toronto Maple Leafs (8W)
16. Edmonton Oilers (9W)
17. Montreal Canadiens (8E)
18. Buffalo Sabres (9E)
19. Winnipeg Jets (10W)
20. NY Islanders (10E)
21. Tampa Bay Lightning (11E)
22. San Jose Sharks (11W)
23. Los Angeles Kings (12W)
24. Anaheim Mighty Ducks (13W)
25. Florida Panthers (12E)
26. Ottawa Senators (13E)

I think St. Louis will win the Stanley Cup - with some changes to their current lineup through the season - over either New Jersey or Philadelphia. Sounds like a tough, fast, exciting final, eh?

But the great thing about this sport is its unpredictability, so don't hold me to it. Anything can happen, as last season clearly illustrated.

A couple of quick acknowledgments: thank's first and foremost to Bob McKenzie, who developed this book's concept with Warwick Publishing, and authored the first Hockey Annual, three years ago. Also thank's to Jim Williamson, Nick Pitt and Kimberley Davison at Warwick for all their efforts and support.

Murray Townsend,
August 16, 1995
Toronto

WESTERN CONFERENCE

Anaheim Mighty Ducks

Why do ducks fly south?

Answer: Because it's too far to walk.

That was my favorite joke as a kid, and the only duck joke I've ever known. Well, there was one other, but I can't say it here.

The Mighty Ducks of Anaheim have certainly been no joke on the ice. They've been at least respectable in their first two seasons, this year staying in the playoff race to the end.

Okay, but at least their name was fair game, and we could have some fun with that. The Ducks get the last laugh in that one too, because for the one-year period ending in June of 1994 they were the top merchandising team in the NHL.

Everything off the ice in Anaheim is just ducky and on it things are coming along.

The Ducks didn't have quite as good a winning percentage last season as in their first year, but that's not unusual. Consider the following chart showing expansion teams in their first two seasons. WHA entries and "original" expansion in 1967-68 are not included because they're not typical expansion teams.

Team	First Season	Second Season	Point Difference
San Jose	17-58-5	11-71-2	-15
Buffalo	24-39-15	16-43-19	-12
Vancouver	24-46-8	20-50-8	- 8
Anaheim	33-46-5	16-27-5 (28-47-9)*	- 6*
Kansas City	15-54-11	12-56-12	- 5
Florida	33-34-17	20-22-6 (35-38-11)*	- 2*
Atlanta	25-38-15	30-34-14	+ 9
Washington	8-67-5	11-59-10	+11
Ottawa	10-70-4	14-61-9	+13
Tampa Bay	23-54-7	30-43-11	+18
NY Islanders	12-60-6	19-41-18	+26

* projected over an 84 game schedule

Six of the 11 true expansion teams had worse second seasons. I have a theory about that, but it's probably a combination of factors. And in a couple instances teams couldn't have possibly been as bad as their first season.

The theory follows along the lines of a recently traded player whose point production goes up with a new team for the first year (especially if he's traded during the season) and then reverts to form afterwards.

With a new team every single player is trying to make an impression and earn or keep a spot. By the second year, places are a little more settled and players have a little backup in terms of performance. In other words, they may not be as desperate to perform as well.

A couple Ducks fit into that category, most notably Bob Corkum who came to camp out of shape. He had a poor season, but had already shown management his capabilities in their first year and knew his job wasn't in jeopardy.

Once the initial adreneline wears off, the team has to build talent. At some point draft picks start to pay off, trades are made for need as opposed to just filling empty holes, and an identity starts to take shape.

That happened with the Ducks towards the end of last year. They changed from a strictly defensive clutch-and-grab type team to one with some offensive promise and some good young potential.

Draft selections Paul Kariya and Oleg Tverdovsky started to pay dividends; younger, more offensive players, such as Mike Sillinger, Milos Horan, and Jason York were obtained in trades during the season; and even a rare supplemental draft pick made the grade in Steve Rucchin.

The team showed their improvement later in the season. After the trading deadline they had a record of 7-6-2. Before it they were 11-19-4.

Good news? Quick-thinking people would think so, but there are a few curious elements. Before the trading deadline (TD) they didn't have a game where they gave up 40 shots. In three of their next eight after the TD they did.

Also, they were outshot by at least 15 shots in seven of the 15 post TD games, and by at least 20 in four of them. Before TD, they were never outshot by 20.

The slightly good news was that their goals per game went up to 2.9 from 2.6. That's an increase of only 26 over an 84 game schedule.

The other good news, of course, was that they won more often.

Obviously, they sacrificed defense for offense. There has to be some kind of acceptable mix between the two. Weak teams can win by playing strictly defensive, but they don't get much better than mediocre.

The Ducks are on their way to finding the right balance. It's a decent beginning.

TEAM PREVIEW

GOAL: Guy Hebert is still the number one man, and there aren't a lot of complaints. He went through his good times and his bad times and the end result was that his stats were pretty similar to his initial year in the Ducks net. His goals against average dropped to 3.13 from 2.83, but his save percentage remained close, going to .904 from .907.

With a little less team attention being paid to defense, the Troy, New York native did all that could be expected of him.

The disturbing thing was that the team GAA dropped from eighth place all the way down to 22nd. That's not Hebert's fault, it's a team thing. That and the fact that backup Mikhail Shtalenkov wasn't very good.

Even though Shtalenkov was drafted by the Ducks just two years ago, he will be 30 this year. He got into 18 games and posted a poor GAA of 3.61. He's only played 28 NHL games so it's too early to make any conclusions. But, older Russians usually have a more difficult time adapting.

	GP	MIN	GA	AVG	W	L	T	SO
Hebert	39	2092	109	3.13	12	20	4	2
Shtalenkov	18	810	49	3.63	4	7	1	0

DEFENCE: There's a problem associated with having a mobile defense corps – often they're not as good defensively because they've got other things on their mind. They're thinking about scoring at the other end, not just stopping the opposition in their own end.

The Ducks have more offensive-minded defensemen now with the emergence of rookie Oleg Tverdovsky, and the acquisitions of Jason York from Detroit and Milos Holan from Philadelphia near the trading deadline last year.

They needed some offense from their backliners, especially to help out the woeful power play. Tom Kurvers was supposed to fill that role but his defensive shortcomings made him unsuited for regular duty. And eventually, he wasn't suited for any duty at all.

Milos Holan, a 24-year-old Czech player of the year in 1993, came over to the Ducks from Philadelphia for Anatoli Semenov. The Ducks like him because he shoots a lot. In just 25 games, he had 94 shots on net, third highest on the team. Over 48 games, he would have led the Ducks by a big margin, and those numbers projected over 84 games would have given him 312, which is 106 more than the team high of 206 by Joe Sacco in their first season.

That's the good news. The bad news is that he didn't score very much. In fact, check out shooting percentages for players with at least 80 shots on the season.

Lowest Shooting Percentage
(80 or more shots)

	Team	Shots	Goals	Shooting %
Sean Hill	Ott.	107	1	0.9
Glen Wesley	Hfd.	125	2	1.6
Scott Stevens	N.J.	111	2	1.8
Steve Chiasson	Cgy.	110	2	1.9
MILOS HORAN	ANA.	93	2	2.2

Interesting, but no big deal. A defenseman who gets a lot of shots on net is providing an opportunity for others to deflect the puck or poke in the rebound. That didn't happen with Ducks, but it could with the right players up front.

Tverdovsky, Holan, York and Dollas are probably the top four power play point men, in order.

Dollas had a regular spot there last year, but was mostly a stop-gap performer, who is valuable enough to the team just concentrating on defense.

Tverdovsky will play there full-time eventually, once he gets the necessary experience and gets clued in. Tverdovsky has some amazing skills, and he's probably going to pile up some big point totals. But, the second draft pick overall in 1994 sometimes looks and plays like he's out to lunch. What he lacks in instinct will probably be made up with his pure offensive talent, and we'll probably see him on an all-star team within three or four years.

Dollas (30-years-old) heads up the veterans on defense. He's joined by captain Randy Ladouceur (35), Robert Dirk (29) and Don McSween (31).

McSween made news last year by being the first player to file for unemployment during the labor stoppage. Somebody else, and maybe we would have made fun of him – like we can with Kurvers, who also filed. McSween, who has spent most of his career in the minors, had a legitimate claim.

Once the players got back into action, however, McSween was cut on the wrist and had to undergo surgery, missing the remainder of the season.

Pesky Dave Karpa provides some toughness and made a solid contribution to the Ducks. Quebec originally dealt him to Los Angeles, who had the trade invalidated when they felt the medical reports on his injured wrist weren't good. The Kings' loss was the Ducks' gain.

Among the prospects, big Russian Nikolai Tsulgin has a spot waiting for him when he's ready. Darren Van Impe and Jason Marshall, both obtained in deals last year, also have an opportunity, but maybe not for a while. There's already too much youth on the blueline, and it's important to have the right number of veterans in the lineup.

Overall, not a top-flight defense, and certainly not one that would be on a contender. But, when Tverdovsky makes his mark and becomes a premier offensive defenceman, less will be needed or expected from the others and they can concentrate on their roles.

FORWARD: Start with Paul Kariya, and uh, you can pretty much end with him too. The right wing/left wing/centre is the franchise and likely one of the few that will still be around in three years.

But, is he a scorer or a playmaker? Or is he everything? Apparently, that's caused him some confusion as well. He's a natural playmaker, but when nobody else on the team can score it's natural to use your goal scoring abilities as well.

Besides being able to do all that, Kariya can juggle. He does it to balance the left and right side of his brain to help improve his hockey. And to think some guys just do it to be fun at parties.

That improvement might be accelerated were there anyone else on the team who could score. The Ducks want, and need, a Brendan Shanahan type player.

Mike Sillinger was a nice addition to the team at the trading deadline. He was too far down the depth chart in Detroit, but he's the number one center in Anaheim. He's small, but he's quick and he's a nice playmaker. If only he had Brendan Shanahan to pass to.

Stephan Lebeau, another small playmaking centre is off to Switzerland, leaving Shaun Van Allen, a bigger playmaking center, who also needs Shanahan to pass to.

Steve Rucchin is bigger yet, and one of the surprise stories of the NHL last season. A product of Western Ontario University, the supplemental draft selection is one of the few to make the grade from a Canadian University. He's a third or fourth line centre, but his two-way play makes him a good guy to have around. Patrik Carnback, who just happens to be a playmaker, also plays center when he's not playing wing. David Sacco, another center obtained for the Duck's first year's leading scorer Terry Yake, only played eight games with the big club.

Chad Kilger was selected fourth overall in the draft. He's a big, powerful center and just might eventually be the perfect linemate for Kariya.

Todd Krygier, a press box regular with Washington, was picked up and played on the top line with Sillinger and Kariya late in the year.

That says a lot when a couple players who couldn't get into other lineups make up two-thirds of the first line.

Krygier is the subject of one of my pet stats. He has earned exactly 30 points in four of his six NHL seasons.

Wingers Gary Valk, Bob Corkum and Joe Sacco had disappointing years after promising initial campaigns. Sacco's a wacko in the scoring department. He's all over the place. Two years ago, he had three goals in the first half season and 16 in the second. Last year he had five points in the first half and 13 in the second. The split in the goal department was three and 10. Maybe they should just play him in the second half of each season.

Guys like Valk (free agent), Corkum, Peter Douris, Jim Thomson and Todd Ewen are role players and will perform best when they're not expected to score much.

Valeri Karpov looked good in training camp, but was eventually sent for a stint in the minors and only scored four goals in limited action with the Ducks.

John Lilley might be able to provide some

punch. He made the team in training camp, but was sent to the minors during the lockout. He wasn't all that impressive there, however, scoring nine times and adding 15 assists in 45 games.

We're not sure what Steven King can do because he's hurt all the time. But, you see, he's got this great name, and it's fun to keep mentioning that he's had another nightmare season.

There's not nearly enough scoring on the Anaheim forward lines, plain and simple.

SPECIAL TEAMS:

Please hold your nose when reading this. The Ducks stunk at special teams. They were last in power play percentage and last in penalty killing.

For much of the season the Ducks had actually allowed more goals against while on the power play than they scored themselves. After 20 games they had six power play goals and had given up six short-handed goals.

That's some power play.

We already know what they need. *Someone who can put the puck in the net.*

The Ducks attempted to get some help at the trading deadline for the power play, Holan and York, but the team still didn't score, even though they looked better. Their power play percentage after the trading deadline was 11.7, not much of an improvement from 11.4 percent.

The failure of the penalty killing unit was a little more curious because after finishing eighth in their initial season, they dropped to dead last.

They have enough defensive-type players that this shouldn't have happened. Maybe Steven King could provide the answer to the mystery.

Power Play	G	ATT	PCT
Overall	23	202	11.4% (26th NHL)
Home	13	98	13.3% (23rd NHL)
Road	10	104	9.6% (25th NHL)

8 SHORT HANDED GOALS ALLOWED (T-21st NHL)

Penalty Killing	G	TSH	PCT
Overall	47	193	75.6% (26th NHL)
Home	17	92	81.5% (20th NHL)
Road	30	101	70.3% (26th NHL)

4 SHORT HANDED GOALS SCORED (T-17th NHL)

Penalties	GP	MIN	AVG
MIGHTY DUCKS	48	731	15.2 (1st NHL)

TOP SPECIAL TEAM SCORERS

Power play	G	A	PTS
KARIYA	7	8	15
VAN ALLEN	1	7	8
DOLLAS	3	3	6
LEBEAU	1	4	5
YORK	0	5	5
SILLINGER	2	2	4
SACCO	2	2	4
HOLAN	1	3	4
Short handed	**G**	**A**	**PTS**
VAN ALLEN	1	1	2
TVERDOVSKY	1	0	1
KARIYA	1	0	1
DOLLAS	1	0	1
LADOUCEUR	0	1	1
HOLAN	0	1	1
CARNBACK	0	1	1

COACHING AND MANAGEMENT:

Both coach Ron Wilson and GM Jack Ferreira were to have their contracts extended this summer. That means Michael Eisner and the Disney folks think they're doing a good job.

Everything appears to be on track. Ferreira's made some good trades, some good draft selections, and is showing the necessary patience.

As for Wilson, normally I think one of the marks of a good coach is how the special teams perform, but St. Louis' special teams weren't so great and I think Mike Keenan is the best coach in the game.

Also, in defence of Wilson, he didn't have a goal scorer on the power play.

Wilson is also a bit of whiner. He's not afraid to speak out about refereeing or anything else. When your team is a loser you're a whiner. When your team is a winner, you're outspoken.

DRAFT

1995 DRAFT SELECTIONS

Round	Sel.	Player	Pos	Amateur Team
1	4	Chad Kilger	C	Kingston (OHL)
2	29	Brian Wesenberg	RW	Guelph (OHL)
3	55	Mike Leclerc	LW	Brandon (WHL)
5	107	Igor Nikulin	LW	Russia
6	133	Peter Leboutillier	RW	Red Deer (WHL)
7	159	Mike Laplante	D	Calgary (AJHL)
8	185	Igor Karpenko	G	Ukraine

Chad Kilger, the son of a former NHL referee was the number one forward taken in the draft. The Ducks like his size, 6-3 204, and his character, and consider him an all-round player. He has been compared to Ron Francis and Jason Arnott. With Kingston in the OHL last season he was 42-53-95.

Brian Wesenberg was 17-27-44 with Guelph in his first junior year. That was a talented team that has some major players moving on so he will be given more responsibility and his scoring totals should increase quite a bit. He's a big guy at 6-3, but a lightweight at 173 pounds.

PROGNOSIS: If you're a Mighty Duck fan you don't have to worry much about this season because it doesn't matter. The future is when it should be...in the future.

Can the Ducks make the playoffs? Anything is possible, but I don't think so yet. And oddly enough, that may be a good thing.

You've heard the old adage about mortgaging the future for the present? The Ducks aren't doing that, to their credit.

They'll be patient, fit the puzzle pieces together, and one day the young players will be not so young.

The best organizations build first and then do maintenance. In only their third season, the Ducks are just putting in the foundation. The only danger is if they skimp on the building codes.

PREDICTION:
Pacific Division: 7th
Western Conference: 13th
Overall: 24th

STAT SECTION

	Conference Rank (12)		League Rank
Record	16-27-5	12	25
Home	11-9-4	5	14
Away	5-18-1	12	24
Team Plus\Minus	-20	7	19
Goals For	125	12	22
Goals Against	164	9	22

PLAYERS	1994-95 OVERALL				PROJECTED 84 GAME TOTALS		
	GP	G	A	PTS	G	A	PTS
P.KARIYA	47	18	21	39	32	38	70
S.VAN ALLEN	45	8	21	29	15	39	54
S.LEBEAU	38	8	16	24	18	35	53
T.KRYGIER	35	11	11	22	26	26	52
P.DOURIS	46	10	11	21	18	20	38
P.CARNBACK	41	6	15	21	12	31	43
B.DOLLAS	45	7	13	20	13	24	37
B.CORKUM	44	10	9	19	19	17	36
J.SACCO	41	10	8	18	20	16	36
S.RUCCHIN	43	6	11	17	12	21	33
M.SILLINGER	28	4	11	15	12	33	45
O.TVERDOVSKY	36	3	9	12	7	21	28
V.KARPOV	30	4	7	11	11	20	31
M.HOLAN	25	2	8	10	7	27	34
J.YORK	24	1	9	10	3	32	35
G.VALK	36	3	6	9	7	14	21
T.KURVERS	22	4	3	7	15	11	26
R.LADOUCEUR	44	2	4	6	8	8	16
D.KARPA	28	1	5	6	3	15	18
J.LILLEY	9	2	2	4	19	19	38
D.WILLIAMS	21	2	2	4	8	8	16
D.LAMBERT	13	1	3	4	6	19	25
R.DIRK	38	1	3	4	2	7	9
T.SWEENEY	13	1	1	2	6	6	12
D.SACCO	8	0	2	2	0	21	21
D.VAN IMPE	1	0	1	1	0	84	84
J.MARSHALL	2	0	1	1	0	42	42
D.MCSWEEN	2	0	0	0	0	0	0
T.EWEN	24	0	0	0	0	0	0
M. SHTALENKOV	18	0	0	0	0	0	0
G. HEBERT	39	0	0	0	0	0	0

Note - The projected totals aren't what the player would score if he played 84 games. Rather, they are point totals pro-rated over 84 games.

Players don't score at the same rate all season long. They can get hot and cold; injuries to them and teammates affect points; players are traded and take on different roles; etc.

Obviously, the fewer actual games played, the less likely his projected point total will be accurate.

MISCELLANEOUS STATS

One Goal Games	7-4
Times outshooting opponent	15
Times outshot	33
Even shots	0
Average Shots For	28.0
Average Shots Against	33.0
Overtime	2-0-5
Longest Winning streak	2
Longest Undefeated streak	2
Longest Losing streak	3
Longest winless streak	5
Versus Teams Over .500	5-18-3
Versus Teams Under .500	11-9-2
First Half Record	7-12-2
Second Half Record	9-12-3

All-Time Rankings - INDIVIDUAL

Goals

Bob Corkum	33
Peter Douris	22
Joe Sacco	21

Assists

Shaun Van Allen	46
Bob Corkum	37
Peter Douris	33

Points

Bob Corkum	70
Shaun Van Allen	62
Peter Douris	55
Joe Sacco	55

BEST INDIVIDUAL SEASONS

Goals

Bob Corkum	93/94	23
Terry Yake	93/94	21
Joe Sacco	93/94	19

Assists

Terry Yake	93/94	31
Bob Corkum	93/94	28
Garry Valk	93/94	27
Tim Sweeney	93/94	27

Points

Terry Yake	93/94	52
Bob Corkum	93/94	51
Garry Valk	93/94	45

Calgary Flames

The good news is that only five other teams have won the Stanley Cup since the Flames in 1989.

The bad news is that 18 teams have won a playoff series over that span and none of them have been Calgary.

The Flames have teased their fans into thinking they had a legitimate shot five of those six seasons. Every year they're full of promise during the regular season and then when it's time to get serious they make a joke out of the playoffs.

Best Regular Season Records
knocked out in first round (last six years)

Quebec	1994-95	30-13-5	.677
Chicago	1990-91	49-23-8	.663
Boston	1992-93	51-26-7	.649
Chicago	1992-93	47-25-12	.631
CALGARY	1990-91	46-26-8	.625
CALGARY	1989-90	42-23-15	.619
Quebec	1992-93	47-27-10	.619
Buffalo	1989-90	45-27-8	.613
Detroit	1992-93	47-28-9	.613
Washington	1991-92	45-27-8	.613
Pittsburgh	1993-94	44-27-13	.601
Detroit	1993-94	46-30-8	.595
Boston	1994-95	27-18-3	.594
CALGARY	1992-93	43-30-11	.577
CALGARY	1993-94	42-29-13	.577
CALGARY	1994-95	24-17-7	.573

The list was much longer than expected, but it tells us two things: good teams get knocked out early frequently, and none of the good teams have been knocked out as often as Calgary. They make the list five times; nobody else is on it more than twice.

There's a reason for Calgary's dismal playoff performance, a very sound, scientific reason.

It's called bad luck. That's right, just plain old bad luck.

Last year, they lost twice to San Jose in overtime, including game seven in double OT. In that one they outshot the Sharks 18-9 in extra time and 60-30 overall.

The year before, the Flames held a 3-1 lead on Vancouver before losing the final three games in overtime. The Canucks went on to the Stanley Cup finals.

In 1991 they lost game seven in overtime to Edmonton, and in 1990 they also lost the deciding game in overtime.

Overtime goals are often a matter of luck and the Flames haven't had any. A bounce here or there and they might have had another couple of Stanley Cups under their belt.

And don't forget the terrible time they've had with injuries. Not only all season long, but into the playoffs for the last two years.

GM Doug Risebrough went about changing their luck after the season when he fired Dave King. Too bad, I think King is one of the best coaches in the game and the Flames are unlikely to do better.

Last year in the *Hockey Annual* I listed who I thought were the 10 best coaches in the NHL. The top six were Mike Keenan, Roger Neilson, John Muckler, Jacques Lemaire, Pat Burns and Dave King. Three of the six - Neilson, Muckler and King - no longer handle the duties with the same teams. That means either I'm dumb or the teams that fired them are (Note: Muckler fired himself).

Since we're, uh, fairly certain I'm not dumb, then it must be the teams.

It all comes down to expectations. Teams get spoiled and think they can go on to the next level by changing coaches. The elevator also goes down as often as not and the next level isn't so good.

I'm telling you, just a couple lucky bounces and King would be mentioned with the top coaches in the game. At last report, he had been hired as a short-term consultant for the Japanese hockey program.

TEAM PREVIEW

GOAL: This was the big question mark before last season, whether or not the Flames would be able to compensate for the loss of Vernon. Kidd answered that question in a big way and kept on answering it, setting a team record by playing in 28 consecutive games.

But, then the Flames developed a different problem of sorts - too many goalies. Andrei Trefilov and Jason Muzzatti were supposed to fight it out with Kidd for the number one job, but instead ended up fighting it out for playing time in Saint John.

Meanwhile, Dwayne Roloson, a free agent signee, was handling the number one chores down there just fine, playing the majority of the regular season games and all of the playoffs.

Meanwhile, again, the Flames acquired Rick Tabaracci from Washington, who did an outstanding job with a 1.49 GAA in five Calgary games, and was 2.11 overall.

Kidd faltered somewhat in the playoffs, but that isn't unusual in Calgary, and he'll still be the number one man. You have to figure Tabaracci will be number two, if he signs. That leaves Rolason, who will be happy to play again in Saint John, and Muzzatti who won't. Trefilov showed his displeasure in the summer, shuffling off to Buffalo.

1994/95	GP	MIN	GA	AVG	W	L	T	SO
Muzzatti	1	10	0	.00	0	0	0	0
Tabaracci	5	202	5	1.49	2	0	1	0
Kidd	43	2463	107	2.61	22	14	6	3
Trefilov	6	236	16	4.07	0	3	0	0

DEFENCE: Mobility is their strength, strength is their weakness. A good, fast, puck-handling defence is great when you have the puck, but the other team is going to get it too, and that's where the Flames run into problems.

When most of your defensemen are candidates for the Lady Byng Trophy, you know opposing forwards aren't going to get too worried about standing in front of the net or digging in the corners.

The concept of a mobile defense corps is good, for two reasons I can think of: one, they get the puck out of their own end sooner and can move it faster to the forwards; two, they can contribute offensively themselves. The Flames defensemen certainly didn't have a problem in that area.

Top Three Point Scoring Defensemen - Each Team

	Points	Defensive Rank
Detroit	99	2
CALGARY	96	10
St. Louis	96	13

NY Rangers	89	12
Chicago	88	1
Boston	81	7
Pittsburgh	74	20
Buffalo	66	3
Toronto	64	16
Dallas	63	11
Washington	63	4
New Jersey	62	5
Vancouver	62	17
Winnipeg	62	25
Los Angeles	61	23
Philadelphia	56	8
Hartford	54	14
NY Islanders	54	19
Quebec	51	9
San Jose	50	21
Montreal	44	18
Edmonton	43	26
Florida	43	6
Anaheim	42	22
Tampa Bay	35	15
Ottawa	29	24
Average	58	

According to the chart, many of the teams with high point totals from their top three defensemen also rank high defensively. As well, many of the poorer offensive teams ranked poor defensively. Of the top 14 teams, 10 were also among the top 14 defensively.

That could lead to the conclusion that a good defence is a good offense, but I'd hesitate on that one. There are too many other factors - injuries, strong backchecking opposition - which we won't go into now, which could have a more direct correlation.

Phil Housley was second in the league in scoring for defensemen, behind Paul Coffey, and finished first on the Flames with a plus 17. For a guy with noted defensive shortcomings, that's pretty good.

Zarley Zalapski is another strictly offensive type, as is James Patrick. Steve Chiasson is an all round player who also contributes offensively.

The Flames have a couple of defense-first types around as well in Frank Musil and Trent Yawney.

Others who should get playing time are Kevin Dahl and Dan Keczmer. Youngsters with an opportunity are Jamie Allison, a stay-at-home type, and Joel Bouchard, not a stay-at-home type.

The Flames have offensive types and defensive types, but what they lack are physical, tough types.

FORWARD: There's certainly no shortage of toughness in the Calgary forwards. Six of them had at least 100 PIM. Washington had three, but no other team had more than two.

They've also got plenty of scoring, plenty of good defensive players, and plenty of depth.

The latter is important because the Flames are one of the most injury-prone teams. Consider the following list of Flames who missed at least 10 games last season, or just over one-quarter of the season.

Michael Nylander	42
Gary Roberts	40
Kelly Kisio	34
Todd Hlushko	25
Sheldon Kennedy	18
Sandy McCarthy	11
Mike Sullivan	10
Dan Keczmer	10
Frank Musil	10

The biggest concern is Gary Roberts, who has had serious neck problems and had to undergo surgery. If he's ready to go it makes for an imposing first line of Roberts on the left side, Joe Nieuwendyk at centre and Theoren Fleury at right wing.

Fleury had an outstanding year. After leading the pre-season in scoring and playing in Europe, he finished sixth in scoring. His 29 goals and 58 points project a 50 goal, 100 point season. People used to worry about Fleury's durability because of his size (listed at 5-6, 160) but geez the guy rarely even misses a game. Over the last six seasons, he's missed just three.

Reichel is a dependable first unit power play man and second line centre. He's also a dependable second half player. For some reason, he gets off to a slow start and then comes on big-time.

Fleury is a restricted free agent (which usually means they don't go anywhere). Reichel wasn't happy with his contract and was threatening to go to Europe (which also means they don't usually go anywhere).

Joel Otto was with the Flames for 11 years, and even though he was a free agent, guys like that also don't usually go anywhere either. But, he did anyway, signing with Philadelphia. He was a valuable member of the Flames - big, tough, excellent on faceoffs, but he will turn 34 years old this year.

Kelly Kisio and Mike Sullivan are also centremen, who can play wing. Both are veterans who can contribute. Kisio had a six game goal-scoring streak, longest of the year for the Flames, but still spent most of his time on the injury list. Sullivan is a legendary shadow-pest who's handy to have around, especially at playoff time.

Yet another centre is Michael Nylander, who spent almost the whole season out with a broken wrist.

In the minors is a center waiting for an opportunity, which he should get now that Otto is gone. Cory Stillman, the sixth pick overall in 1992, and rated the Number 1 Flames prospect by *The Hockey News,* is a playmaker, who has put together two good seasons in Saint John. Last year he had 28 goals and 53 assists in 63 games.

Roberts and Fleury lead the wingers, although Fleury can play centre like most of the Calgary players.

Also at wing is German Titov (who can also play centre) one of the streakiest scorers in the league. He jumped out of the gate with nine goals in his first 10 games and then scored just three in his next 30. The year before he pulled off a similar feat.

Other wingers include tough guys Ronnie Stern (163 PIM) Sandy McCarthy (101 PIM), Alan May (119 PIM) and Paul Kruse (141 PIM). Kruse surprised some with a bit of a scoring touch, putting in 11 goals, or three more than his 112 previous NHL games. Jim Peplinski, who attempted a comback late last season, is still on their roster, so it looks like he'll give it another go.

Sheldon Kennedy and Wes Walz (also a center) are a couple of other small forwards who can contribute, and Vesa Viitakoski is a big forward who plays small, but is expected to play regularly in Calgary at some point.

Speaking of small, the Flames acquired Nikolai Borschevsky from Toronto during last season. He played surprisingly well, earning five points in eight games before, no surprise, getting injured. Borschevsky, who once scored 34 goals for Toronto, is an interesting guy to watch because you've never seen anyone so timid. Although he has some speed, he has a knack of making sure he's not first into a corner, and if he happens to have the puck and someone comes near him, he'll just throw it away. His whole game plan is to ensure he doesn't get hit, so there's absolutely no chance any of Fleury's fearlessness will rub off.

If the key Calgary forwards can stay off the injury list and Fleury and Reichel return, they'll once again be among the better forward units in the league.

They have four potential 40-goal men, size, toughness, good checkers, character, plenty of playmakers, and lots of secondary depth.

SPECIAL TEAMS: The Flames were the most penalized team in the league last season and had the most short handed situations for the second year in a row. It's a good thing their penalty killing is so good. Or is it that their penalty killing is so good because they get so much practise?

The power play success percentage dropped only slightly from the previous season so the loss of Al MacInnis was far from devastating. They've got a bunch of guys who can play the point on the power play, along with snipers and playmakers up front. Incidentally, Calgary's power play finished ahead of MacInnis' new team in St. Louis.

Power Play	G	ATT	PCT
Overall	39	211	18.5% (12th NHL)
Home	18	106	17.0% (16th NHL)
Road	21	105	20.0% (7th NHL)

3 SHORT HANDED GOALS ALLOWED (T-3rd NHL)

Penalty Killing	G	TSH	PCT
Overall	37	249	85.1% (4th NHL)
Home	21	122	82.8% (15th NHL)
Road	16	127	87.4% (2nd NHL)

7 SHORT HANDED GOALS SCORED (T-6th NHL)

Penalties	GP	MIN	AVG
FLAMES	48	1249	26.0 (26th NHL)

Top Scorers
FLAMES SPECIAL TEAMS SCORING

Power play	G	A	PTS
FLEURY	9	11	20
HOUSLEY	3	17	20
NIEUWENDYK	3	12	15
REICHEL	5	8	13
CHIASSON	1	11	12

ZALAPSKI	1	6	7

Short handed	G	A	PTS
TITOV	2	1	3
OTTO	2	1	3
FLEURY	2	1	3
KISIO	1	0	1
PATRICK	0	1	1

COACHING AND MANAGEMENT: GM Doug Risebrough said the number one quality he was looking for in the new coach was communication skills with the players.

What's the big deal about communicating, anyway? Some of the best coaches in the business don't sit their players down for chit-chats.

Coaches aren't babysitters. You never hear players who are going well complain about a lack of communication with the coach. It's the ones who aren't, and need excuses. If the coach is sitting them out, they're not going to be happy with what he has to tell him anyway. In fact, if a player doesn't know what he's doing wrong, he's apt to try and improve every part of his game.

Okay, so it's the nineties, and we're big on communication, but show me where that translates into a winning hockey team.

The new coach/communicator is Pierre Page, who has had a couple kicks of the can with Minnesota and Quebec.

Page, upon his return, said he had improved himself and that, "The Flames will get the best of me."

You can take that quote two ways.

The man who would be King's replacement is probably very good at winning playoff series because that's a big reason King was let go.

Let's see how Page's teams have done in the playoffs over his eight year professional coaching career - five in the NHL, four in the minors.

Uh... he's never won a series.

DRAFT

1995 DRAFT SELECTIONS

Round	Sel.	Player	Pos	Amateur Team
1	20	Denis Gauthier	D	Drummondville (QMJHL)
2	46	Pavel Smirnov	C	Russia
3	73	Rocky Thompson	D	Medicine Hat (WHL)
4	98	Jan Labraatan	LW	Sweden
6	150	Clark Wilm	C	Saskatoon (WHL)
7	176	Ryan Gillis	D	North Bay (OHL)
9	223	Steve Shirreffs	D	Hotchkiss (US HS)

Denis Gauthier is a big, tough defenseman with an attitude. On the ice, that is. He piled up 190 minutes in penalties last year and is considered an outstanding hitter and a supreme shift-disturber. To give you an idea of how tough that Drummondville team was, five players had more than the 190 minutes Gauthier earned. To give you an idea of how tough Gauthier is, he comes from a family of professional wrestlers, which is what he also wanted to be when he was younger.

PROGNOSIS: The Flames have too much talent to fall too far off in the standings, but they don't have enough to challenge the improved clubs in St. Louis and Vancouver, the still-strong Detroit, or Colorado, which has moved over from the Eastern Conference.

But, they have plenty to get into the playoffs where everyone will be waiting to see if they can win a playoff series.

Some of their success will also depend on the return of Reichel and Fleury, and whatever tinkering Risebrough does.

Tinkering isn't much of a factor with a weak club, but when you're up among the better ones, it can make more of a difference.

PREDICTION:
Pacific Division: 3rd
Western Conference: 6th
Overall: 11th

STAT SECTION

Team Rankings 1994/95

		Conference Rank	League Rank
Record	24-17-7	3	7
Home	15-7-2	3	10
Away	9-10-5	4	9
Team Plus\Minus	+26	3	5
Goals For	163	3	5
Goals Against	135	3	11

MISCELLANEOUS STATS

One Goal Games	6-7
Times outshooting opponent	24
Times outshot	22
Even shots	2
Overtime	1-17
Average Shots For	30.2
Average Shots Against	29.3
Longest Winning streak	3
Longest Undefeated streak	5
Longest Losing streak	2
Longest winless streak	3
Versus Teams Over .500	9-8-4
Versus Teams Under .500	15-9-3
First Half Record	11-9-4
Second Half Record	13-8-3

PLAYER	1994-95 OVERALL				PROJECTED 84 GAME TOTALS		
	GP	G	A	PTS	G	A	PTS
T. FLEURY	47	29	29	58	52	52	104
J. NIEUWENDYK	46	21	29	50	38	53	91
P. HOUSLEY	43	8	35	43	16	68	84
R. REICHEL	48	18	17	35	32	30	62
Z. ZALAPSKI	48	4	24	28	7	42	49
S. CHIASSON	45	2	23	25	4	43	47
G. TITOV	40	12	12	24	25	25	50
J. OTTO	47	8	13	21	14	23	37
W. WALZ	39	6	12	18	13	26	39
P.KRUSE	45	11	5	16	21	9	30
S.KENNEDY	30	7	8	15	20	22	42
R.STERN	39	9	4	13	19	9	28
K.DAHL	34	4	8	12	10	20	30
K.KISIO	12	7	4	11	49	28	77
M.SULLIVAN	38	4	7	11	9	15	24
N.BORSCHEVSKY	27	0	10	10	0	31	31
J.PATRICK	43	0	10	10	0	20	20
S.MCCARTHY	37	5	3	8	11	7	18
L.ESAU	15	0	6	6	0	34	34
D.KECZMER	28	2	3	5	6	9	15
A.MAY	34	2	3	5	5	7	12
F.MUSIL	35	0	5	5	0	12	12
G.ROBERTS	8	2	2	4	21	21	42
V.VIITAKOSKI	10	1	2	3	8	17	25
E.WARD	2	1	1	2	42	42	84
M.GREIG	8	1	1	2	11	11	22
C.STILLMAN	10	0	2	2	0	17	17
R.TABARACCI	13	0	2	2	0	13	13
T.YAWNEY	37	0	2	2	0	5	5
T.HLUSHKO	2	0	1	1	0	42	42
J.PEPLINSKI	6	0	1	1	0	14	14
M.NYLANDER	6	0	1	1	0	14	14
T.KIDD	43	0	1	1	0	2	2
S.KONROYD	1	0	0	0	0	0	0
JMUZZATTI	1	0	0	0	0	0	0
J.ALLISON	1	0	0	0	0	0	0
J.BOUCHARD	2	0	0	0	0	0	0
N.EISENHUT	3	0	0	0	0	0	0
B.NIECKAR	3	0	0	0	0	0	0
S.MORROW	4	0	0	0	0	0	0
A.TREFILOV	6	0	0	0	0	0	0

PLAYOFFS

Results: Lost conference quarter-final to San Jose

Record: 3-4

Home: 1-3

Away: 2-1

Goals For: 35

Goals Against: 26

Overtime: 0-2

Power play: 22.6 (4th)

Penalty Killing: 80.6 (9th)

PLAYER	GP	G	A	PTS	+/-	PIM
T.FLEURY	7	7	7	14	8	2
P.HOUSLEY	7	0	9	9	5	0
G.TITOV	7	5	3	8	1	10
M.SULLIVAN	7	3	5	8	5	2
J.NIEUWENDYK	5	4	3	7	0	0
P.KRUSE	7	4	2	6	2	10
R.REICHEL	7	2	4	6	1	4
M.NYLANDER	6	0	6	6	3-	2
K.KISIO	7	3	2	5	0	19
S.KENNEDY	7	3	1	4	3	16
R.STERN	7	3	1	4	4	8
Z.ZALAPSKI	7	0	4	4	7	4
S.CHIASSON	7	1	2	3	9	9
J.OTTO	7	0	3	3	2	2
F.MUSIL	5	0	1	1	0	0
J.PATRICK	5	0	1	1	2-	0
S.McCARTHY	6	0	1	1	2-	17
D.KECZMER	7	0	1	1	0	2
R.TABARACCI	1	0	0	0	0	0
W.WALZ	1	0	0	0	0	0
T.HLUSHKO	1	0	0	0	0	2
T.YAWNEY	2	0	0	0	4-	2
K.DAHL	3	0	0	0	1-	0
T.KIDD	7	0	0	0	0	0

All-Time Rankings - INDIVIDUAL

Goals

Joe Nieuwendyk	314
Gary Roberts	235
Theoren Fleury	232

Assists

Al MacInnis	609
Gary Suter	437
Guy Chouinard	336

Points

Al MacInnis	822
Joe Nieuwendyk	616
Gary Suter	565

Best Seasons

Goals

Lanny McDonald	1982-83	66
Gary Roberts	1991-92	53
Joe Nieuwendyk	1987-88	51
Joe Mullen	1988-89	51
Joe Nieuwendyk	1988-89	51
Theoren Fleury	1990-91	51

Assists

Kent Nilsson	1980-81	82
Al MacInnis	1990-91	75
Bob MacMillen	1978-79	71

Points

Kent Nilsson	1980-81	131
Joe Mullen	1988-89	110
Joe Mullen	1978-79	108

Chicago Blackhawks

It was a strange year for the Chicago Blackhawks.

How strange? Read on.

Dumb and Dumber

During the lockout Chris Chelios suggested Commissioner Gary Bettman should be concerned for his family; Jeremy Roenick said he didn't want the "little man" to win (among other things); and after it was settled, Bernie Nicholls said he hoped the fans stayed away for a couple games in order to stick it to the owners.

Dumbest

The Blackhawks signing Bob Probert and taking on a guy with more personal problems that Wile E. Coyote. Probert was placed on indefinite suspension by the league and ordered to rehabilitation. He never played a game.

Oh, Say Can You Sing

Wayne Messmer, the celebrated anthem singer who was shot outside Chicago Stadium, had his vocal chords back in shape last season but was only needed for the opening game. The Blackhawks relieved him of his duties because he is a vice-president with the rival IHL Chicago Wolves. Rivals?

There's No Place Like Home

The Hawks moved into their brand new building, the United Centre, which proved somewhat less friendly than Chicago Stadium. For the first time since the 1954-55 season, they had a better record on the road than at home.

Take out the Laundry and the Trash

Washed-up hockey players Bernie Nicholls and Denis Savard weren't the type of players in much demand anymore. Nicholls was signed as a free agent when New Jersey no longer wanted him, and Savard was given to the Hawks by Tampa for a sixth round draft pick. All Nicholls did was lead the team in regular season scoring, and all Savard did was lead the team in playoff scoring.

Power Surge

The Blackhawk power play was ranked 19th the year before last, 16th the year before, and 18th the year before that. So, last season, all of a sudden they finish first. The difference? Newcomers Nicholls and Suter, who were one-two in team power play points.

The Saga of J.R.

You could have almost forgot there was a playoff series going on between Chicago and Toronto. The important news was whether or not Roenick would be recovered enough from his injury to return for the playoffs. After a collision with Derian Hatcher of Dallas (and lengthy debates on whether or not Hatcher did it on purpose – he didn't) Roenick was supposed to be out for the season and part of the next one. It was a major distraction, but geez, we really did want to know. He returned in the next round.

Streaking

The biggest streak for the Blackhawks was a 13 game winless one that included eight straight losses. It was their longest winless streak since the 1959-60 season. But, that's just the bad news. They had a five game winning streak on the road, another five gamer, and yet another five game winning streak to finish off the season.

Don't Worry, be Yappy

Jeremy Roenick has something to say about everything, whether he has something to say about it or not. We can't repeat everything he said here because it would make the book considerably larger. Mind you, he's often asked what he thinks of things because of who he is, and if he didn't have anything to say the media would criticize him anyway.

The Fugitive (or Liar Liar Pants on Fire)

Darin (Richard) Kimble quit the team, according to Sutter. Kimble disputed that, saying he was sent home and would never quit on his teammates. Later in the year Sutter was quoted as saying Kimble was sent home because he was causing a disturbance, asking for more ice time.

Now You See Him...

Bernie Nicholls had 21 goals in Chicago's first 30 games, a pace of 59 for a full season. In their last 18 games Nicholls had just one marker, a pace of 5 for a full season.

TEAM PREVIEW

GOAL: Ed Belfour plays most of the games and would be happy playing all of them.

He was sensational for most of the playoffs, give or take an easy overtime goal, and had his hot and cold spurts during the season. The thing about Belfour is when he's hot, he's the hottest, and he carries the team.

The Blachawks finished first in goals against, with Belfour playing in 42 of the 48 games. He had the fifth best goals against average and tied for first with five shutouts. The only downside of Belfour was that he didn't have a comparatively good save percentage and only averaged 24 shots against per 60 minutes. Kelly Hrudey in Los Angeles, by comparison, had 35 shots against him per 60 minutes and a 3.14 GAA, way down the list. But, he had a .910 save percentage, higher than Belfour's.

League Leaders in Shutouts

1994/95	ED BELFOUR	5	
	Dominik Hasek	5	
1993/94	ED BELFOUR	7	
	Dominik Hasek	7	
	Patrick Roy	7	
1992/93	ED BELFOUR	7	
1991/92	ED BELFOUR	5	
	Bob Essensa	5	
	Kirk McLean	5	
	Patrick Roy	5	

Despite only playing five full NHL seasons, Belfour is tops among active goalies with 28 shutouts and is only two away from joining the top 25 of all time. In 1990/91, when he won the Calder Trophy for rookie-of-the-year, he was second in shutouts.

Backup to Belfour is Jeff Hackett, with Jimmy Waite on deck, for some reason.

Two minor league goalies, who didn't have particularly good seasons, are Chris Rogles and Christian Soucy in Indianapolis. But, nobody's gonna get a chance anyway, with Belfour playing all the time.

	GP	MIN	GA	AVG	W	L	T	SO
Belfour	42	2450	93	2.28	22	15	3	5
Hackett	7	328	13	2.38	1	3	2	0
Waite	2	119	5	2.52	1	1	0	0

DEFENCE: They're either old or their experienced, depends on how you look at it. Consider the ages of the main Blackhawk defencemen as of October 1 of 1995.

Chris Chelios	33
Steve Smith	32
Gary Suter	31
Eric Weinrich	28
Cam Russell	26

This group, along with Gerald Diduck, 30, helped make the Blackhawks the top defensive team in the league, and Chelios and Suter helped make them the number one power play team.

Obviously, age isn't a problem – yet. But, just in case you haven't heard this cliche a thousand times – they're not getting any younger.

Pulford likes his veterans – probably the lasting effects from that old-timer team in 1967 that won the Stanley Cup for the Toronto Maple Leafs.

So, we could say that this is a make-it or break-it year for the Blackhawks, but we would probably be saying that next year as well.

Gerald Diduck, for example, was obtained from Vancouver for a song. Vancouver obviously wanted to get rid of him, and Chicago obviously needed him.

I always wonder why a team trades someone so valuable in the midst of a playoff drive. Do they know something others don't? Just curious.

Did the Canucks think differently when the Blackhawks swept them in the playoffs? And what is Hartford thinking after signing him as a free agent during the summer?

The young guys on the Blackhawks don't get much playing time, but they will this year unless Pulford gets another veteran. Among the press box regulars are former prospect Roger Johansson and another offensive prospect in Keith Carney, who's finding it difficult to contribute while not on the ice.

The Blackhawks also signed my favorite junior defenceman, Mike Rusk, who played with Guelph in the OHL last year. (Okay, so maybe he's my favorite because we lived only a couple blocks away from each other in Milton, Ontario.)

The Blackhawks have very little depth in the organization at this position, so hopefully Rusk can get a shot at some point (pun intended). Plus, it may help that Hartsburg was his coach in Guelph last season.

Depth, however isn't a problem with the Blackhawks, even though they drafted a ton of defencemen this year. There's plenty of old-timers around the league that can be had cheap, and Pulford will sign some when he feels the need.

FORWARD: Before the start of last season, there was Jeremy Roenick, and then there was the rest of them. Not so, anymore.

Joe Murphy had a projected (over 84 games) 48 goal season, Tony Amonte and Patrick Poulin had comeback seasons of sorts, Sergei Krivakrasov and Jeff Shantz started to show some stuff on a checking line, big rookie Eric Daze gave them some future promise, and then there were the big surprises.

Bernie Nicholls blew the doors off. At least for the first half of the season. He finished 12th in league scoring, first on the Blackhawks, and was third in the league in power play points. The downside was that he had a 30 game goal drought that extended into the playoffs.

Denis Savard was the other surprise. Give us a break, the guy was on his last legs in Tampa Bay. The Hawks got him to replace Jeremy Roenick when he got hurt, but they didn't really expect him to REPLACE him. All Savard did was lead the Blackhawks in scoring and cause a lot of sore necks from people shaking their heads in wonder.

As per the defence, there are lots of oldsters on the Blackhawk forward line, because that's what Pulford likes. Let's look at the old-timers, with ages as of Oct. 1, 1995.

Dirk Graham	36
Denis Savard	34
Bernie Nicholls	34
Brent Sutter	33
Murray Craven	31

Lots of experience here, folks. Graham isn't a for-sure for this season. He was still pondering it at press time. But, the rest of them are a go. Sutter has a year left on his contract, and despite the fact he doesn't score much anymore, is still valuable for his experience and defensive expertise. Once, perhaps the best faceoff man in the league, those skills have dimished some now, although you'd still put your money on him in an important situation.

It's hard to believe Nicholls and Savard could duplicate last season, but then again, it was hard to believe they could have seasons like last year to begin with.

Elsewhere are the tough guys, Jim Cummins and Bob Probert. Probert, of course, was on indefinite suspension last year and forced to go through rehabilitation again. He's clear to play this year, but you have to wonder how long it can last.

Krivakrasov, Shantz, Poulin and Daze represent the youth, which quite frequently on Chicago isn't represented at all. Shantz is a defensive specialist, and does his job quite well. He may always be a fourth liner, but he's a good fourth liner. Krivakrasov who started to come into his own, also frequented the fourth line. A little guy, who lied when he said he was 5-10, did some scoring as well, but sat out some during the playoffs because of his size. Poulin is a much needed commodity on the left side when he's in the game, but he goes through periods of inactivity, and then finds himself in the press box. Still, he had a decent year, scoring 15 goals and adding 15 assists. He might yet become a consistent major league sniper and live up to his previous hype. Daze is a big guy who cuts an imposing figure on the ice. At 6-4, 200 pounds, he has put up some nice numbers in junior and may continue to do so.

A lot of things went right with the Chicago forwards last year. Whether or not they can do it again, hardly seems the point. Pulford will just go out and grab another oldtimer no longer wanted by his present team, and somehow he'll make a go of it.

SPECIAL TEAMS: Murphy, Nicholls and Sutter up front. Chelios and Suter on the points. Good enough for first overall last year, and still good enough for first.

As well, there are lots of good defensive forward types to make the penalty killing unit effective.

Power Play	G	ATT	PCT
Overall	52	212	24.5% (1st NHL)
Home	22	97	22.7% (T-4th NHL)
Road	30	115	26.1% (2nd NHL)

3 SHORT HANDED GOALS ALLOWED (T-3rd NHL)

Penalty Killing	G	TSH	PCT
Overall	36	228	84.2% (9th NHL)
Home	17	106	84.0% (11th NHL)
Road	19	122	84.4% (7th NHL)

7 SHORT HANDED GOALS SCORED (T-6th NHL)

BLACKHAWKS SPECIAL TEAMS SCORING

Power play	G	A	PTS
NICHOLLS	11	17	28
SUTER	5	19	24
CHELIOS	3	20	23
MURPHY	7	8	15
ROENICK	5	13	18
SAVARD	2	6	8
AMONTE	6	7	13
KRIVOKRASOV	6	0	6
POULIN	4	2	6
WEINRICH	1	3	4

Short handed	G	A	PTS
SHANTZ	2	1	3
NICHOLLS	2	0	2
CHELIOS	1	1	2

COACHING AND MANAGEMENT: There were probably more good things said about new Blackhawk coach Craig Hartsburg last year than any other coach outside the NHL. With the Guelph Storm in the OHL he took them to the finals. Everybody likes him and the players can't say enough good things about him despite the fact he demands 100 percent effort every game and worked them hard.

The key is to get Roenick to like you. He was always spouting off about Sutter, but then again he spouts off about everything. If he has good things to say about Hartsburg then he's in.

Darryl Sutter wasn't a favorite of Roenick because he didn't let him play the way he wanted. Sutter had this thing about winning as a team. Maybe a crazy notion, if you're Roenick.

Under Sutter they finished with the league's best GAA, scored the seventh most goals, had the top power play, survived the loss of their superstar during the season and much of the playoffs, and made it to the conference finals. Sounds pretty close to a coach of the year. Good job, Darryl.

Sutter resigned to spend more time with his family and especially his son, who has Down's Syndrome. You always wonder in these situations if he was just given the opportunity to resign gracefully rather than be fired.

Sutter did have a curious habit about criticizing players through the media. Don't know about that. If it's a motivational tool, I think it's a fairly good one, because then the player is motivated to prove him wrong.

General Manager Pulford is Pulford. He doesn't smile, he smokes, and he gets a lot of criticism from others, but he gets the job done. He even survived the Mike Keenan years, and since coming on the scene in 1977 the team has never failed to make the playoffs.

DRAFT

1995 DRAFT SELECTIONS

Round	Sel.	Player	Pos	Amateur Team
1	19	Dimitri Nabokov	C	Russia
2	45	Christiane Laflamme	D	Beauport (QMJHL)
3	71	Kevin McKay	D	Moose Jaw (WHL)

4	82	Chris Van Dyk	D	Windsor (WHL)
4	98	Pavel Kriz	D	Tri-City (WHL)
6	146	Mark Magliardi	G	Des Moines (USHL)
6	149	Marty Wilford	D	Oshawa
7	175	Steve Tardif	C	Drummondville (QMJHL)
8	201	Casey Hankinson	LW	Minnesota (WCHA)
9	227	Mike Pittman	C	Guelph (OHL)

The Blackhawks aren't high on Europeans, and haven't had many in their lineup. Sergei Krivokrasov has worked out pretty well, so far, so the Hawks dipped into the European pool again for Nabakov.

Nabakov isn't considered flashy and is not projected as a big scorer. He's considered to be a gritty performer who's good in the corners. Mind you, that's against other Europeans, and there's a big difference in the North American corners.

It may just be me, but why the heck waste a first round draft pick on a guy who's projected as a third or fourth line player, if he ever makes it that far? And if that's what you're looking for, a European is even more of a stretch because they're often suspect defensively, and their courage level gets knocked down a level or two against guys who really battle it out in the corners. Why not go for a North American of the same ilk, who's already proven he can handle the tough going?

PROGNOSIS: What we have here is a contender with a sense of urgency. A lot of the key players are old and they want a last kick at the can.

Hungry players make better players and there's no reason to think this group won't have a shot at the big dinner.

They have all the components: goaltending, defense, coaching, mobile defensemen, tough defensemen, a superstar forward in Roenick, tough guys up front, role players up front, secondary scoring up front.

The only thing they don't have is a long future together so time now to do it before the next group of old guys comes along.

PREDICTION:
Central Division: 3rd
Western Conference: 5th
Overall: 9th

STAT SECTION

Team Rankings 1994/95

		Conference Rank	League Rank
Record	24-19-5	4	8
Home	11-10-3	7	16
Away	13-9-2	2	2
Team Plus\Minus	+25	4	6
Goals For	156	5	7
Goals Against	115	1	1

PLAYER	1994-95 OVERALL				PROJECTED 84 GAME TOTALS		
	GP	G	A	PTS	G	A	PTS
BERNIE NICHOLLS	48	22	29	51	38	51	89
JOE MURPHY	40	23	18	41	48	38	86
CHRIS CHELIOS	48	5	33	38	9	58	67
GARY SUTER	48	10	27	37	17	47	64
TONY AMONTE	48	15	20	35	26	35	61
JEREMY ROENICK	33	10	24	34	25	61	86
PATRICK POULIN	45	15	15	30	28	28	56
DENIS SAVARD	43	10	15	25	20	29	49
SERGEI KRIVOKRASOV	41	12	7	19	25	14	39
JEFF SHANTZ	45	6	12	18	11	22	33
BRENT SUTTER	47	7	8	15	13	14	27
DIRK GRAHAM	40	4	9	13	8	19	27
ERIC WEINRICH	48	3	10	13	5	17	22
STEVE SMITH	48	1	12	13	2	21	23
MURRAY CRAVEN	16	4	3	7	21	16	36
BRENT GRIEVE	24	1	5	6	3	17	20
JIM CUMMINS	37	4	1	5	9	2	11
GERALD DIDUCK	35	2	3	5	5	7	12
CAM RUSSELL	33	1	3	4	3	8	11
GREG SMYTH	22	0	3	3	0	11	11
ED BELFOUR	42	0	3	3	0	6	6
ERIC DAZE	4	1	1	2	21	21	42
ROGER JOHANSSON	11	1	0	1	8	0	8
KEITH CARNEY	18	1	0	1	5	0	5
TONY HORACEK	19	0	1	1	0	4	4
JIM WAITE	2	0	0	0	0	0	0
DANIEL GAUTHIER	5	0	0	0	0	0	0
JEFF HACKETT	7	0	0	0	0	0	0
DARIN KIMBLE	14	0	0	0	0	0	0
STEVE DUBINSKY	16	0	0	0	0	0	0

MISCELLANEOUS STATS

One Goal Games	6-6
Times outshooting opponent	33
Times outshot	15
Even shots	0
Overtime	2-0-5
Average Shots For	30.0
Average Shots Against	24.8
Longest Winning streak	5
Longest Undefeated streak	6
Longest Losing streak	8
Longest winless streak	13
Versus Teams Over .500	8-9-5
Versus Teams Under .500	16-10-0
First Half Record	14-8-2
Second Half Record	10-11-3

PLAYOFFS

Results: Defeated Toronto 4-3, Defeated Vancouver 4-0, Lost to Detroit in Conference finals 4-1.
Record: 9-7 Home: 5-3 Away: 4-4
Goals For: 45 (2.8/gm)
Goals Against: 39 (2.4/gm)
Overtime: 3-4
Power play: 12.7% (5th)
Penalty Killing: 13.2% (11th)

Playoff Scoring

	GP	G	A	PTS	+/-	PIM
DENIS SAVARD	16	7	11	18	12	10
JOE MURPHY	16	9	3	12	1-	29
BERNIE NICHOLLS	16	1	11	12	0	8
CHRIS CHELIOS	16	4	7	11	6	12
MURRAY CRAVEN	16	5	5	10	2	4
GARY SUTER	12	2	5	7	1-	10
TONY AMONTE	16	3	3	6	3	10
ERIC WEINRICH	16	1	5	6	8	4
PATRICK POULIN	16	4	1	5	1	8
DIRK GRAHAM	16	2	3	5	6	8
JEFF SHANTZ	16	3	1	4	0	2

GERALD DIDUCK	16	1	3	4	4-	22
JEREMY ROENICK	8	1	2	3	2-	16
BRENT SUTTER	16	1	2	3	1	4
CAM RUSSELL	16	0	3	3	4	8
JIM CUMMINS	14	1	1	2	3	4
KEITH CARNEY	4	0	1	1	0	0
STEVE SMITH	16	0	1	1	2	26
ERIC DAZE	16	0	1	1	4-	4
JEFF HACKETT	2	0	0	0	0	0
SERGEI KRIVOKRASOV	10	0	0	0	0	8
ED BELFOUR	16	0	0	0	0	6

All-Time Rankings - INDIVIDUAL

Goals
Bobby Hull	604
Stan Mikita	541
Steve Larmer	406

Assists
Stan Mikita	926
Denis Savard	666
Doug Wilson	554

Points
Stan Mikita	1,467
Bobby Hull	1,153
Denis Savard	1,021

BEST INDIVIDUAL SEASONS

Goals
Bobby Hull	1968-69	58
Al Secord	1982-83	54
Bobby Hull	1965-66	54

Assists
Denis Savard	1987-88	87
Denis Savard	1981-82	87
Denis Savard	1982-83	86

Points
Denis Savard	1987-88	131
Denis Savard	1982-83	121
Denis Savard	1981-82	119

Dallas Stars

A year ago, the Stars were positioned just right. They had the most points in their franchise history, had improved for the fourth straight season, and were ready to go places.

But, something happened on the way to heaven.

Let's look at some team comparisons:

	1993-94	1994-95
Overall	42-29-13	17-23-8
	.578	.438
Home	23-12-7	9-10-5
	.631	.479
Road	19-17-6	8-13-3
	.524	.396
Goals For	3.4	2.8
Goals Against	3.2	2.8
Shots For	30.4	31.6
Shots Against	30.8	28.9
One Goal Games	17-8	5-14
Overtime	6-3-13	0-1-8
Tied After two periods		
	9-3-7	4-7-3
Power Play (rank)		
	15th	19th
Penalty Killing (rank)		
	4th	7th

Let's start with the obvious. They had a worse winning percentage in 1994-95, both at home and on the road. The real damage came at home where they went from one of the best to one of the worst.

Next, goals scored were down, but that was the same all over the league. Goals against were also down.

Shots for – up. Shots against – down. That's supposed to be something good, you'd think, but not always. I'll explain that some other time.

Power play and penalty killing rankings weren't much different from the previous season.

That leaves three categories that are indeed significant.

The team record when tied after two periods went from good to bad. I think it's an important stat, and somewhat of a character measurer. A team only has to win the one period. Everything's even up to that point. The team that plays the hardest wins the period and the game.

The overtime record went for a skid, as well, which ties in with the final stat shown above – one goal games.

Bill James had a theory (and maybe still does) about one-run games in baseball. He said (I hope I get this right) that a team that loses a lot of one-run games could be due for a big rise in wins the following year. And a team that wins a lot of one-run games could do the opposite.

The idea, I think, is that those wins or losses have a higher percentage of luck involved, and can more easily reverse themselves the following year.

Certainly, in hockey, I believe that overtime records have some basis in luck.

Let's take a look anyway.

ONE-GOAL GAMES

		1993-94			1994-95		
	GP	W	L	%	W	L	%
ANA	84	10	21	.323	7	4	.636
BOS	84	13	11	.542	15	9	.625
BUF	84	7	15	.318	8	8	.500
CGY	84	14	10	.583	6	7	.462
CHI	84	15	14	.517	6	6	.500
DAL	84	17	8	.680	5	14	.263
DET	84	8	8	.500	7	7	.500
EDM	84	7	14	.333	6	6	.500
FLA	84	16	20	.444	8	8	.500
HFD	84	11	10	.524	10	10	.500
L.A	84	9	15	.375	6	3	.667
MTL	84	11	9	.550	6	8	.429
N.J	84	9	10	.474	7	11	.389
NYI	84	10	16	.385	8	12	.400
NYR	84	16	9	.640	9	13	.409
OTT	84	8	13	.381	5	13	.278
PHI	84	13	9	.541	14	5	.737
PIT	84	20	7	.741	11	6	.647
QUE	84	8	11	.400	10	5	.667
S.J	84	19	11	.633	8	6	.571
STL	84	19	12	.613	8	8	.500
T.B	84	13	18	.419	6	10	.375
TOR	84	15	14	.517	12	3	.800
VAN	84	17	15	.531	1	3	.250
WSH	84	10	10	.500	7	6	.538
WPG	84	10	15	.400	6	11	.353

Lots of mixed messages here, but the three teams with the worst one-goal records in 1993-94 – Anaheim, Buffalo and Edmonton – all improved to at least .500 in 1994-95 in one goal games. But only Edmonton, of the three, improved their overall winning percentage, and that was only slightly.

The three highest one-goal winning percentages in 1993-94 were Pittsburgh, Dallas and the New York Rangers. Pittsburgh were the only ones to stay above .500 in that stat in 1994-95.

So, what does all that mean? Hard to say. Defensive teams are going to have a lot more one-goal games, offensive teams are not. Good teams are going to win a lot more games, whether by a goal or two goals; and poor teams are going to do the opposite. Good teams often win games by two goals or more, which is more telling than one-goal games; and again poor teams are going to do the opposite.

I would say this: a mediocre team that loses a lot of games by one-goal could, in fact, be in for a rise in the standings; and a mediocre team that won a lot of one-goal games could be in for a drop. Thank you, Bill James.

Keeping in mind that teams often are doing complete make-overs from one season to the next, I'd say there are two teams we can keep on eye on in the coming season that fit the specs.

Toronto had a 12-3 mark in one-goal games, but they were mediocre at best last season. Change that 12-3 mark to, say, 7-8, and they wouldn't have made the playoffs last year.

Dallas, on the other hand, lost so many close games, I think we can expect them to reverse that, to at least .500, and that makes them a considerably better team.

One more item of business: the Stars penalty shot jinx. In franchise history 24 penalty shots have been taken and only three resulted in goals – one in 1971, one in 1975 and the last goal in 1985. They're currently on a ten-shot scoreless drought that included last year's most amusing attempt when Dave Gagner lost the puck in a pile of snow.

Opponents have been successful on 13 of 27 penalty shot attempts.

TEAM PREVIEW

GOAL: Both Andy Moog and Darcy Wakaluk had injury problems last season, including a broken hand to Wakaluk after he slammed his hand on a door after a loss.

Moog is 35 years old, but had his best goals against average ever in the NHL. Comparatively, his 2.44 mark wasn't spectacular in the defensive conscious short-season NHL last year, but his save percentage of .915 was. It was fourth best in the league.

Wakaluk, who challenged for the number one job prior to last season, has dropped in value some and his job may be jeopardy.

That's because they have a future star in waiting. His name is Manny Fernandez, yet another gem out of the Quebec Junior League. His rights were obtained from the Nordiques (Colorado) for a useless power play specialist (Tommy Sjodin) and a third round pick in the 1994 draft.

After leading the Quebec League in goals against average and earning a first team all-star berth, he spent last season in Kalamazoo where he had another great year, posting a 21-9-9 mark, and a GAA of 2.72, up among the leaders all season.

He shared those duties with Mike Torchia, who was traded to Washington in the off-season for futures.

GM Bob Gainey likes to bring along rookies slowly, in the old Montreal Canadiens tradition, but it's going to be hard to keep Fernandez down on the farm.

	GP	MIN	GA	AVG	W	L	T	SO
Moog	31	1770	72	2.44	10	12	7	2
Fernandez	1	59	3	3.05	0	1	0	0
Wakaluk	15	754	40	3.18	4	8	0	2
Torchia	6	327	18	3.30	3	2	1	0

DEFENCE:

Derian Hatcher	6-5, 225
Kevin Hatcher	6-4, 225
Craig Ludvig	6-3, 222
Doug Zmolek	6-2, 225
Grant Ledyard	6-2, 195
Richard Matvichuk	6-2, 190
Paul Cavallini	6-1, 210

Get the picture? These are big boys.

	Pts	Pts/84gms
Derian Hatcher	16	37
Kevin Hatcher	29	52
Craig Ludvig	9	16
Doug Zmolek	5	10
Grant Ledyard	18	40
Richard Matvichuk	2	9
Paul Cavallini	12	23

Get the picture? Big boys, some with scoring punch, some with none.

	PIM	PIM/84gms
Derian Hatcher	105	204
Kevin Hatcher	66	118
Craig Ludvig	61	109
Doug Zmolek	67	134
Grant Ledyard	20	44
Richard Matvichuk	14	84
Paul Cavallini	28	53

Big boys with scoring punch, who play it physical.

Smile, that's about all you need.

FORWARD: Take away Mike Modano and the next leading goal scorer, projected over 84 games, would have had only 24 goals. So, take away Modano and the Stars would fall apart?

Not exactly.

Modano missed 18 games last season – four with a bruised ankle, and then the final 14 with ruptured tendons in his ankle. Let's compare the Dallas record with and without Modano.

	With Modano	Without Modano
Record	10-15-5	7-8-3
Average goals scored	2.8	2.8
Average goals against	3.0	2.8

Curiously, the Stars played better without Modano, and their scoring remained exactly the same.

I think at times that when a team's star player goes down, the others pick up the slack and then some. The same thing happened with the Sabres two seasons ago when LaFontaine was injured.

In Modano's absence, Todd Harvey scored seven of his 11 goals on the season, Kevin Hatcher eight of his 10, and Derian Hatcher three of his five.

I think, however, that it's just a short term phenomenon, that eventually wears off.

So, what the Stars need is more scoring. A no-brainer, correct?

That's what you heard about the Stars all season long. And then they went and got rid of Russ Courtnall, one of the few scorers. And

the year before they dumped off Ulf Dahlen to San Jose.

And Gainey did make some light-hearted attempts to pick up some scoring power, obtaining Mike Donnelly from Los Angeles, Greg Adams from Vancouver, and Corey Millen from New Jersey.

So, more scoring power? Well, consider this, Dallas scored the same number of goals as New Jersey. Do they need more scoring to be successful? Ah... I don't think so.

There's more than one way to be successful. The Dallas blueprint runs along the same lines as New Jersey – a good defense, forwards who know both ends of the rink and can put up average goal production, good coaching and decent goaltending.

The Stars have the right approach, they just need the right players to make it go. And, of course, the players to buy into the system instead of whining about too much line juggling or power play unit changes.

They were successful the year before without many scorers, and with Gainey using the same tactics. Gainey knows character players, he will find them and somehow get the right mix with the forwards.

During the off-season he signed Bob Bassen, who's a perfect fit for this team.

Another character player is Todd Harvey – an oustanding talent who showed flashes of brilliance last season, and will only get better. He's been compared in playing style to Bobby Clarke.

Another young talent is Jamie Langenbrunner who led the Peterborough Petes in scoring in the OHL, and was 12th in the league with 34-43-77 in just 46 games.

A couple of young Europeans who are supposed to add scoring touch are Jarkko Varvio and Jere Lehtinen, who played last year in Finland. They don't fit the Dallas mold, however, so it will be interesting to see if they get any playing time. Gainey has already discarded other Europeans who didn't pay attention to their defense.

Gainey will continue to mix and match his forwards, hoping to come up with the right recipe. He's done it before, and he can do it again.

SPECIAL TEAMS: Some of the players took time out to complain last year that they couldn't get the power play moving if Gainey kept switching the players all the time. So, Gainey left it alone and they did all right, for a while.

With Kevin Hatcher on one point, you want Modano and Gagner somewhere up front, and probably Harvey. Millen could certainly play there, as can Donnelly, Adams, and Klatt.

Matvichuk is projected as more of an offensive force from the defense, but otherwise there are still some guys back there, including Ledyard, who can handle things.

With Gainey and assistant coach Doug Jarvis, two of the best penalty-killers of all-time, predictably that unit was good again last year and will be right up there this year as well.

Power Play	G	ATT	PCT
Overall	39	248	15.7% (T-19th NHL)
Home	24	136	17.6% (15th NHL)
Road	15	112	13.4% (20th NHL)

7 SHORT HANDED GOALS ALLOWED (T-18th NHL)

Penalty Killing	G	TSH	PCT
Overall	34	218	84.4% (T-7th NHL)
Home	16	113	85.8% (5th NHL)
Road	18	105	82.9% (10th NHL)

4 SHORT HANDED GOALS SCORED (T-17th NHL)

Penalties	GP	MIN	AVG
STARS	48	1117	23.3 (21st NHL)

STARS SPECIAL TEAMS SCORING

Power play	G	A	PTS
GAGNER	7	12	19
HATCHER,K	3	10	13
MODANO	4	7	11
LEDYARD	4	6	10
KLATT	5	3	8
HARVEY	2	6	8
DONNELLY	3	4	7
ADAMS	3	4	7

Short handed	G	A	PTS
GILCHRIST	3	0	3
ADAMS	2	0	2
EVASON	0	2	2

COACHING AND MANAGEMENT: A bit of a setback last season, but prior to that the Stars had been improving steadily. The betting is they'll get back on track again this year.

Gainey likes to get his people on board, and with the program. And as both coach and general manager it makes the job easier.

DRAFT

1995 DRAFT SELECTIONS

Round	Sel.	Player	Pos	Amateur Team
1	11	Jarome Iginia	RW	Kamloops (WHL)
2	37	Patrick Cote	LW	Beauport (QMJHL)
3	63	Petr Buzek	D	Czechoslovakia
3	69	Sergei Gusev	D	Russia
5	115	Wade Strand	D	Regina (WHL)
6	141	Dominic Marleau	D	Victoriaville (QMJHL)
7	173	Jeff Dewer	RW	Moose Jaw (WHL)

8	193	Anatoli Kovesnikov	LW	Russia
8	202	Sergei Luchinkin	LW	Russia
9	219	Steve Lowe	C	Sault Ste Marie(OHL)

Jarome Iginia wasn't ranked nearly as high as the Stars selected him by Central Scouting, but you know Bob Gainey, he likes certain players and Iginia fits.

Same thing with their second pick. Patrick Cote, who amassed 314 penalty minutes last season, was ranked 142nd by the CSB, but Dallas took him 37th.

Third round pick Petr Buzek is an interesting story. He was ranked fifth among Europeans and expected to go around the middle of the first round. A car accident just before the draft that left Buzek with a shattered kneecap and a broken femur, scared most teams off.

PROGNOSIS: The Stars are going to be in one of the toughest divisions with Detroit and St. Louis both predicted as powerhouses, and Chicago also with a good club. That probably means the Stars can finish no higher than fourth, and no higher than sixth or seventh in the conference.

But, they will be improved over last year and by the time they get to the post-season will have a playoff type team. Anything can happen in the playoffs, which Gainey knows very well from their finals appearance in 1991.

PREDICTION:
Central Division: 4th
Western Conference: 7th
Overall: 12th

STAT SECTION

Team Rankings 1994/95

		Conference Rank	League Rank
Record	17-23-8	8	19
Home	9-10-5	10	21
Away	8-13-3	8	21
Team Plus\Minus	-4	6	14
Goals For	136	8	13
Goals Against	135	3	11

MISCELLANEOUS STATS

One Goal Games	5-14
Times outshooting opponent	29
Times outshot	17
Even shots	2
Overtime	0-1-8
Average Shots For	31.6
Average Shots Against	28.9
Longest Winning streak	5
Longest Undefeated streak	5
Longest Losing streak	4
Longest winless streak	7
Versus Teams Over .500	7-15-6
Versus Teams Under .500	10-8-2
First Half Record	9-12-3
Second Half Record	8-11-5

PLAYER	1994-95 OVERALL				PROJECTED 84 GAME TOTALS		
	GP	G	A	PTS	G	A	PTS
DAVE GAGNER	48	14	28	42	24	49	73
MIKE MODANO	30	12	17	29	34	48	82
KEVIN HATCHER	47	10	19	29	18	34	52
MIKE DONNELLY	44	12	15	27	23	29	52
COREY MILLEN	45	5	18	23	9	34	43
TRENT KLATT	47	12	10	22	21	18	39
GREG ADAMS	43	8	13	21	16	25	41
TODD HARVEY	40	11	9	20	23	19	42
MIKE KENNEDY	44	6	12	18	11	23	34
GRANT LEDYARD	38	5	13	18	11	29	40
PAUL BROTEN	47	7	9	16	13	16	29
DERIAN HATCHER	43	5	11	16	10	21	31
DEAN EVASON	47	8	7	15	14	13	27
BRENT GILCHRIST	32	9	4	13	24	11	35
PAUL CAVALLINI	44	1	11	12	2	21	23
PETER ZEZEL	30	6	5	11	17	14	31
CRAIG LUDWIG	47	2	7	9	4	13	17
DOUG ZMOLEK	42	0	5	5	0	10	10
SHANE CHURLA	27	1	3	4	3	9	12
JARKKO VARVIO	5	1	1	2	17	17	34
RICHARD MATVICHUK	14	0	2	2	0	12	12
GORD DONNELLY	16	1	0	1	5	0	5
GRANT MARSHALL	2	0	1	1	0	42	42
ANDY MOOG	31	0	1	1	0	3	3
ZAC BOYER	1	0	0	0	0	0	0
EMMANUEL FERNANDEZ	1	0	0	0	0	0	0
TRAVIS RICHARDS	2	0	0	0	0	0	0
MARK LAWRENCE	2	0	0	0	0	0	0
JAMIE LANGENBRUNNER	2	0	0	0	0	0	0
MIKE TORCHIA	6	0	0	0	0	0	0
MIKE LALOR	12	0	0	0	0	0	0
DARCY WAKALUK	15	0	0	0	0	0	0

PLAYOFFS

Results: Lost opening round 4-1 to Detroit.
Record: 1-4 Home: 1-1 Away: 0-3
Goals For: 10 (2.0/gm)
Goals Against: 17 (3.4/gm)
Overtime: 0-0
Power play: 11.5% (14th)
Penalty Killing: 70.0% (16th)

POS	NO.	PLAYER	GP	G	A	PTS
D	4	KEVIN HATCHER	5	2	1	3
R	21	PAUL BROTEN	5	1	2	3
C	16	DEAN EVASON	5	1	2	3
L	23	GREG ADAMS	5	2	0	2
C	15	DAVE GAGNER	5	1	1	2
D	14	PAUL CAVALLINI	5	0	2	2
D	24	RICHARD MATVICHUK	5	0	2	2
C	25	PETER ZEZEL	3	1	0	1
C	6	COREY MILLEN	5	1	0	1
R	22	TRENT KLATT	5	1	0	1
D	3	CRAIG LUDWIG	4	0	1	1
L	11	MIKE DONNELLY	5	0	1	1
C	41	BRENT GILCHRIST	5	0	1	1
G	34	DARCY WAKALUK	1	0	0	0
R	37	*ZAC BOYER	2	0	0	0
D	18	MIKE LALOR	3	0	0	0
D	12	GRANT LEDYARD	3	0	0	0
R	27	SHANE CHURLA	5	0	0	0
G	35	ANDY MOOG	5	0	0	0
D	5	DOUG ZMOLEK	5	0	0	0
L	39	*MIKE KENNEDY	5	0	0	0
C	10	*TODD HARVEY	5	0	0	0

All-Time Rankings - INDIVIDUAL

Goals

Brian Bellows	342
Dino Ciccarelli	332
Bill Goldsworthy	267

Assists

Neal Broten	586
Brian Bellows	380
Bobby Smith	369

Points

Neal Broten	852
Brian Bellows	722
Dino Ciccarelli	651

BEST INDIVIDUAL SEASONS

Goals

Brian Bellows	1989-90	55
Dino Ciccarelli	1981-82	55
Mike Modano	1993-94	50

Assists

Neal Broten	1985-86	76
Bobby Smith	1981-82	71
Tim Young	1976-77	66

Points

Bobby Smith	1981-82	114
Dino Ciccarelli	1981-82	106
Neal Broten	1985-86	105

Detroit Red Wings

The thing about getting zonked in the Stanley Cup finals in four games is that you're thought of as a bunch of losers, rather than one of the two best teams.

The Buffalo Bills were a good football team that earned the same type of reputation.

The toughest part for the Detroit braintrust is to figure out what to do about it. On one hand, they know they can't stand pat because they were hopelessly outmatched by the Devils last year. On the other, they're so close they don't want to do too much to spoil it. If the Wings had Claude Lemieux or Martin Brodeur, the outcome would likely have been different.

But, they're going to have to do something, even if it's to add just one player or two. Vancouver and St. Louis figure to be greatly improved in the Western Conference. And the Red Wings have a fair number of older players who can't be counted on to repeat their production. Especially over a full season.

I suppose we could go into what a great season the Red Wings had, but what fun would that be? Let's look at how they got stiffed in the finals.

The most startling thing was how one of the NHL's best offensive team were shut down so completely. They were outscored 16-7 and had only three even strength goals.

They were outshot 106 to 75. A team that averaged 32.7 shots per game during the regular season was reduced to 18.8. In only one period they even reached double figures. And in the final period of the finals, which they went into down just one goal, they managed one shot!

Shots by game were 17, 18, 24 and 16. Not once during the regular season, did they have fewer than 20 shots during a game.

Also, during the regular season, Detroit was the better defensive team, finishing second in goals against, compared to fifth for New Jersey.

Not that we wouldn't want to give the Devils their due. It was no accident what they were able to accomplish.

And it was no accident the Red Wings put together such an outstanding regular season record. In fact, it was the 12th best over the last 50 years.

They might take some comfort from the fact that everyone on the list, and most of them directly below, won a Stanley Cup at or around the time they posted such a high winning percentage.

Best Winning percentage since 1954-55 (when Detroit last won Stanley Cup)

1.	Montreal	1976-77	60-8-12	.825*
2.	Montreal	1977-78	59-10-11	.800*
3.	Montreal	1975-76	58-11-11	.794*

4. Boston	1970-71	57-14-7	.776
5. Montreal	1972-73	52-10-16	.769*
6. Boston	1971-72	54-13-11	.763*
7. Edmonton	1983-84	57-18-5	.744*
8. Edmonton	1985-86	56-17-7	.744
9. NY Islanders	1981-82	54-16-10	.738*
10. Philadelphia	1975-76	51-13-16	.738
11. Calgary	1988-89	54-17-9	.731*
12. DETROIT	1994-95	33-11-4	.729

* won Stanley Cup

Since 1955-56, first place teams overall during the regular season have won the Stanley Cup 19 of 39 times. In the last six years only one team (1993-94 Rangers) that finished first overall has gone on to win the Cup.

When there were six teams it was considerably easier, but now with 26, getting through the playoffs is a completely different grind than the regular season.

They really are two different seasons. The playoffs, of course, are more intense, with tighter checking, better teams, more defense.

A team can be built to excel in one or the other, or both. Sometimes teams have great regular season marks, but are smoked in the playoffs – see Boston, or Buffalo, or Calgary and others.

That's what is important to keep in mind. The Red Wings made it down to the last two. They're not far away.

TEAM PREVIEW

GOAL: The goaltending problems in Detroit never seem to end. First, they needed a goalie, then they got him, then they didn't want him.

Who the heck knows.

Mike Vernon was supposed to be the savior and you could argue that he did just about everything asked of him, at least until the finals when he let in some bad goals.

Vernon, who is a free agent, supposedly had a contract offer from the Red Wings, which was supposedly withdrawn after his disappointing finals performance. At that point, supposedly, Vernon was said to rethink his position on the contract and accept it, knowing he wouldn't do better.

Stay tuned.

Meanwhile, perhaps the best number two goalie in hockey, Chris Osgood, bides his time, putting up impressive numbers. He has a 37-15-5 record in the Red Wing nets over the last two years as second banana. Last season, his .917 save percentage was second best in the league.

His lack of experience is what worries people. What if they hand the number one job to him and he doesn't come through? Then they're right back where they started from, looking for a reliable veteran netminder to lead them to the promised land.

Here's what I would do. Give the job to Osgood and find a backup somewhere around the NHL. There's lots of dependable veterans of that ilk that can be had cheap. Heck, they could even get Bob Essensa, exiled right out of the Red Wing organization and loaned to another team.

Osgood's served his apprenticeship and served it well. Time to give him a shot.

	GP	MIN	GA	AVG	W	L	T	SO
Osgood	19	1087	41	2.26	14	5	0	1
Vernon	30	1807	76	2.52	19	6	4	1

DEFENCE: Sometimes there's only room for so many living legends. And it's often difficult to remember their status when its late in their careers.

But, Paul Coffey did a little reminding last season, tying for sixth in overall scoring, and earning his third Norris Trophy.

And, of course, his numbers do a lot of talking for him, as well.

Top 10 Defensemen All-Time Point Leaders

1. PAUL COFFEY	1,336	
2. Ray Bourque	1,253	
3. Denis Potvin	1,052	
4. Larry Robinson	958	
5. Larry Murphy	945	
6. Bobby Orr	915	
7. Brad Park	896	
8. Phil Housley	882	
9. Al MacInnis	850	
10. Doug Wilson	827	

Top 10 All-Time Point Leaders

1. Wayne Gretzky	2,506
2. Gordie Howe	1,850
3. Marcel Dionne	1,771
4. Phil Esposito	1,590
5. Stan Mikita	1,467
6. Bryan Trottier	1,425
7. Mark Messier	1,379
8. John Bucyk	1,369
9. Guy Lafleur	1,369
10. PAUL COFFEY	1,336

Top 10 All-Time Playoff Point Leaders

1. Wayne Gretzky	346
2. Mark Messier	272
3. Jari Kurri	222
4. Glenn Anderson	209
5. Bryan Trottier	184
6. Jean Beliveau	176
7. PAUL COFFEY	172
*also top ranked defenseman	
8. Denis Savard	170
9. Denis Potvin	164
10. Mike Bossy	160
Gordie Howe	160
Bobby Smith	160

Coffey and Nicklas Lidstrom take care of the offence for the Wings, and they've got plenty of veteran types to take care of the defensive part.

But, it's not a young defense and it's not a very physical one, either.

Mark Howe and Mike Ramsey are so ancient, it's illegal for us to print their ages. At press time, they were still in the fold, but neither will play a full schedule if they play at all.

Vladimir Konstantinov and veteran Bob Rouse are other regulars. Viacheslav Fetisov was obtained late last season and made a nice contribution, but he's an old-timer as well, and a free agent to boot.

Terry Carkner is still around and provides a back-up measure of toughness and size, but it's not enough.

There is some size on the prospect list, however. Anders Ericksson (6-3, 218), Jamie Pushor (6-3, 205) and Aaron Ward (6-2, 200) will give the veterans a run for their jobs.

Who the Wings would really like (and you can say the same for any team in the league) is a Scott Stevens.

Give them Scott Stevens and give them the Stanley Cup.

FORWARD: Easily the best one-two-three centre punch in the league with Sergei Fedorov, Steve Yzerman and Keith Primeau. They've got an oustanding sniper in Ray Sheppard; good youthful talent in Slava Kozlov, Martin Lapointe, Kris Draper and Greg Johnson; the ever-present Dino Ciccarelli; toughness in Darren McCarty, Stu Grimson and Shawn Burr; defensive forwards in Bob Errey and Doug Brown; and they have Mike Krushelnyski, whatever he does.

Pretty much everything they need, and more.

The "more" was a committment to an overall type game, meaning they came behind their blueline more than once in a while, and not everyone went too far behind the other team's.

It worked well, because they didn't sacrifice their offense (they were only five goals behind league leading Quebec) and they improved tremendously on defense. The best thing about it was even the stars, such as Yzerman, bought into the system. (This despite a 15 game streak without scoring a goal, the longest of Yzerman's career.)

The difference between last year and the year before, however, is that his only value to the team wasn't with his offense. If he wasn't scoring goals, he was at least helping prevent them.

Fedorov was still preventing goals, and still scoring, but there was a difference in him last season. Questions started to arise about his attitude – his level of committment and level of selfishness. Not too many questions in the playoffs, though, and that's where it counts.

Keith Primeau is the third centre – or left winger, or centre, or left winger. Depends on the month. He prefers centre to left wing and seems better suited there, although it wasn't long ago we were saying he was better suited to left wing. Who knows, maybe right wing is the place he oughta be.

Right wing is in pretty good hands in Detroit. Ray Sheppard doesn't look like he's doing much until you look at the scoresheet. He was third in the league with 32 goals (behind Peter Bondra and Jaromir Jagr) and was on pace for his second consecutive 50 goal season.

Dino Ciccarelli is 35 years old, but refuses to go out to pasture. Bowman has even tried benching him on occasion to give him the hint, but all that does is make him play that much harder when he comes back. There have been all kinds of rumors about him heading down to Florida to finish his career.

With tough guy Darren McCarty and handy defensive specialist Doug Brown also on right wing, and with the rest of the talent on this team, it makes it tough for Martin Lapointe to get quality playing time.

Lapointe, who spent the lockout in Adirondack, was tearing up that league with his goal scoring. He's a character-type who's probably going to be an extremely valuable player when he gets the opportunity.

On the left side is Kozlov, Errey, Burr, Grimson and Krushelnyski.

You wouldn't want to do much with this group except tinker a bit and make another run at the Stanley Cup.

SPECIAL TEAMS: The Red Wings had the best special team units in the league last season, finishing second on the power play and in penalty killing.

There's just too much offensive talent for the power play not to remain on top, and just too much defensive talent for the penalty killing not to remain on top as well.

Power Play	G	ATT	PCT
Overall	52	215	24.2% (T-2nd NHL)
Home	32	119	26.9% (1st NHL)
Road	20	96	20.8% (5th NHL)

7 SHORT HANDED GOALS ALLOWED (T-18th NHL)

Penalty Killing	G	TSH	PCT
Overall	28	206	86.4% (2nd NHL)
Home	16	104	84.6% (8th NHL)
Road	12	102	88.2% (1st NHL)

5 SHORT HANDED GOALS SCORED (T-13th NHL)

Penalties	GP	MIN	AVG
RED WINGS	48	932	19.4 (14th NHL)

RED WINGS SPECIAL TEAMS SCORING

Power play	G	A	PTS
COFFEY	4	27	31
YZERMAN	4	15	19
CICCARELLI	6	11	17
FEDOROV	7	9	16
SHEPPARD	11	2	13
KOZLOV	5	7	12
LIDSTROM	7	4	11
PRIMEAU	1	8	9

Short handed	G	A	PTS
FEDOROV	3	0	3
BROWN	1	1	2

COACHING AND MANAGEMENT: You sometimes get the impression Scotty Bowman has gone off the deep end, but who the heck ever said successful coaches have to be normal guys. All they have to do is win, and he has no problem doing that.

Guess how many losing seasons he's had in 23 years with five different teams?

None. Well, one if you count the 12 games he coached Buffalo in 1986-87.

Only Al Arbour has coached more games, but Bowman could catch him this year. If he remains as coach, that is. Before last season started, he vowed that it would be his last no matter what. Don't bet on it.

ALL-TIME GAMES COACHED

1. Al Arbour	1,606	
2. Scotty Bowman	1,572	
3. Dick Irvin	1,437	
4. Billy Reay	1,102	
5. Jack Adams	982	
6. Sid Abel	963	
7. Punch Imlach	959	
8. Bryan Murray	916	
9. Toe Blake	914	
10. Bob Berry	860	

DRAFT

1995 DRAFT SELECTIONS

Round	Sel.	Player	Pos	Amateur Team
1	26	Maxim Kuznetsov	D	Russia
2	52	Phillippe Audet	LW	Granby (QMJHL)
3	58	Darryl Laplante	C	Moose Jaw (WHL)
4	104	Anatoly Ustagov	LW	Russia
5	125	Chad Wilchynski	D	Regina (WHL)
5	126	David Aresenault	G	Drummondville (QMJHL)
6	156	Tyler Perry	C	Seattle (WHL)
7	182	Per Eklund	LW	Sweden
8	208	Andrei Samokvalov	RW	Russia
9	234	David Englblom	C	Sweden

Kuznetsov is a big, rough Russian who was ranked 21st by he CSB for Europeans. He's considered a questionable prospect. Perhaps the Red Wings, with so much talent, can afford to waste a pick, or take a chance on one. After all, Sergei Fedorov was selected 74th overall in the 1989 draft.

PROGNOSIS: They're so close they won't let it get away from them without a fight. The problem is St. Louis and Vancouver have improved, and Quebec has moved to Colorado and the Western Conference. Making it to the Stanley Cup finals is going to be difficult.

They could use some bigger, tougher guys on defense and the goaltending situation has to be cleared up, but they'll be there. One of the problems facing Stanley Cup winners and finalists the next year is getting motivated for so many meaningless regular season encounters. Bowman has never had much time for unmotivated players, however, so expect to see the Wings among the top three or four teams in the league – during the regular season.

Last year's Stanley Cup finals will be weighing heavily on their minds, come play-off time, so that may be enough motivation when the games start to count for real.

PREDICTION:
Central Division: 2nd
Western Conference: 2nd
Overall: 2nd

STAT SECTION

Team Rankings 1994/95

		Conference Rank	League Rank
Record	33-11-4	1	1
Home	17-4-3	1	3
Away	16-7-1	1	1
Team Plus\Minus	+39	1	1
Goals For	180	1	3
Goals Against	117	2	2

MISCELLANEOUS STATS

One Goal Games	7-7
Times outshooting opponent	36
Times outshot	12
Even shots	0
Overtime	0-0-4
Average Shots For	32.7
Average Shots Against	25.1
Longest Winning streak	6
Longest Undefeated streak	11
Longest Losing streak	2
Longest winless streak	2
Versus Teams .500 or over	14-7-1
Versus Teams Under .500	19-4-3

First Half Record   16-6-2
Second Half Record 17-5-2

PLAYOFFS

Results: Defeated Dallas 4-1, defeated San Jose 4-0, defeated Chicago 4-1, lost in finals to New Jersey 4-0.
Record: 12-6-0 Home: 8-2-0 Away: 4-4-0
Goals For: 61 (3.4/game)
Goals Against: 44 (2.4/game)
Overtime: 3-0
Power play: 24.7 (3rd)
Penalty Killing: 82.1% (8th)

Playoff Scoring

PLAYER	GP	G	A	PTS
SERGEI FEDOROV	17	7	17	24
PAUL COFFEY	18	6	12	18
VYACHESLAV KOZLOV	18	9	7	16
NICKLAS LIDSTROM	18	4	12	16
STEVE YZERMAN	15	4	8	12
DOUG BROWN	18	4	8	12
DINO CICCARELLI	16	9	2	11
KEITH PRIMEAU	17	4	5	9
VIACHESLAV FETISOV	18	0	8	8
RAY SHEPPARD	17	4	3	7
BOB ERREY	18	1	5	6
KRIS DRAPER	18	4	1	5
DARREN MCCARTY	18	3	2	5
BOB ROUSE	18	0	3	3
VLAD. KONSTANTINOV	18	1	1	2
SHAWN BURR	16	0	2	2
STU GRIMSON	11	1	0	1
MARTIN LAPOINTE	2	0	1	1
TIM TAYLOR	6	0	1	1
MIKE RAMSEY	15	0	1	1
GREG JOHNSON	1	0	0	0
CHRIS OSGOOD	2	0	0	0
MARK HOWE	3	0	0	0
MIKE KRUSHELNYSKI	8	0	0	0
MIKE VERNON	18	0	0	0

PLAYERS	1994-95 OVERALL				PROJECTED 84 GAME TOTALS		
	GP	G	A	PTS	G	A	Pts
P.COFFEY	45	14	44	58	26	82	108
S.FEDOROV	42	20	30	50	40	60	100
D.CICCARELLI	42	16	27	43	32	54	86
K.PRIMEAU	45	15	27	42	28	51	79
R.SHEPPARD	43	30	10	40	59	20	79
S.YZERMAN	47	12	26	38	21	46	67
V.KOZLOV	46	13	20	33	24	37	61
N.LIDSTROM	43	10	16	26	20	31	51
D.BROWN	45	9	12	21	17	22	39
B.ERREY	43	8	13	21	16	25	41
V.FETISOV	18	3	12	15	14	56	70
S.BURR	42	6	8	14	12	16	28
V.KONSTANTINOV	47	3	11	14	5	20	25
D.MCCARTY	31	5	8	13	14	22	36
M.LAPOINTE	39	4	6	10	9	13	22
G.JOHNSON	22	3	5	8	11	19	30
K.DRAPER	36	2	6	8	5	14	19
B.ROUSE	48	1	7	8	2	12	14
M.HOWE	18	1	5	6	5	23	28
M.KRUSHELNYSKI	20	2	3	5	8	13	21
*T.TAYLOR	22	0	4	4	0	15	15
T.CARKNER	20	1	2	3	4	8	12
M.RAMSEY	33	1	2	3	3	5	8
*A.WARD	1	0	1	1	0	84	84
M.FERNER	17	0	1	1	0	5	5
S.GRIMSON	42	0	1	1	0	2	2
A.MCKIM	2	0	0	0	0	0	0

ALL-TIME RANKINGS - INDIVIDUAL

Goals
Gordie Howe	786
Steve Yzerman	481
Alex Delvecchio	456

Assists
Gordie Howe	1,023
Alex Delvecchio	825
Steve Yzerman	679

Points
Gordie Howe	1,809
Alex Delvecchio	1,281
Steve Yzerman	1,160

BEST INDIVIDUAL SEASONS

Goals
Steve Yzerman	1988-89	65
Steve Yzerman	1989-90	62
Steve Yzerman	1992-93	58

Assists
Steve Yzerman	1988-89	90
Steve Yzerman	1992-93	79
Marcel Dionne	1974-75	74

Points
Steve Yzerman	1988-89	155
Steve Yzerman	1992-93	137
Steve Yzerman	1989-90	127

Edmonton Oilers

When last season was finally ready to get underway I wrote in *The Hockey News* something about Edmonton challenging Ottawa for last overall in the NHL.

An Edmonton radio station, with a panel that included Dave Semenko (he didn't scare me) took me to task, and even went so far as to suggest the Oilers would make the playoffs. I said they didn't have a chance.

See guys, you bunch of homers, I was right. The Oilers missed the playoffs by, uh, a full four points.

Mind you, they were still 22 of 26 overall, so they weren't far out of last, either.

This year they would have made the playoffs if Quebec hadn't moved to Colorado, and into their division.

The Oilers have an exciting team. At least in terms of potential, where they are loaded with some of the best young forwards in the league.

I wouldn't mind being an Edmonton fan right now, except for one thing – I know that the Oilers can't afford their youngsters to get too good. In terms of salaries, that is.

That, of course, is sad, but you won't find me among those who think the small market teams should just die off. It's not that I'm entirely sure they shouldn't, just that I don't want them to.

We're all sick of labor disputes in sports. And fans have grown increasingly restless about players making exhorbitant amounts of money who still find something to complain about. After all, it's the fans who pay the freight, and it's come to the point where many can no longer afford it.

I watched, listened, and read carefully while the labor dispute was on, and became increasingly intrigued with the media coverage. For the most part it was objective and the reports just spouted out the propoganda of the day.

From what I can figure, Joe Fan doesn't ever want to side with the owners, but didn't want to side with the players this time either. It had reached the point where enough was enough, and relating with the players had reached an impossible state.

To be perfectly honest, I don't care how much money the players make as a group, and I don't pay any attention to their individual salaries. I do find it distasteful when a player who has signed a contract that was perfectly good at the time, decides to holdout for renegotiation after he puts up some better numbers. I don't see any of them agreeing to renegotiate the contract downwards when they have an off year. And I don't like the overall good of the game being threatened just so that more money can be made by either side.

At any rate, the best thing about last year's labor dispute was that by playoff time all was almost forgotten, and the Stanley Cup victory by the New Jersey Devils didn't seem tainted in the least.

TEAM PREVIEW

GOAL: During the summer, St. Louis signed Shayne Corson to an offer sheet and then the two teams worked out their own compensation with Curtis Joseph going to Edmonton along with forward Mike Grier.

Both Joseph and Bill Ranford won't fit in the Oiler net, so expect one of them, probably Joseph, to be traded. Or the Oilers can just let free agent Ranford sign with another team and collect the compensation.

Only Ed Belfour has played more games than Ranford over the last five years (see chart below). While the statistics of a goalie on a weak team don't measure up to the others, Ranford is certainly one of the best in the game. There's no way to tell how many games he's won just on his own, but it's lots, and maybe a higher percentage than any other goalie.

Fred Braithwaite is the backup, but it's difficult to tell how good he is because he doesn't play very much. He wasn't drafted by an NHL team, and is just two years removed from junior hockey. Whether or not his apprenticeship is best served by being a rarely used backup is questionable, but the Oilers already have two youngsters who took their lumps with a weak team in Cape Breton, and sported the league's worst goals against average. Steve Passmore, hampered by a mysterious cramping ailment, and Joaquin Gage. Both were first year pros.

Most NHL Games Last Five Years

Ed Belfour	309
Bill Ranford	305
Patrick Roy	288

Tim Cheveldae	278
Mike Vernon	259
Kelly Hrudey	256
Andy Moog	254
Kirk McLean	252

	GP	MIN	GA	AVG	W	L	T	SO
Ranford	40	2203	133	3.62	15	20	3	2
Brathwaite	14	601	40	3.99	2	5	1	0
Gage	2	99	7	4.24	0	2	0	0

DEFENCE: Luke Richardson is the only Oiler regular defenseman who's been with the team for longer than two and a half seasons, and don't be surprised if you can say the same thing next year, and the year after that.

The Oilers used 12 defensemen last year and 15 the year before that. They'll no doubt hit double figures again this year.

Richardson is the one in the group you'd like most to stay home. He's solid, dependable, and one of the best open-ice hitters in the league.

Sather likes his Europeans and they're pretty much interchangable – castoffs from other teams who don't stick around long, and invariably get attached to the power play. Last year, he had Boris Mironov, Igor Kravchuk, Jiri Slegr and Fredrik Olausson.

Kravchuk is the top power play point man from that group, although Olausson used to be when he was with Winnipeg. He had two season highs of 72 points, as well as a couple in the 50-point range. He even had a 20 goal season. Last year, however, he had no goals and just 10 assists. After 26 games, he had just 3 points but came on stronger at the end with five points in his last seven games.

Nick Stadjuhar is projected as the offensive future for the Oilers and should get a shot to stick this year. He had 38 points in 54 game for Cape Breton last year, but needs to improve defensively.

Bryan Marchment is the most valuable Oiler rearguard, at least in terms of trade value, and it's somewhat of a surprise that Sather held onto him last season. Tough, mean and dirty, he's just the kind of guy teams hate to play against, but would love to have on their side. Marchment is on the frequent-suspended list and missed six games last year as payment for dirty deeds.

Other dependable stay-at-home include Ken Sutton and Dean Kennedy. With such a young forward unit, more of this type is needed instead of the guys that want to join the party in the other team's end.

Ryan McGill is another defensive defenseman who earned playing time last year after being obtained from Philadelphia, but he suffered a detached retina after taking a puck in the eye, and it's not known if and when he can recover from that.

It could be that Sather is settling into more of a stable lineup now that they're improving, but don't bet on it quite yet. By the end of the season, there will likely be a lot of different faces patrolling the Oiler blueline.

FORWARD: The Oilers have a bit of a problem at this position – they have so much young talent they don't have room for it all. That's a dilemma they haven't experienced for quite a while.

Last season, the Oilers led the league with most goals scored by rookies, and the year before they led the league in most games played by rookies.

Most Goals by Rookies - 1994/95

Edmonton	43
Anaheim	35
St. Louis	32
Quebec	26
Montreal	23
Boston	21
San Jose	21
Dallas	18
Los Angeles	17
Ottawa	17
Tampa Bay	15
Vancouver	14
Chicago	13
New Jersey	13
NY Islanders	13
Washington	11
Hartford	9
Philadelphia	7
Pittsburgh	6
Buffalo	4
NY Rangers	3
Toronto	2
Winnipeg	2
Calgary	1
Detroit	1
Florida	1

David Oliver led Edmonton rookies with 16 goals, and while you didn't hear about him too much last year, he was right up there among the top rookies in various scoring categories. He was tied for second with his 16 goals, first in power play goals (10), first in power play points (16), and third overall in total points (30). He has a knack for getting the garbage goals, which makes him a natural on the power play. Don't underestimate that skill, a lot of guys have made careers of picking up the garbage.

Todd Marchant wasn't too far behind Oliver in terms of production. He was tied for fourth in the league with 27 points, sixth in goal scoring (13), and tied for first in short-handed goals and short-handed points (2).

This year's rookie forward crop could be even better. Mats Lindgren has been projected in some quarters as a big scorer. He joined the Oilers from Sweden, but couldn't play after it was determined he had a slightly cracked disc in his lower back. He is a first round pick of Winnipeg's in the 1993 draft and came to Edmonton in a trade that saw Dave Manson go the other way. Lindgren is a center, just like all the rest of the Oiler forwards, so he'll probably end up on the wing.

Jason Bonsignore is a big center who will almost certainly be with the team this year. The Oilers obtained the Jets' first round draft pick in the Manson deal and selected Bonsignore fourth overall in the 1994 draft. He seems to have oodles of ability, and is a big guy at 6-4, but at times he has had problems putting it together. He got into one game with the Oilers last season and scored his first NHL goal.

Next potential top rookie candidate is Ryan Smith, a left-winger selected sixth overall by the Oilers in 1994. His had 41 goals and 45 assists for Moose Jaw in the WHL last season, in just 50 games. He's considered a character-type player.

There are others. Miroslav Satan, a left-winger, scored 24 goals in 25 games for Cape Breton. Peter White led the AHL in scoring with 105 points, Marko Tuomainen had a big season at Clarkson University, and Tyler Wright is another first round draft selection who has been up and down with the big team the last couple years.

And we're not taking into account the Oilers first round pick this season, speedy Steve Kelly, taken sixth overall.

Others on the Oiler attack units aren't that old either.

Jason Arnott, the seventh overall pick in the 1993 draft, vied for the number one center spot with Doug Weight, who is an oldster on this team at just 24. Weight, incidentally, started last season by scoring zero goals in his first 20 games. Any return to normalcy should increase his goal production considerably.

Scott Thornton, yet another first rounder,

number three overall for Toronto in 1989, started to play more up to potential last season. He's only 24. Right-winger, Kirk Maltby, played all but one game and is still only 22. Dean McAmmond (another first rounder), also just 22, missed almost the entire season when his achilles tendon was severed by a skate.

Mike Stapleton played 46 games last year, but is an unrestricted free agent.

Shayne Corson, the walking police blotter, is off to St. Louis and won't be missed much in Edmonton. He was stripped of his captaincy last season, didn't endear himself to his teammates, and certainly can't count fired coach George Burnett among his close friends.

Kelly Buchberger is valuable guy to have around for his toughness and even contributes some goals every so often. In 1991-92 he had 20 of them. Last year, Buchberger only scored seven, but he got more value out of those seven goals than anyone else in the league. Five of them were game-winners, putting him seventh in the league, only three behind leader Owen Nolan. Twice he had the game winner in consecutive games.

Zdeno Ciger is also in the mix somewhere. He was a holdout at the start of training camp last year, apparently wanting to renegotiate his contract. Later, it was learned he was tired of the NHL and just wanted to stay home. Isn't that just the type of guy you want on your team?

There's just so much prospective talent here. Mind you, not a lot of defensive talent, but it should be an interesting season seeing how the Oilers are able to fit them all in.

SPECIAL TEAMS: With a young team you expect inconsistency in this area. There's no reason to think they will get any better.

But, considering they were one of the lowest scoring teams in the league, 18th on the power play isn't too bad. Oliver's 10 goals were up among the league leaders and Doug Weight's 20 power play assists were tied for third.

Power Play	G	ATT	PCT
Overall	42	259	16.2% (18th NHL)
Home	22	138	15.9% (19th NHL)
Road	20	121	16.5% (12th NHL)

8 SHORT HANDED GOALS ALLOWED (T-21st NHL)

Penalty Killing	G	TSH	PCT
Overall	52	233	77.7% (25th NHL)
Home	25	118	78.8% (26th NHL)
Road	27	115	76.5% (T-23rd NHL)

8 SHORT HANDED GOALS SCORED (T-4th NHL)

Penalties	GP	MIN	AVG
OILERS	48	1183	24.6 (25th NHL)

OILERS SPECIAL TEAMS SCORING

Power play	G	A	PTS
WEIGHT	1	20	21
ARNOTT	7	11	18
OLIVER	10	6	16
CORSON	2	9	11
KRAVCHUK	3	5	8
STAPLETON	3	4	7
MARCHANT	3	4	7
MIRONOV	0	5	5

Short handed	G	A	PTS
BUCHBERGER	1	2	3
MARCHANT	2	0	2
MALTBY	2	0	2
RICHARDSON	1	1	2

COACHING AND MANAGEMENT: Glen Sather always looks like the cat who swallowed the mouse.

It's difficult to judge him, considering the financial contraints he's been under recently, but he put together some outstanding teams in the past, and it looks like he's going to do it again.

It won't be with George Burnett, who was fired after just 35 games last season. Speculation before last year's hiring of Burnett was that it would be a co-coach arrangement with assistant Ron Low. Neither one of them apparently liked that idea, preferring that one man be in charge. As it turned out they were both in charge, albeit at different times. Low took over the club late in the season after Burnett was fired.

The firing of Burnett came directly after he took the captaincy away from Corson. Burnett, apparently didn't have the respect of the players, and certainly not Corson's. And, he wasn't a great communicator.

The team was 12-20-3 under Burnett, and 5-7-1 with Low at the helm.

DRAFT

1995 DRAFT SELECTIONS

Round	Sel.	Player	Pos	Amateur Team
1	6	Steve Kelly	C	Prince Albert (WHL)
2	1	Georges Laraque	RW	St. Jean (QMJHL)
3	57	Zib Lukas	D	Czechoslovakia
4	83	Mike Minard	G	Chilliwack (BCJHL)
5	109	Jan Snopek	D	Oshawa (OHL)
7	161	Martin Cerven	C	Slovakia
8	187	Stephen Douglas	D	Niagara Falls (OHL)
9	213	Jiri Antonen	D	Czechoslovakia

Steve Kelly was considered by many to be the speediest player in the draft. Speed kills, but it doesn't always translate into goals. He had 31 of them with Prince Albert in the WHL last season, not a particularly high total considering it was his third year in the league.

The Oilers were successful sticking Jason Arnott immediately into the fire after he was drafted, but now with so much young talent the Oilers may choose to allow Kelly another year to develop.

PROGNOSIS: The Oilers will continue to improve and there's an outside chance they can make the playoffs. But, they're still too young and unpredictable. That means good stretches and bad stretches.

Even if the Oilers don't make the playoffs, they will be improved, and as long as they can keep the nucleus together, it won't be long before we can start talking about them as contenders.

PREDICTION:
Pacific Division: 4th
Western Conference: 9th
Overall: 16th

STAT SECTION

TEAM RANKINGS 1994/95

		Conference Rank	League Rank
Record	17-27-4	11	22
Home	11-12-1	9	19
Away	6-15-3	11	22
Team Plus\Minus	-37	12	25
Goals For	125	12	22
Goals Against	183	12	26

MISCELLANEOUS STATS

One Goal Games	6-6
Times outshooting opponent	20
Times outshot	26

Even shots	2
Overtime	1-2-4
Average Shots For	29.7
Average Shots Against	30.6
Longest Winning streak	3
Longest Undefeated streak	6
Longest Losing streak	9
Longest winless streak	10
Versus Teams .500 or over	7-18-1
Versus Teams Under .500	10-9-3
First Half Record	9-13-2
Second Half Record	8-14-2

All-Time Rankings - INDIVIDUAL

Goals

Wayne Gretzky	583
Jari Kurri	474
Glenn Anderson	413

Assists

Wayne Gretzky	1,086
Mark Messier	642
Jari Kurri	569

Points

Wayne Gretzky	1,669
Jari Kurri	1,043
Mark Messier	1,034

BEST INDIVIDUAL SEASONS

Goals

Wayne Gretzky	1981-82	92
Wayne Gretzky	1983-84	87
Wayne Gretzky	1984-85	73

Assists

Wayne Gretzky	1985-86	163
Wayne Gretzky	1984-85	135
Wayne Gretzky	1982-83	125

Points

Wayne Gretzky	1985-86	215
Wayne Gretzky	1981-82	212
Wayne Gretzky	1984-85	208

PLAYERS	1994-95 OVERALL				PROJECTED OVER 84 GAMES		
	GP	G	A	PTS	G	A	Pts
D.WEIGHT	48	7	33	40	12	58	70
J.ARNOTT	42	15	22	37	30	44	74
S.CORSON	48	12	24	36	21	42	63
*D.OLIVER	44	16	14	30	31	27	58
*T.MARCHANT	45	13	14	27	24	26	50
K.BUCHBERGER	48	7	17	24	12	30	42
S.THORNTON	47	10	12	22	18	21	39
I.KRAVCHUK	36	7	11	18	16	26	42
M.STAPLETON	46	6	11	17	11	20	31
L.RICHARDSON	46	3	10	13	5	18	23
J.SLEGR	31	2	10	12	5	27	32
K.MALTBY	47	8	3	11	14	5	19
D.KENNEDY	40	2	8	10	4	17	21
F.OLAUSSON	33	0	10	10	0	25	25
B.MIRONOV	29	1	7	8	3	20	23
K.SUTTON	24	4	3	7	14	11	25
*P.WHITE	9	2	4	6	19	37	56
B.MARCHMENT	40	1	5	6	2	11	13
Z.CIGER	5	2	2	4	33	33	66
I.FRASER	13	3	0	3	19	0	19
L.DEBRUSK	34	2	0	2	5	0	5
G.MARK	18	0	2	2	0	9	9
*J.BONSIGNORE	1	1	0	1	84	0	84
K.NILSSON	6	1	0	1	14	0	14
T.WRIGHT	6	1	0	1	14	0	14
*R.INTRANUOVO	1	0	1	1	0	84	84
M.AIVAZOFF	21	0	1	1	0	4	4
*D.BONVIE	2	0	0	0	0	0	0
*R.SMYTH	3	0	0	0	0	0	0
*M.TUOMAINEN	4	0	0	0	0	0	0
D.MCAMMOND	6	0	0	0	0	0	0
R.MCGILL	20	0	0	0	0	0	0

Los Angeles Kings

There was as much action off the ice as on it in Los Angeles last year. Maybe more.

The mess was substantial in both cases.

If you're looking for a bright spot, it could be new coach Larry Robinson. He wasn't even considered an option for the cash-strapped Kings, and was quoted himself as saying he wanted no part of the situation there.

It was funny watching the coaching derby over the summer. Robinson was rumored to be up for every one of the openings. As each team hired someone else, he became even more of a favorite for the next one. Finally, with only Los Angeles left, everyone pretty much conceded he wouldn't be coaching in the NHL this year.

So much for rumors.

Now, he needs a miracle. If it was a challenge he was looking for, he certainly found one.

GM Sam McMaster won't be much help. Virtually all of his deals have been questionable, and one of them borders on the insane.

Maybe if you're an Kings fan you could live with trading Luc Robitaille, a 60 goal scorer and four time 100 point man who wasn't very old, to Pittsburgh for Rick Tocchet, a guy with major injury problems.

Maybe you could live with him trading Mike Donnelly, a regular left winger and two-time 29 goal scorer, for a fourth round draft pick.

Maybe you could live with them giving up Alexei Zhitnik, a hot young defenseman, as part of a deal for Grant Fuhr, a washed up former star goalie they didn't need anyway.

Maybe.

But trading the Kings number one draft pick next year and a fourth rounder to Washington for 12 goal scorer Dimitri Khristich and Byron Dafoe is entirely too ridiculous.

That draft pick could very well be number one overall.

I bet Washington GM David Poile had to keep pinching himself to make sure he wasn't dreaming.

Long ago, the Kings used to regularly hand their number one picks over to Montreal for questionable talent. In fact, they've distributed those picks out like candy to anyone with their hands open.

And after all this time, and all that history, they still haven't learned.

The following chart lists the players chosen by teams in first round draft picks obtained from Los Angeles.

1969	Dick Redmond
1970	Reg Leach
1971	Ron Jones
1972	Steve Shutt
1973	Andre Savard
1974	Mario Tremblay

1975 - Pierre Mondou
1976 - Rod Schutt
1977 - Ron Duguay
1978 - Danny Geoffrian
1979 - RAY BOURQUE
1980 - none
1981 - Gilbert Delorme
1982 - SCOTT STEVENS
1983 - John MacLean
1984 - Ed Olczyk
1985 - none
1986 - none
1987 - Dave Archibald
1988 - none
1989 - Jason Miller
1990 - none
1991 - Martin Rucinsky
1992 - Jason Bowen
1993 - Nick Stadjuhar
1994 - none
1995 - none
1996 - ?

Quite an impressive list. I went back and checked the transactions that led to giving up the above picks. Some of them are pretty convoluted deals, but be assured most of the trades were ridiculous. For example, the spot where they might have taken Ray Bourque was given up so the Kings could obtain Ron Grahame. And Jerry Korab was obtained in the spot Scott Stevens was selected.

Larry Robinson is going to make the team more of a contender on the ice, but can he contend with a front office with a rich history of ineptitute?

TEAM PREVIEW

GOAL: After years of being a number one goalie, maybe Kelly Hrudey has finally proven that he is, in fact, a number one goalie. He had a great season for the Kings.

Oh, he wasn't anywhere near the league goals against leaders. The Kings finished twenty-third in the league, but he was up there with the save percentage leaders and he managed to post a winning 14-13 record for the Kings. The other goalies were a combined 1-10.

Hrudey also found something else he was good at. After the season he became a television commentator and did a great job. We make allowances for a lot of athletes who take to the airwaves, but none needed for Hrudey. He was articulate, intelligent, and had a definite stage presence.

The Kings went out and got Grant Fuhr last season thinking he would help them in the stretch drive and playoffs. He was a disaster and if the Kings had done their homework or scouting they would have known.

Let's face it, the guy was probably one of the best playoff goaltenders in the history of the NHL. But the keyword there is WAS. He's not any longer and hasn't been for a while. He's not that old for a netminder at age 33, but he was always a reflex goaltender as opposed to a technical one. The reflexes aren't what they used to be.

And get this, he finished last in the league among goaltenders with at least 540 minutes played.

He signed during the off-season with St. Louis, which makes you wonder what's going on in Keenan's head.

The Kings obtained goalie Byron Dafoe in the Khristich deal. He's kicked around the Washington organization for a number of years.

And, of course they have Jamie Storr, their superstar in waiting, the seventh selection overall in the 1994 draft. He probably won't have to wait long. He should be with the Kings this year, but will have a tough time living up to expectations, especially with the current edition of the Kings.

Defense was a foreign word in the Kings vocabulary last season. The following shows the average number of shots per game each team surrendered last year.

Los Angeles	34.8
Anaheim	33.0
Pittsburgh	32.9
Ottawa	32.5
Winnipeg	32.2
Montreal	31.9
Toronto	31.9
San Jose	31.6
Hartford	30.7
Edmonton	30.6
Buffalo	30.4
Quebec	30.3
NY Islanders	30.2
Vancouver	29.6
Calgary	29.3
Dallas	28.9
Florida	28.5
St. Louis	28.3
Tampa Bay	27.6
Philadelphia	26.9
NY Rangers	26.3
New Jersey	25.4
Detroit	25.1
Chicago	24.9
Washington	24.8
Boston	24.3

	GP	MIN	GA	AVG	W	L	T	SO
Jaks	1	40	2	3.00	0	0	0	0
Hrudey	35	1894	99	3.14	14	13	5	0
Storr	5	263	17	3.88	1	3	1	0
Fuhr	14	698	47	4.04	1	7	3	0
Stauber	1	16	2	7.50	0	0	0	0

DEFENCE: It makes a lot of sense to have a group of young, offensive defensemen, and then go hire a coach who's going to concentrate on defense.

But, you wouldn't expect much different in Los Angeles these days.

Their first draft selection, third overall, Aki-Petteri Berg, is another offensive minded defenseman who is supposed to hit like Scott Stevens and skate like Paul Coffey. We'll see.

Rob Blake, touted a couple years ago as a future Norris Trophy winner, is being touted this season as a possible Comeback Player of the Year winner. He's coming off a poor season, but should be able to bounce back.

Darryl Sydor is another offensive force who has improved his point production each year.

Chris Snell is a minor league scoring dynamo, earning 96 points in St. John's for the Toronto organization two years ago. Rob Cowie, same thing with Springfield in the Hartford organization, 74 points two years ago.

Michel Petit was third in Kings defensemen scoring last season, and Marty McSorley was second. Philippe Boucher, obtained from Buffalo, is also an offensive-minded defenseman.

Fortunately, they also obtained Denis Tsygurov in the Buffalo deal, and he scored zero points in 25 games.

It would be possible for the defense to outscore the forwards if you could put them all out on the ice at the same time and on the power play.

Kings defensemen watched their goaltenders face more shots than any other team in the league, but it's all going to be different now. Yes, indeed.

This group of offensive-minded defensemen are going to play defense (wink, wink) under new coach Robinson.

Stay-at-home defensemen? Who needs them.

FORWARD: There isn't much more time for viewing of perhaps the greatest hockey player in the history of the game, so get your tickets early.

Wayne Gretzky will turn 35 years old this season and is showing signs of wear and tear. He finished 19th in the league this season in scoring, still good but he can't play forever.

It's sad that he has to play on this team to finish out his career. Why don't the Kings do him a favor and ship him off to a respectable team. St. Louis, apparently, had some interest. Don't let his last left winger be Eric Lacroix.

At the same time they can send Jari Kurri and Rick Tocchet. All three deserve better. Especially at their ages. Kurri is 35 and Tocchet is 31.

Take away those three players and what you have left is a mediocre American Hockey League lineup.

Everybody wants off a sinking ship. Take troubled Dan Quinn, not the most eligible of free agents last season. Los Angeles took a chance on him, though, and he did a decent job.

Quinn repaid the gesture by signing with Ottawa this year again, a team that didn't want him anymore last year. Curiously, one of the reasons Quinn gave for his exit was the unsettled situation in Los Angeles.

Tony Granato is still a decent commodity and made a comeback of sorts from a dismal previous season.

John Druce had a decent season with 15 goals and Eric Lacroix a good rookie season with nine goals.

And, of course, there's Dimitri Khristich, obtained from Washington. He scored 12 goals and had 14 assists last season, fifth best on the Capitals. The previous year he was 29-29-58. He could play the left side on Gretzky's line and prove to be of value, but so could a lot of guys and you don't have to give up a first round pick to get him.

One good prospect is right winger Kevin Brown who is supposed to be a power forward. But, he's not an overwhelming scorer and not a big penalty man. He played 23 games with the Kings last season scoring twice and adding three assists.

Jeff Shavalier, a left winger, was 31-39-70 with Phoenix last season, his first as a pro. Swede Daniel Rydmark is supposed to get a shot as well.

Matt Johnson will be the enforcer if he can get in the lineup. He only got into 14 games last year but still led the team with 104 penalty minutes. Given the chance he could be the heavyweight champion of the league.

The rest are retreads, never-has-beens and never-will-be's. A bunch of them are free agents or weren't offered contracts. Just shuffle the deck and see who comes out on top.

SPECIAL TEAMS: The power play can be better with all the offensive defensemen and Wayne Gretzky in the middle. But, they had pretty much the same people last year so it will probably remain mediocre.

The penalty killing was mediocre as well. You might expect that to improve under Robinson.

Power Play	G	ATT	PCT
Overall	35	200	17.5% (13th NHL)
Home	21	112	18.8% (13th NHL)
Road	14	88	15.9% (14th NHL)

8 SHORT HANDED GOALS ALLOWED (T-21st NHL)

Penalty Killing	G	TSH	PCT
Overall	42	221	81.0% (17th NHL)
Home	19	109	82.6% (T-16th NHL)
Road	23	112	79.5% (18th NHL)

5 SHORT HANDED GOALS SCORED (T-13th NHL)

Penalties	GP	MIN	AVG
KINGS	48	978	20.4 (15th NHL)

Top Scorers

KINGS SPECIAL TEAMS SCORING

Power play	G	A	PTS
GRETZKY	3	19	22
KURRI	2	13	15
TOCCHET	7	5	12
McSORLEY	1	6	7
BLAKE	4	2	6
QUINN	2	4	6
BURRIDGE	2	3	5

Short handed	G	A	PTS
McSORLEY	0	3	3
GRETZKY	0	3	3
SNELL	2	0	2
CONACHER	1	1	2

COACHING AND MANAGEMENT: Rogie Vachon took over as interim coach after Barry Melrose was fired, a few weeks into a slump, and a few weeks after Sam McMaster said nobody's job was in danger.

Who knows about Melrose. He took the team to the Stanley Cup finals and raised expectations for a mediocre team. They couldn't live up to them. And the team made a bundle of bad trades during his reign as coach. Before McMaster took over, Paul Coffey and Tomas Sandstrom were shipped out in deals they'd like to have back.

As for McMaster, about the only smart thing he's done is hire Larry Robinson. Once the ownership situation gets settled and people have an idea what's going on, McMaster will probably be fired. He probably has some inkling of that because he's not doing anything to build a team for the future by giving up a first round draft pick for a middle of the road NHL player. He knows they have to start winning right away.

Robinson's chance for success is limited because of the team he has inherited. But, the good thing for him is that they can't get much worse.

DRAFT:

1995 DRAFT SELECTIONS

Round	Sel.	Player	Pos	Amateur Team
1	3	Aki-Petteri Berg	D	Finland
2	33	Donald MacLean	C	Beauport (QMJHL)
2	50	Pavel Rosa	RW	Russia
3	59	Vladimir Tsyplakov	LW	Fort Wayne (IHL)
5	118	Jason Morgan	C	Kingston (OHL)
6	137	Igor Melyakov	LW	Russia
7	157	Benoit Larose	D	Sherbrooke (QMJHL)
7	163	Juha Vuorivirta	C	Finland
9	215	Brian Stewart	D	S.S.Marie (OHL)

GM Sam McMaster said Berg was the best, young defenseman ever to come out of Europe. He's supposed to be the whole package – offence, defence, and physically imposing.

We should find out soon because it won't take much to make the Kings this year.

PROGNOSIS: The Kings can make the play-offs. But, so can Ottawa and any other team.

Will they? No.

Everything is wrong, especially if Robinson wants to try and make this team a carbon copy of the New Jersey Devils. Most of the players are offensive-minded, and they weren't even good at that.

Robinson or not, this team is going nowhere.

PREDICTION:
Pacific Division: 6th
Western Conference: 12
Overall: 23

STAT SECTION

PLAYERS	OVERALL				PROJECTED OVER 84 GAMES		
	GP	G	A	PTS	G	A	Pts
W.GRETZKY	48	11	37	48	19	65	84
R.TOCCHET	36	18	17	35	42	40	82
D.QUINN	44	14	17	31	27	32	59
J.KURRI	38	10	19	29	22	42	64
T.GRANATO	33	13	11	24	33	28	61
D.SYDOR	48	4	19	23	7	33	40
M.McSORLEY	41	3	18	21	6	37	43
J.DRUCE	43	15	5	20	29	10	39
R.BURRIDGE	40	4	15	19	8	32	40
M.PETIT	40	5	12	17	11	25	36
*E.LACROIX	45	9	7	16	17	13	30
P.CONACHER	48	7	9	16	12	16	28
R.LANG	36	4	8	12	9	19	28
R.BLAKE	24	4	7	11	14	24	38
K.TODD	33	3	8	11	8	20	28
G.SHUCHUK	22	3	6	9	11	23	34
*C.SNELL	32	2	7	9	5	18	23
R.COWIE	32	2	7	9	5	18	23
*Y.PERREAULT	26	2	5	7	6	16	22
P.BOUCHER	15	2	4	6	11	22	33
*K.BROWN	23	2	3	5	7	11	18
T.CROWDER	29	1	2	3	3	6	9
*S.O'DONNELL	15	0	2	2	0	11	11
*J.SHEVALIER	1	1	0	1	84	0	84
*M.JOHNSON	14	1	0	1	6	0	6
A.BLOMSTEN	5	0	1	1	0	17	17
D.THOMLINSON	1	0	0	0	0	0	0
T.WATTERS	1	0	0	0	0	0	0
*E.LAVIGNE	1	0	0	0	0	0	0
R.BROWN	2	0	0	0	0	0	0
*D.TSYGUROV	25	0	0	0	0	0	0

Team Rankings 1994/95

		Conference Rank	League Rank
Record	16-23-9	9	20
Home	7-11-6	12	25
Away	9-12-3	7	13
Team Plus\Minus	-25	11	24
Goals For	142	7	11
Goals Against	174	10	23

MISCELLANEOUS STATS

One Goal Games	6-3
Times outshooting opponent	17
Times outshot	30
Even shots	1
Average Shots For	30.0
Average Shots Against	34.7
Overtime	0-0-9
Longest Winning streak	3
Longest Undefeated streak	4
Longest Losing streak	5
Longest winless streak	8
Versus Teams Over .500 plus	7-13-5
Versus Teams Under .500	9-10-4
First Half Record	8-12-4
Second Half Record	8-11-5

All-Time Rankings - INDIVIDUAL
Goals

Marcel Dionne	550
Dave Taylor	431
Luc Robitaille	392

Assists

Marcel Dionne	757
Dave Taylor	638
Wayne Gretzky	606

Points

Marcel Dionne	1,307
Dave Taylor	1,069
Wayne Gretzky	837

Best Individual Seasons

Goals

Bernie Nicholls	1988-89	70
Luc Robitaille	1992-93	63
Marcel Dionne	1978-79	59

Assists

Wayne Gretzky	1990-91	122
Wayne Gretzky	1988-89	114
Wayne Gretzky	1989-90	102

Points

Wayne Gretzky	1988-89	168
Wayne Gretzky	1990-91	163
Bernie Nicholls	1988-89	150

Rocky Mountain Avalanche

The news wasn't all bad in Quebec last season.

Well, maybe it was. They're off to Denver which means for Nords fans, no news is all the news they have from now on.

That doesn't mean we can't do a season in review and a season in preview - good news, bad news style.

Good News: Their winning percentage of .677 was the best ever in Quebec.
Bad News: It was the last ever in Quebec.

Good News: Their mark of 30-13-5 was good enough for first in the Eastern Conference and the first seed in the playoffs.
Bad News: They had to face the defending Stanley Cup champions in the first round and lost.

Good News: The team got some valuable playoff experience.
Bad News: They'd be better off forgetting it.

Good News: Marc Crawford was coach of the year and Peter Forsberg was rookie-of-the year.
Bad News: Neither one can win the same award this year.

Good News: They've moved to the Western Conference which has been the easier conference in the past.

Bad News: The Western Conference is much improved this year, while the Eastern Conference is weaker.

Good News: The new COMSAT group in Denver scrapped the nickname Colorado Extreme after public disgust.
Bad News: You have to wonder about an organization that would come up with such a dumb name and think it was a good one.

Good News: The team finally settled on a nickname - the Avalanche.
Bad News: It's better than the Extreme, but only slightly.

Good News: Alexei Kovalev wasn't seriously hurt in that playoff incident that cost the Nordiques a goal and maybe a chance to win the series.
Bad News: Kovalev wasn't hurt at all, faking the injury to get a whistle, which he got.

Good News: The Nords won't have to worry about players who don't want to play for them because of the culture, high Quebec taxes and Canadian dollar.
Bad News: It's too late to get Eric Lindros back.

Good News: The power play was excellent, good enough for second in the league.
Bad News: In the playoffs the power play ranked last.

Good News: The Nords had one three-game losing streak, but otherwise didn't lose two games in a row.

Bad News: They matched their regular season three-game losing streak in the playoffs.

TEAM PREVIEW

GOAL: Fiset...Thibault...Fiset...Thibault...

Who's better?

Who cares? They're both two of the best young goaltenders in the NHL today.

Thibault is 20 years old, five years younger than Fiset. Both are former Canadian Major Junior Goaltender of the Year award winners, and both have had their ups and downs at the professional level.

Crawford seemed to go with the hot hand and stick with him for awhile. Fiset got most of the early action, playing in 15 of the first 19 games. Then Thibault played in 13 of the next 15. After that Thibault injured his shoulder and it was Fiset the rest of the way, except for a couple games by Garth Snow.

All three goalies played some in the playoffs, but none distinguished themselves.

Snow is gone, which is good, because now if he plays against the Avalanche, the headlines can read, "Snow Stops Avalanche."

If he had stuck around and played, I can only think of negative possible headlines such as, "Avalance Slides with Snow in Net."

As for Thibault and Fiset, deciding how to use them is difficult for the coach because they're both young and need work.
If Crawford sticks with the hot goalie, the other gets colder and colder.

A good strategy might be to just alternate them game to game. That's been done with success on other teams. There's no danger of them missing the playoffs anyway, so give them both lots of work and then go with the better one in the playoffs.

	GP	MIN	GA	AVG	W	L	T	SO
Thibault	18	898	35	2.34	12	2	2	1
Fiset	32	1879	87	2.78	17	10	3	2
Snow	2	119	11	5.55	1	1	0	0

DEFENCE: With so much offense from the forwards, less is needed from the defence and they can concentrate on doing the job in their own end of the rink.

Few have a reputation for doing that better than Sylvain Lefebvre. If they had a defensive defenseman award, as many have suggested, he might have won it for the last two years in a row.

In fact, because we can do pretty much whatever we want, we're going to make our own award. It's called The Hockey Annual Defensive Defenseman of the Year Award.

There's no actual trophy (yet) and no monetary award (ever) but at least the winner won't have to make a speech.

The vote has been tabulated and by a landslide, Sylvain Lefebre is this year's winner.

The rest of the Quebec defense isn't particularly distinguished, but they're young and willing. They don't have an offensive force either, with Krupp their top scorer and not a very big one at that.

You'd have a hard time coming up with a good reason why they absolutely have to have a quarterback on the point considering they were the top scoring team in the league. But, you'd think they would still like to have one.

Besides Lefebvre and Krupp, the Avalanche have their regulars from last year back in Steven Finn, Adam Foote, Curtis Leschyshyn, Craig Wolanin.

Others vying for ice-time include Janne Laukkanen, Jon Klemm and Aaron Miller.

One of the oddities of the Nords high-power offensive season was that they were outshot in total. It was only by seven for the whole year, but it's still curious.

It didn't hurt them much, though. In games that they were outshot they had a 15-7-2 record.

I don't really understand why they were outshot on the season. On many good teams they can get a lead, and force the other team to open it up. It's not unusual for winning teams to get outshot in the third period of games.

In the Nords case, they were almost even in third period shots. It was the first period where they outshot the most. It was also the period when Quebec had their fewest goals.

SHOTS BY PERIOD

	1	2	3	OT	T
NORDIQUES (30.1 avg.)	459	497	473	19	1448
Opponents (30.3 avg.)	489	481	475	10	1455

GOALS BY PERIOD

	1	2	3	OT	T
NORDIQUES	51	68	65	1	185
Opponents	41	47	46	0	134

One possible explanation could be that they got off to slow starts. But, perhaps a better one might be that their opponents went into the game knowing that they had to stop the Quebec offence with a defensive style. Often, individual game plans can work well at first when it's fresh in the players' minds, but fade in effectiveness and intensity as the game goes on.

I checked the next two highest scoring teams, Detroit and Pittsburgh, to see if they experienced any similar tendencies. Detroit was almost the exact opposite, and while Pittsburgh had some tendencies that were slightly similar, they weren't close enough.

FORWARD: It doesn't get any better than this. There isn't another team in the league that can put out four lines this good.

They've got it all - scoring, youth, size, toughness, and speed.

Best of all, they're perfectly suited to the more offensive-minded Western Conference.

Down the middle they have Joe Sakic, Peter Forsberg, Mike Ricci, Claude Lapointe and Troy Murray, a character player who was signed as a free agent over the summer.

Sakic, the team MVP, had a point in 38 of the 47 games he played, and his 62 points were good for fourth best in the league. Those points, pro-rated over 84 games would have given him his fourth 100 point season in seven NHL seasons.

Peter Forsberg got off to a slow start with only 14 points in the first half of the season but in the second half, he was just one away from the league lead. That was enough to earn him the Calder Trophy for best rookie, propelling him ahead of Washington goalie Jim Carey.

Top Second Half Scorers

Jagr	Pit.	37
Forsberg	Que.	36
Lindros	Phi.	36
Renberg	Phi.	33
Zhamnov	Wpg.	33
Recchi	Mtl.	32
Nolan	Que.	32
Francis	Pit.	32
Fleury	Cgy.	31
Coffey	Det.	30

Forsberg came to Quebec in the Eric Lindros deal, as did Mike Ricci who finished fifth on the team despite being the third line center. Ricci, however, was valuable on the power play where he had nine goals to put him in the top 10 in the league in that category.

On left wing is Wendel Clark, who gives the team character, although once again he spent time sidelined with an injury. He also slowed down considerably after a great start. He had 10 of his 12 goals in the team's first 13 games. He only had two afterward and finished off the season with zero goals in his last 13 games.

Also on the left side is tough guy Chris Simon, another one from the Lindros deal, along with Valeri Kamensky and Martin Rucinsky. Kamensky was still a free agent at press time and had been making some noise about playing in Europe. Bob Bassen, who was an important member of the Nords last year was signed as a free agent by Dallas.

On the right side is Andrei Kovalenko, Owen Nolan, Scott Young and Adam Deadmarsh. Young was also a restricted free agent.

Nolan is one of the best snipers in the game when he's not injured. His 30 goals were third most in the league and his 13 power play markers were second most.

Deadmarsh, a first round draft choice in 1993, had a decent rookie season.

Bill Huard and Paul MacDermid should also get some ice-time. Huard is a character player, which is why Ottawa gave him up.

Down on the farm is an outstanding prospect who could be ready to join the team sooner than expected. Right winger Landon Wilson was obtained in the Wendel Clark - Mats Sundin deal, and left school early to play pro. He made an impact in the short time he was with Cornwall late in the season and during the playoffs.

So what about that deal? Who wins?

Just to recap, Toronto gave Quebec Wendel Clark, Sylvain Lefebvre, Landon Wilson and their first round choice in 1994 for Mats Sundin, Garth Butcher, Todd Warriner and a first round choice in 1994.

Mats Sundin was Toronto's best player last year, Butcher was a disappointment, Warriner was terrible and the first round choice was used in another deal.

The Maple Leafs missed Lefebvre badly, and it could be argued Clark's character as well.

Clark and Lefebvre were valuable members of the Nordiques who didn't miss Sundin or Butcher in the least. But, it's Wilson who may turn out to be the big prize. He's a solid, major league power forward prospect who can make a big impact in the NHL as early as this year.

In terms of getting what they wanted and giving up what they wanted Quebec has the big edge, but Toronto is very happy with Sundin and he should star in the league for years to come.

SPECIAL TEAMS:

Power Play	G	ATT	PCT
Overall	45	186	24.2% (T-2nd NHL)
Home	23	104	22.1% (7th NHL)
Road	22	82	26.8% (1st NHL)

3 SHORT HANDED GOALS ALLOWED (T-3rd NHL)

Penalty Killing	G	TSH	PCT
Overall	38	203	81.3% (T-14th NHL)
Home	15	97	84.5% (T-9th NHL)
Road	23	106	78.3% (21st NHL)

9 SHORT HANDED GOALS SCORED (3rd NHL)

Penalties	GP	MIN	AVG
NORDIQUES	48	770	16.0 (T-5th NHL)

NORDIQUES SPECIAL TEAMS - TOP SCORERS

Power play	G	A	PTS
SAKIC	3	19	22
NOLAN	13	4	17
RICCI	9	7	16
FORSBERG	3	12	15
KAMENSKY	5	7	12
YOUNG	3	9	12
KRUPP	3	9	12
CLARK	5	3	8

Short handed	G	A	PTS
YOUNG	3	0	3
SAKIC	2	1	3
NOLAN	2	0	2
LESCHYSHYN	0	2	2

COACHING AND MANAGEMENT: Crawford won the coach of the year award so that speaks for his season. It's not unusual for a coach to do well their first year. One reason is that the previous guy usually gets fired because the team had a lousy year and because the GM thinks the team under-achieved. As well, whatever motivational techniques a coach uses are still fresh and useful in year one. Their effectiveness often fades in direct correlation to the coach's tenure.

General Manager Pierre Lacroix has done an outstanding job turning this team into a winner in such a short time. He didn't create a huge turnover, but the moves he did make were excellent.

DRAFT

1995 DRAFT SELECTIONS

Round	Sel.	Player	Pos	Amateur Team
1	25	Marc Denis	G	Chicoutimi (QMJHL)
2	51	Nic Beaudoin	LW	Detroit (OHL)
3	77	John Tripp	RW	Oshawa (OHL)
4	81	Tomi Kallio	LW	Finland
5	129	Brent Johnson	G	Owen Sound (OHL)
6	155	John Cirjak	RW	Spokane (WHL)
7	181	Dan Smith	D	UBC (CIAU)
8	207	Tomi Hirvonen	C	Finland
9	228	Chris George	RW	Sarnia (OHL)

Colorado already has two young goalies in Jocelyn Thibault and Stephane Fiset, so choosing another one with their first round pick is a curious decision.

But, who knows what will happen to those two a couple years down the road, so taking the best player available is the way to go nowadays.

Quebec League goaltenders are in vogue right now. Denis was the third from that league to go in the first round.

PROGNOSIS: This team is so talented that they could sleepwalk through the regular season. That, in fact, is a danger. The Avalanche could slide in the standings.

They played hard all last year during the regular season and then experienced the playoffs for just the second time in eight seasons. All of a sudden they realize there was something more important than winning all their regular season contests.

That might affect their regular season intensity, and their point total.

Another thing that may cause a slide is that they're playing in a new arena. Their record in the old one was 19-1-4. They won't be able to duplicate those numbers. They're playing in a building unfamiliar to them and it's going to take some time to gain that home advantage. Chicago learned that when they moved to a new arena last year,

On the plus side, there are far fewer defensive teams in the Western Conference which means there's less stopping their offensive stars.

PREDICTION:
Pacific Division: 1st
Western Conference: 3rd
Overall: 3rd

STAT SECTION

MISCELLANEOUS STATS

One Goal Games	10-5
Times outshooting opponent	23
Times outshot	24
Even shots	1
Average Shots For	30.1
Average Shots Against	30.3
Overtime	1-0-5
Longest Winning streak	7
Longest Undefeated streak	7
Longest Losing streak	3
Longest winless streak	4
Versus Teams Over .500	14-7-3
Versus Teams Under .500	16-6-2
First Half Record	16-5-3
Second Half Record	14-8-2

PLAYOFFS
Results: Lost to NY Rangers 4-2 in Conference quarter-finals
Record: 2-4 Home: 2-1 Away: 0-3
Goals For: 19 (3.2/gm)
Goals Against 25 (4.2/gm)
Overtime: 0-1
Power play: 8.0 (16th)
Penalty Killing: 75.9 (12th)

	GP	G	A	PTS
SCOTT YOUNG	6	3	3	6
BOB BASSEN	5	2	4	6
PETER FORSBERG	6	2	4	6
JOE SAKIC	6	4	1	5
OWEN NOLAN	6	2	3	5
MIKE RICCI	6	1	3	4
WENDEL CLARK	6	1	2	3
CRAIG WOLANIN	6	1	1	2
CHRIS SIMON	6	1	1	2
UWE KRUPP	5	0	2	2
SYLVAIN LEFEBVRE	6	0	2	2
VALERI KAMENSKY	2	1	0	1
JANNE LAUKKANEN	6	1	0	1
RENE CORBET	2	0	1	1
CURTIS LESCHYSHYN	3	0	1	1
STEVEN FINN	4	0	1	1
ADAM FOOTE	6	0	1	1
ANDREI KOVALENKO	6	0	1	1
ADAM DEADMARSH	6	0	1	1
BILL HUARD	1	0	0	0
GARTH SNOW	1	0	0	0
PAUL MACDERMID	3	0	0	0
JOCELYN THIBAULT	3	0	0	0
STEPHANE FISET	4	0	0	0
CLAUDE LAPOINTE	5	0	0	0

Team Rankings 1994/95

		Conference Rank	League Rank
Record	30-13-5	1	2
Home	19-1-4	1	1
Away	11-12-1	5	8
Team Plus\Minus	+44	1	2
Goals For	185	1	1
Goals Against	134	6	8

PLAYERS	OVERALL				Projected over 84 games		
	GP	G	A	PTS	G	A	Pts
J.SAKIC	47	19	43	62	34	77	111
*P.FORSBERG	47	15	35	50	27	63	90
O.NOLAN	46	30	19	49	55	35	90
S.YOUNG	48	18	21	39	32	37	69
M.RICCI	48	15	21	36	26	37	63
W.CLARK	37	12	18	30	27	41	68
V.KAMENSKY	40	10	20	30	21	42	63
B.BASSEN	47	12	15	27	21	27	48
A.KOVALENKO	45	14	10	24	26	19	45
U.KRUPP	44	6	17	23	11	32	43
*A.DEADMARSH	48	9	8	17	16	14	30
C.LESCHYSHYN	44	2	13	15	4	25	29
S.LEFEBVRE	48	2	11	13	3	19	22
C.LAPOINTE	29	4	8	12	12	23	35
C.SIMON	29	3	9	12	9	26	35
M.RUCINSKY	20	3	6	9	13	25	38
C.WOLANIN	40	3	6	9	6	13	19
A.FOOTE	35	0	7	7	0	17	17
B.HUARD	33	3	3	6	8	8	16
P.MACDERMID	14	3	1	4	18	6	24
*D.NORRIS	13	1	2	3	6	13	19
A.GUSAROV	14	1	2	3	6	12	18
*R.CORBET	8	0	3	3	0	32	32
*A.MILLER	9	0	3	3	0	28	28
*J.LAUKKANEN	11	0	3	3	0	23	23
S.FINN	40	0	3	3	0	6	6
*J.KLEMM	4	1	0	1	21	0	21

All-Time Rankings - Individual

Goals

Michel Goulet	456
Peter Stastny	380
Anton Stastny	252

Assists

Peter Stastny	668
Michel Goulet	489
Joe Sakic	391

Points

Peter Stastny	1,048
Michel Goulet	945
Anton Stastny	636

Best Individual Seasons

Goals

Michel Goulet	1982-83	57
Michel Goulet	1983-84	56
Michel Goulet	1984-85	55

Assists

Peter Stastny	1981-82	93
Peter Stastny	1985-86	81
Peter Stastny	1982-83	77

Points

Peter Stastny	1981-82	139
Peter Stastny	1982-83	124
Peter Stastny	1985-86	122

San Jose Sharks

When the NHL expands to Europe, the San Jose Sharkovs will be ready.

In fact, maybe they'll just move there themselves, they love it so much.

The team has a strange fixation with European players.

There's no proof that having a lot of them makes NHL teams into winners, although there is some evidence to the opposite.

So, what is this, some big experiment or something? We can't even say the Sharks are a group with a superior vision because we don't know that yet. They're just taking a big chance.

Consider the following chart which shows the use of Europeans by NHL teams last season.

European players on NHL teams - 1994-95

	Minimum 25 games	1-24 gms played	Total
San Jose	6	5	11
Winnipeg	7	2	9
Buffalo	5	3	8
Edmonton	4	4	8
Philadelphia	6	1	7
Vancouver	5	2	7
Ottawa	4	3	7
Quebec	4	3	7
Calgary	4	3	7
Hartford	3	4	7
New Jersey	3	4	7
NY Islanders	1	6	7
NY Rangers	5	1	6
Anaheim	5	1	6
Washington	5	1	6
Pittsburgh	4	2	6
Tampa Bay	5	0	5
Boston	4	1	5
Detroit	4	1	5
Toronto	3	2	5
St. Louis	2	3	5
Los Angeles	3	1	4
Florida	2	2	4
Montreal	2	2	4
Chicago	1	2	3
Dallas	0	1	1

(If a player was traded during the season, and at least 25 games in total, he counts as a regular with his last team - e.g. Alexei Zhitnik had 11 games with Los Angeles and 21 with Buffalo. He counts in the minimum 25 game category with Buffalo and the under 24 game category with Los Angeles.)

The Sharks expect to add more Europeans this season, and in the draft took virtually every eligible Finns.

You get the impression that the Sharks think they're rather clever. They have their unique scouting methods, special camps, interview sessions. But, what exactly have they done?

It's not as if they're a good team. They just barely made the playoffs last year and caught a break to win a round before being trounced by Detroit. And the year before they had a nice playoff run as well.

Both of those occasions aren't true indicators of the talent on this team.

Many do, however, consider them the team with the best young potential in the league.

They only have two draft selections that you can consider successes so far: Jeff Friesen, who had a good rookie year, and Sandis Ozolinsh, who tailed off a bit last season.

That's not to say, positively, that it won't all work out for them. I have my doubts, though. I think they just fall in love with their own players.

I don't think everybody recognizes the difference between skill players and winning players. They can take their video camera over to Finland and tape all these guys playing against other Finns. They look awfully good because they're usually excellent skaters and puckhandlers. But, those are only two ingredients of a successful hockey player. The qualities that determine whether a skilled player makes it or not can't be caught on tape.

The Sharks have made virtually no changes in the off-season and are just counting on waiting for the prospects to come through. If they ever do.

TEAM PREVIEW

GOAL: Two years ago, Arturs Irbe was one of the best goalies in the league. Last year, he might not have even been the best on the Sharks.

Wade Flaherty arrived via Kansas City where he had led the IHL in games played in three different seasons. He posted a better GAA, a better save percentage and a better win-loss record.

There's no doubt that when Irbe is on, he's still one of the best in the league, as evidenced by his four shutouts, one away from the most in the league.

The problem last year was that he wasn't "on" enough of the time, and not at all during the playoffs.

Still, Irbe has to be considered number one, with Flaherty the backup. Irbe has shown the talent before so the chances of him bouncing back are good.

	GP	MIN	GA	AVG	W	L	T	SO
Flaherty	18	852	44	3.10	5	6	1	1
Irbe	38	2043	111	3.26	14	19	3	4

DEFENCE: They're big and they're bad. Uh, but not bad in the vernacular, more like bad in the true sense of the word.

The top seven defencemen last year averaged 6-2, 212. Their problem is they don't use their size and they don't physically intimdate anyone.

Certainly not 6-6 220, Mike Rathje; or 6-3 205, Sandis Ozolinsh; or 6-5 225, Michal Sykora. Makes you wonder why the priority on size on the Sharks. Tom Pederson, 5-9 180, had more penalty minutes than Rathje.

Jim Kyte gives them some toughness, however, as does Shawn Cronin and Jayson More sometimes.

Vlastimir Kroupa is another big teddy bear who split his time between Kansas City and San Jose. Another who who will challenge for a job this year is Marcus Ragnarsson.

The Teddy Bear Defence. That's a good name for them.

Ozolinsh supplies the offence, the little they get from the blueline. He can give them 20 goals a season and more which is excellent for a defenceman. Not so much last year, but the season before he shone with 26 goals.

Often, high scoring defencemen get their

points on the power play. But, since San Jose doesn't have one, a high percentage of Ozolinsh's points came at even strength. That means his offensive talent isn't situational. He can do it any time. If the power play ever did start to click he would be up among the leading scorers among defencemen.

FORWARD: If they don't score, don't hit, don't intimidate and don't check, just what is it that they do?

Not much.

Rookie Jeff Friesen was a pleasant surprise, leading the team in goal scoring with 15, placing him up among the league rookie leaders. Paul Kariya, of Anaheim, led with 18. Friesen showed some flashes of brilliance at times throughout the season and might already be their best forward.

Not that it would take much. Sergei Makarov took the year off pretty much, and there's some question of whether he'll be back.

Craig Janney did okay in a Sharks uniform. He, of course, was spurned by Mike Keenan in St. Louis who doesn't like soft players. Those type are okay in San Jose, however, since that's the type they have most of anyway.

You wouldn't call Jeff Odgers soft. The captain shows a lot of heart, and while it's extremely unusual for a team to have a captain who doesn't get a lot of ice-time, he's well respected and a big fan favorite.

Andrei Nazarov is the only other forward who plays much of a physical game. He's one of the Sharks' big men, 6-6, 230, who actually uses his size.

The Sharks tried to sign free agent Joel Otto, who would have been a nice addition, but Otto appeared to have a closed-mind about playing in San Jose – he chose Philly.

Ulf Dahlen was their top point-getter with 34. Only a couple teams had a leading scorer with fewer points. Over a full season, you'd expect Janney to be on top. It's his heart that's questioned, not hs scoring ability.

Ray Whitney and Pat Falloon were junior teammates in Spokane when they were drafted by the Sharks. Falloon was taken second second overall, while Whitney was selected 23rd.

Last year Whitney outscored Falloon, who has never come close to living up to his earlier promise. Oh, every once in a while he teases a little, and people start saying it's time, but then the clock strikes twelve and he turns back into a pumpkin.

Igor Larionov turns 35 this season, but still makes a contribution.

Down the middle are Janney, Freisen, Larionov and Jamie Baker, who handles the defensive duties until they get somebody more suited to that role.

On the left side is Nazarov, Whitney, Kevin Miller and Chris Tancill. Viktor Kozlov, who has been slowed by injuries is expected to be a major contributor there, and Ville Peltonen is expected to get a shot.

Somebody might well move over to the right side which consists of Dahlen, Falloon, Odgers and maybe Makarov. Shean Donovan might get an opportunity for more playing time, as well.

More size and strength, plus a couple goal-scorers, are just two of the things the Sharks need to move up to the ranks of the mediocre.

SPECIAL TEAMS: The power play last season was second worst in the league just slightly ahead of last place Anaheim. This, on a team with many offence-only type forwards, which makes the prospects for improvement very slim. They appear to have lots of set-up men but few who can hammer it home.

Power Play	G	ATT	PCT
Overall	24	203	11.8% (25th NHL)
Home	14	114	12.3% (24th NHL)
Road	10	89	11.2% (24th NHL)

5 SHORT HANDED GOALS ALLOWED (T-11th NHL)

Penalty Killing	G	TSH	PCT
Overall	39	208	81.3% (T-14th NHL)
Home	17	96	82.3% (18th NHL)
Road	22	112	80.4% (17th NHL)

6 SHORT HANDED GOALS SCORED (T-11th NHL)

SHARKS SPECIAL TEAMS TOP SCORERS

Power play	G	A	PTS
DAHLEN	4	9	13
JANNEY	3	9	12
WHITNEY	4	4	8
FRIESEN	5	2	7
OZOLINSH	3	2	5
PEDERSON	0	5	5

Short handed	G	A	PTS
FRIESEN	1	1	2
BAKER	1	1	2
LARIONOV	0	2	2

COACHING AND MANAGEMENT: Personally, I don't think they quite get it. Vice-Presidents Chuck Grillo and Dean Lombardi run the hockey operation and could prove me wrong, but I doubt it. We won't know anyway for a couple years and by then they might change their strategy.

I suppose we could give them credit for trying something different. Unless it doesn't work.

I don't think a European team in the NHL is going to be a winner.

Kevin Constantine is considered one of the hardest working coaches in the game. He appears to set high expectations for his team, but may have gone overboard early last year.

The Sharks opened the season with a record of 5-1-1 at which time Constantine said he didn't think the team was playing as well as the record showed. So, he went a little snaky. Lines were changed, players were dressed down in practice. Some of the players went public with their complaints. After that, the Sharks went 14-23-1. Opps...

DRAFT

1995 DRAFT SELECTIONS

Round	Sel.	Player	Pos	Amateur Team
1	12	Teemo Riihjarvi	LW	Finland
2	38	Peter Roed	C	White Bear Lake (US HS)
3	64	Marko Makinen	RW	Finland
4	90	Vesa Toskala	G	Finland
5	116	Mikka Kiprusoff	G	Finland
5	130	Michal Bros	C	Czechoslovakia
6	140	Timo Hakanen	C	Finland
6	142	Jaroslav Kudrna	LW	Penticton (BCJHL)
7	167	Brad Mehalko	RW	Lethbridge (WHL)
7	168	Robert Jindrich	D	Czechoslovakia
8	194	Ryan Kraft	C	U. of Minn. (WCHA)
9	220	Miiko Markkanen	RW	Finland

Teemu Riihijarvi wasn't rated nearly as high by Central Scouting as he was selected by San Jose. But, the Sharks really liked him and didn't want to take a chance he'd still be around by the second round. He's big at 6-6, 202, can skate and likes to hit. He has at least two more years of committment in Finland.

The Sharks strategy is at least understandable in Riihijarvi's case, because other clubs had him ranked highly too. But, their second round pick is baffling. Actually, most of them are, but this one particularly so. Peter Roed was ranked 121st by Central Scouting.

Okay, the Sharks wanted him, but they could still have got him much, much later. It's rare to be that out of whack with CSB, unless there's good reason, so it was a pretty safe bet that Roed, from the hockey hotbed of White Bear Lake, would be around at a much later round. The Sharks could have got another player and still got him later.

The Sharks went big on Finns in the draft. They even got Riihijarvi's linemates. Must have had the video camera in Finland a lot this year.

Consider the draft table, which shows which country their draft selections were born. Below it shows draft selections on the roster and a percentage of draft selections between 1991 and 1994 from that country that were on the roster.

	Finland	Czech.	Russia	U.S.	Canada	Sweden
1995	6	3	0	2	1	0
1994	0	3	4	2	3	0
1993	2	1	4	1	3	2
1992	0	2	4	1	3	1
1991	0	1	2	3	6	1
Total	8	10	14	9	16	4

Roster of May 5, 1995 draft selections (1991-1994):

	0	2	2	0	4	0
Percentage	0%	14%	14%	0%	27%	0

Even though the club's only draft success so far has been with Canadian players, it appears they aren't taking them much anymore. I guess it all depends where the video camera goes. Next year, it's rumored they're going to tap the hockey talent in Lichenstein.

PROGNOSIS: The Sharks are weak at forward, weak on defence, and weak in goal. But hey, they've got great potential. Yeah, right.

The Sharks won't make the playoffs, which are more difficult to get into this year because the Quebec franchise moved to Colorado and the Western Conference.

But, they're going to lead the league in potential. And will again the following year, and the one after that, and the one after that.

And they'll be darn happy about it, too.

PREDICTION
Pacific Division: 5th
Western Conference: 11th
Overall: 22nd

STAT SECTION

Team Rankings 1994/95

		Conference Rank	League Rank
Record	19-25-4	7	18
Home	10-13-1	11	22
Away	9-12-3	6	12
Team Plus\Minus	-17	8	20
Goals For	129	11	18
Goals Against	161	8	21

MISCELLANEOUS STATS

One Goal Games	8-6
Times outshooting opponent	6
Times outshot	38
Even shots	4
Average Shots For	24.0
Average Shots Against	31.6
Overtime	1-0-4
Longest Winning streak	5
Longest Undefeated streak	6
Longest Losing streak	5
Longest winless streak	5
Versus Teams Over .500	7-16-2
Versus Teams Under .500	12-9-2
First Half Record	9-13-2
Second Half Record	10-12-2

PLAYERS	1994-95 OVERALL				Projected over 84 games			
	GP	G	A	PTS	G	A	PTS	
U.DAHLEN	46	11	23	34	20	42	62	
C.JANNEY	35	7	20	27	17	48	75	
J.FRIESEN	48	15	10	25	26	17	43	
R.WHITNEY	39	13	12	25	28	26	54	
S.OZOLINSH	48	9	16	25	16	28	44	
S.MAKAROV	43	10	14	24	20	27	47	
I.LARIONOV	33	4	20	24	10	51	61	
K.MILLER	36	8	12	20	19	28	47	
P.FALLOON	46	12	7	19	22	13	35	
T.PEDERSON	47	5	11	16	9	20	29	
C.TANCILL	26	3	11	14	10	36	46	
J.BAKER	43	7	4	11	14	8	22	
M.RATHJE	42	2	7	9	4	14	18	
A.NAZAROV	26	3	5	8	10	16	26	
J.ODGERS	48	4	3	7	7	5	12	
J.KYTE	18	2	5	7	9	23	32	
J.MORE	45	0	6	6	0	11	11	
I.BYAKIN	13	0	5	5	0	32	32	
M.SYKORA	16	0	4	4	0	21	21	
V.BUTSAYEV	6	2	0	2	28	0	28	
V.KOZLOV	16	2	0	2	11	0	11	
D.WOOD	9	1	1	2	9	9	18	
V.KROUPA	14	0	2	2	0	12	12	
S.CRONON	29	0	2	2	0	6	6	
S.DONOVAN	14	0	0	0	0	0	0	

PLAYOFFS
Results: defeated Calgary 4-3
lost to Detroit 4-0
Record: 4-7
Home: 1-4
Away: 3-3
Goals For: 32 (2.9/gm)
Goals Against 59 (5.4/gm)
Overtime: 2-0
Power play: 18.8% (8th)
Penalty Killing: 71.7 (14th)

PLAYER	GP	G	A	PTS
U. DAHLEN	11	5	4	9
I. LARIONOV	11	1	8	9
R.WHITNEY	11	4	4	8
M.RATHJE	11	5	2	7
C. JANNEY	11	3	4	7
S.MAKAROV	11	3	3	6
J.FRIESEN	11	1	5	6
S.OZOLINSH	11	3	2	5
T. PEDERSON	10	0	5	5
P.FALLOON	11	3	1	4
J. BAKER	11	2	2	4
J.MORE	11	0	4	4
C.TANCILL	11	1	1	2
J. ODGERS	11	1	1	2
J.KYTE	11	0	2	2
S. DONOVAN	7	0	1	1
K.MILLER	6	0	0	0
A.IRBE	6	0	0	0
A.NAZAROV	6	0	0	0
V.KROUPA	6	0	0	0
W. FLAHERTY	7	0	0	0
S.CRONIN	9	0	0	0

All-Time Rankings - INDIVIDUAL

Goals
Pat Falloon	73
Johan Garpenlov	45
Sandis Ozolinsh	42

Assists
Pat Falloon	86
Johan Garpenlov	85
Kelly Kisio	78

Points
Pat Falloon	159
Johan Garpenlov	130
Kelly Kisio	115

Best Individual Seasons

Goals
Sergei Makarov	1993-94	30
Sandis Ozolinsh	1993-94	26
Kelly Kisio	1992-93	26

Assists
Kelly Kisio	1992-93	52
Johan Garpenlov	1992-93	44
Todd Elik	1993-94	41

Points
Kelly Kisio	1992-93	78
Sergei Makarov	1993-94	68
Todd Elik	1993-94	66
Johan Garpenlov	1992-93	66

St. Louis Blues

If someone other than Mike Keenan made the changes he did in the off-season, you might consider many of them suspect. But it was Keenan, resident NHL genius, so even if you don't know exactly what he's doing, you can be assured HE knows what he's doing.

Let's review the changes, keeping in mind some of them were for the sake of cost-cutting measures insisted on by the St. Louis owners.

In: Dale Hawerchuk - free agent center from Buffalo.
Out: Peter Stastny - seldom used center, his contract was bought out.

In: Brian Noonan - free agent center who was with Keenan on the Stanley Cup Rangers and in Chicago.
Out: Todd Elik, center signed as a free agent with Boston.

In: Geoff Cournall - free agent left-winger from Vancouver.
Out: Tremendously popular (except with Keenan) left winger Brendan Shanahan, traded to St. Louis.

In: Grant Fuhr - free agent goalie from Los Angeles.
Out: Tremendously popular (except with Keenan) goalie Curtis Joseph traded to Edmonton.

In: Possible future star defenceman Chris Pronger.
Out: Steve Duchesne, top scoring defenceman, traded to Ottawa.

In: Free agent power forward Shayne Corson from Edmonton.
Out: Free spirit Glenn Anderson.

In: Jay Wells, defenceman from the Rangers, who was with Keenan on the Rangers.
Out: Doug Lidster, who was also with Keenan on the Rangers, back to the Rangers.

Out: Bill Houlder, offered termination contract, signed by Tampa Bay.

So, now Keenan is on his way to making the Blues his team. Keenan has only one goal in mind with his changes: to bring a Stanley Cup to St. Louis. He doesn't settle for good seasons.

Last year was a pretty good year in St. Louis, however. At least until the playoffs, when they lost to Vancouver in the opening round, four games to three.

There were a couple of excuses, though. Brendan Shanahan broke his ankle during the series, and according to Keenan, Curtis Joseph blew it for them.

During the regular season, St. Louis had a record of 28-15-5, second best in the Western

Conference and fourth in the league. Their winning percentage was the second best in club history.

Isn't it amazing what one coach can do?

Now, they have a completely revamped lineup. We'll see this year what one coach and one general manager can do with a whole different team.

The Blues were also tops in the league in team plus/minus. Maybe not so co-incidentally New Jersey led the league in that category the season before they won the Cup.

It's a telling stat, because it says, all things being equal, who the best team in the league was. Naturally, power plays and penalty killing are important, but most teams would rather be the best team at even strength. The special teams components are easier to fix.

Team Plus/Minus Records - 1994-95

	GP	GF	PGF	NET	GA	PGA	NET	+/-
STL	48	178	36	142	135	46	89	53
QUE	48	185	45	140	134	38	96	44
DET	48	180	52	128	117	28	89	39
PIT	48	181	42	139	158	46	112	27
CGY	48	163	39	124	135	37	98	26
CHI	48	156	52	104	115	36	79	25
N.J	48	136	22	114	121	28	93	21
PHI	48	150	40	110	132	37	95	15
WSH	48	136	45	91	120	34	86	5
BOS	48	150	46	104	127	24	103	1
NYR	48	139	40	99	134	34	100	1-
BUF	48	130	45	85	119	32	87	2-
VAN	48	153	47	106	148	39	109	3-
DAL	48	136	39	97	135	34	101	4-
HFD	48	127	30	97	141	37	104	7-
FLA	48	115	29	86	127	32	95	9-
NYI	48	126	28	98	158	46	112	14-
MTL	48	125	28	97	148	37	111	14-
ANA	48	125	23	102	164	47	117	15-
S.J	48	129	24	105	161	39	122	17-
T.B	48	120	25	95	144	32	112	17-
TOR	48	135	37	98	146	28	118	20-
WPG	48	157	42	115	177	40	137	22-
L.A	48	142	35	107	174	42	132	25-
EDM	48	136	42	94	183	52	131	37-
OTT	48	117	31	86	174	39	135	49-

TEAM PREVIEW

GOAL: He's just kidding. You ARE just kidding, Mike? Right?

Keenan said during the summer that he's happy with his goaltending duo of Grant Fuhr and Jon Casey. He, he, he, he...good one.

Fuhr has been washed up for years and Casey's in the same boat. Both are 33-years-old and just barely suited for backup duty anymore.

You'd think Keenan had cracked a few brain cells or something, if you didn't know he was just kidding.

Keenan, of course, is the hardest coach to please when it comes to goalies. He pulls goalies out of games faster and more often than any other coach in NHL history.

Consider the number of times he used more than one goaltender in a game last year keeping in mind St. Louis had one of the best records in the league.

ST. LOUIS	11
Anaheim	9
Winnipeg	8
Edmonton	8
San Jose	8
Los Angeles	8
New Jersey	7
Boston	6
Washington	6
NY Rangers	5
NY Islanders	5
Hartford	5
Tampa Bay	5
Ottawa	5
Calgary	4

Florida	4
Dallas	4
Quebec	4
Vancouver	3
Chicago	3
Pittsburgh	3
Buffalo	2
Philadelphia	2
Montreal	2
Detroit	1
Toronto	1

The other teams near St. Louis in times pulling the goalie, except for New Jersey, are the weaker teams in the league, the ones you would expect to change often.

Keenan already has no patience, so what's going to happen with these two. He might have to pull them every game.

But, he won't, because he was just kidding. Wasn't he?

	GP	MIN	GA	AVG	W	L	T	SO
Casey	19	872	40	2.75	7	5	4	0
Joseph	36	1914	89	2.79	20	10	1	1
Sarjeant	4	120	6	3.00	1	0	0	0

DEFENCE: The Blues defence was considered to be too soft last season, especially in the playoffs. They didn't clear the front of the net very well and opposing forwards could muscle their way around.

Non-physical types Steve Duchesne and Bill Houlder are gone, but they still haven't added much in that area. And they'll need to with the goalies they're planning to employ.

Duchesne is big-time offensive threat whose salary was dumped off on Ottawa. Houlder was an offensive-type as well, and signed with Tampa Bay as a free agent.

The top three defencemen remaining are all offensive types, so that part is covered, but none are going to intimidate anyone physically.

Al MacInnis, with the booming shot, is one of the best offensive defencemen in the league, although he didn't show it too much last year because he was injured for 16 games.

Jeff Norton won't scare anyone, but he can contribute points.

The third defenceman, Chris Pronger, is huge at 6-5, but he isn't particularly physical either. Keenan really likes Pronger, or says so because he has to. He says Pronger is going to be a star, something they got tired of saying in Hartford.

Jay Wells will be considerably more of a physical presence than Doug Lidster, although he's also 36 years old. Keenan likes him for his leadership abilities.

Murray Baron's another physical force, while other veterans battling for playing time are not - Rick Zombo and Donald Dufresne.

One rookie who could make the team is Jamie Rivers, yet another offensive defenseman. Two years ago, Rivers had an amazing 121 points for Sudbury in the OHL. Last year, he had 65 points in 46 games.

Jeff Batters and Terry Hollinger got into some games as well last year.

FORWARD: Here we go again. If this were another team besides Keenan's I wouldn't be overly impressed with this forward unit.

The first line should have Dale Hawerchuk between Geoff Courtnall and Brett Hull.

Hawerchuk is 32-years-old and has started to show it. He had some injury problems with Buffalo last year, but his projected 84 game point total from the games he played is only 58.

Courtnall's not young either, at 33, although he hasn't started to show it. He's had some good numbers in recent years.

Brett Hull is still a 50 goal scorer, so that doesn't change.

If that line becomes a reality, you'd have to consider the serious defensive deficiencies as well. But, in other ways they compliment each other very well. Courtnall has the speed, Hawerchuk the playmaking ability and Hull the goal-scoring responsibility.

The Blues do have some good depth at forward and what should be an excellent second line with Noonan, Corson and Tikkanen. Those players are winners, which is exactly why Keenan has them. They're all mid-range scorers, which is what a second line is all about, but they bring lots more to the party, including checking ability, size, and feistiness (I'd use "grit" but I hate that word).

They could do a little mixing and matching with their first two lines and may find that Corson fits better on the first unit than Courtnall.

If they keep a line they used last year, which was very effective, it would put Ian Laperriere between Keenan favorite Greg Gilbert and Denis Chasse. Laperriere and Chasse were rookies, and contributed not only with their scoring but with some good toughness.

Adam Creighton played well last year and will be a regular again this year, probably on the fourth line, but possibly as high as the second.

Basil McRae and Tony Twist are still around to fill the enforcer rolls, but there's only so much room. Still, on a team bound for the Stanley Cup, character players are valuable resources.

Others who should play, in varying degrees of time, are youngsters David Roberts, Patrice Tardif, and Craig Johnson. Maybe even Guy Carbonneau, although it appears he's not an integral part of the team anymore. He could be the designated press box sitter, the same as Stastny was last year.

The Blues fans will miss Brendan Shanahan, who was a big fan favorite. It's odd how he and Keenan didn't get along, especially considering it was supposed to be Hull and Keenan who would have conflicts.

If you're a player, and you don't get along with Keenan, you can punch your ticket goodbye. If you're a player, and you do get along with Keenan and play his style, you can punch your ticket at the same time as Keenan and be assured of going where he goes. Not to mention always being close to winning the Stanley Cup.

SPECIAL TEAMS: Apparently, Mike Keenan doesn't work much with his special teams, which could account for the poor rankings.

It's difficult to see the power play improving without Brendan Shanahan, a major league sniper, and Steve Duchesne on the point. But since they weren't that good to begin with, they probably won't get any worse. Maybe they don't need Shanahan's sniping ability anyway, with Brett Hull fully capable of handling those responsibilities. If they get the playmakers out with him and MacInnis on the point, they should be okay.

Can you imagine Brett Hull killing penalties? Well, he did, even scoring a rare goal on a 3 on 5 situation. Hull also tied for the league lead in shorthanded points. Who would have thought it?

Power Play	G	ATT	PCT
Overall	36	220	16.4% (16th NHL)
Home	20	121	16.5% (17th NHL)
Road	16	99	16.2% (13th NHL)

2 SHORT HANDED GOALS ALLOWED (T-1st NHL)

Penalty Killing	G	TSH	PCT
Overall	46	233	80.3% (21st NHL)
Home	25	120	79.2% (25th NHL)
Road	21	113	81.4% (13th NHL)

7 SHORT HANDED GOALS SCORED (T-6th NHL)

Penalties	GP	MIN	AVG
BLUES	48	1077	22.4 (19th NHL)

BLUES SPECIAL TEAMS TOP SCORERS

Power play	G	A	PTS
HULL	9	7	16
TIKKANEN	5	8	13
DUCHESNE	1	12	13
MACINNIS	2	10	12
SHANAHAN	6	5	11
ELIK	4	3	7
CREIGHTON	3	4	7
NORTON	0	6	6

Short handed	G	A	PTS
HULL	3	3	6
TIKKANEN	2	1	3
SHANAHAN	2	1	3
MACINNIS	0	1	1
DUCHESNE	0	1	1
CARBONNEAU	0	1	1
BARON	0	1	1

COACHING AND MANAGEMENT: One thing bothers me a little. Mike Keenan has been talking a lot and making a lot of moves with consideration to a budget.

He never had to worry about stuff like that when he was just a coach. He could just say gimme, gimme, gimme and not have to worry about the consequences of their salaries.

Uh, like last year. Now, he's shaping his own team, all right, but you can bet he would do things differently were he not worrying about the salaries.

Keenan, in my mind, is the best coach in the NHL. He's no great communicator, and some of his tendencies are strange to us mortals, but his results show no matter what anybody thinks, he's a winner. And that's the name of the game.

Stanley Cup final appearances since Keenan began coaching in the NHL in 1985

Mike Keenan	4
Glen Sather	3
Scotty Bowman	2
Bob Johnson	2
Jacques Lemaire	1
Pat Quinn	1
Jacques Demers	1
Barry Melrose	1
Bob Gainey	1
John Muckler	1
Mike Milbury	1
Terry Crisp	1
Pat Burns	1
Terry O'Reilly	1
Jean Perron	1

DRAFT

1995 DRAFT SELECTIONS

Round	Sel.	Player	Pos	Amateur Team
2	49	Jochen Hecht	C	Germany
3	75	Scott Roche	G	North Bay (OHL)
4	101	Michal Handzus	C	Slovakia
5	127	Jeff Ambrosio	LW	Belleville (OHL)
6	153	Denis Hamel	LW	Chicoutimi (QMJHL)
7	179	J Grand-Pierre	D	Val D'or (QJMHL)
8	205	Derek Bekar	C	Powell River (BCJHL)
9	209	Libor Zabransky	RW	Czechoslovakia

There haven't been many German players selected in the draft. Only 18 before last year. Few have ever made the grade, with the number one player being Uwe Krupp, who played in Quebec last year.

As usual, the Blues didn't get their first pick until the second round. The last time they had a first rounder was in 1989.

PROGNOSIS: I've made some pretty lofty predictions for the Blues, finishing first in everything, but I'm not totally convinced. If they don't get a real number one NHL goal-tender, I'd move them down in the standings.

There are some other worries, it's not a lock. Many of the forwards they're counting on to lead the way are in dangerous territory, age-wise. Players don't just keep on producing year after year despite their age. At some point, it doesn't work anymore.

Plus, their defence isn't all that great. Adequate might be the term used there.

The one thing you do know is that if one or more of the components aren't working, it won't be long before Keenan finds better ones that do work.

They'll be better than the lineup they currently have. Keenans says they're already better than last year. Last year I picked them to win the Stanley Cup, so I better stick with them again.

PREDICTION:
Central Division: 1st
Western Conference: 1st
Overall: 1st

STAT SECTION

Team Rankings 1994/95

		Conference Rank	League Rank
Record	28-15-5	2	4
Home	16-6-2	2	4
Away	12-9-3	3	3

Team Plus\Minus	+53	1	1
Goals For	178	2	4
Goals Against	135	3	11

MISCELLANEOUS STATS

One Goal Games	8-8
Times outshooting opponent	26
Times outshot	19
Even shots	3
Average Shots For	29.3
Average Shots Against	28.2
Overtime	1-1-5
Longest Winning streak	4
Longest Undefeated streak	7
Longest Losing streak	2
Longest winless streak	3
Versus Teams Over .500	11-8-3
Versus Teams Under .500	17-7-3
First Half Record	14-8-2
Second Half Record	14-7-4

PLAYOFFS

Results: lost in conference quarter-finals 4-3 to Vancouver
Record: 3-4
Home: 1-3
Away: 2-1
Goals For: 27 (3.9/gm)
Goals Against: 27 (3.9/gm)
Overtime: 0-1
Power play: 13.3% (10th)
Penalty Killing: 74.4 (13th)

PLAYERS	OVERALL				Projected over 84 Games		
	GP	G	A	PTS	G	A	PTS
B.HULL	48	29	21	50	51	37	88
B.SHANAHAN	45	20	21	41	37	39	76
S.DUCHESNE	47	12	26	38	21	46	67
E.TIKKANEN	43	12	23	35	23	45	68
A.CREIGHTON	48	14	20	34	24	35	59
J.NORTON	48	3	27	30	5	47	52
A.MACINNIS	32	8	20	28	21	53	74
I.LAPERRIERE	37	13	14	27	30	32	62
G.ANDERSON	36	12	14	26	28	33	61
G.GILBERT	46	11	14	25	20	26	46
T.ELIK	35	9	14	23	22	33	55
B.HOULDER	41	5	13	18	10	27	37
D.CHASSE	47	7	9	16	13	16	29
G.CARBONNEAU	42	5	11	16	10	22	32
P.TARDIF	27	3	10	13	9	31	40
D.ROBERTS	19	6	5	11	27	22	49
V.KARAMNOV	26	3	7	10	10	23	33
D.LIDSTER	37	2	7	9	5	16	21
C.JOHNSON	15	3	3	6	17	17	34
R.ZOMBO	23	1	4	5	4	15	19
B.MCRAE	21	0	5	5	0	20	20
M.BARON	39	0	5	5	0	11	11
T.TWIST	28	3	0	3	9	0	9
D.DUFRESNE	22	0	3	3	0	13	13
P.STASTNY	6	1	1	2	14	14	28
P.BOZON	1	0	0	0	0	0	0
V.PROKHOROV	2	0	0	0	0	0	0
D.FELSNER	3	0	0	0	0	0	0
T.HOLLINGER	5	0	0	0	0	0	0
J.BATTERS	10	0	0	0	0	0	0

Playoff Scoring

PLAYER	GP	G	A	PTS
B.SHANAHAN	5	4	5	9
B.HULL	7	6	2	8
D.CHASSE	7	1	7	8
T.ELIK	7	4	3	7
A.MACINNIS	7	1	5	6
E.TIKKANEN	7	2	2	4
S.DUCHESNE	7	0	4	4
I.LAPERRIERE	7	0	4	4
B.MCRAE	7	2	1	3
G.CARBONNEAU	7	1	2	3
G.GILBERT	7	0	3	3
A.CREIGHTON	7	2	0	2
B.HOULDER	4	1	1	2
G.ANDERSON	6	1	1	2
M.BARON	7	1	1	2
J.NORTON	7	1	1	2
C.JOSEPH	7	0	1	1
T.TWIST	1	0	0	0
C.JOHNSON	1	0	0	0
J.CASEY	2	0	0	0
V.KARAMNOV	2	0	0	0
D.DUFRESNE	3	0	0	0
R.ZOMBO	3	0	0	0
D.LIDSTER	4	0	0	0
D.ROBERTS	6	0	0	0

All-Time Rankings - INDIVIDUAL

Goals

Brett Hull	415
Bernie Federko	352
Brian Sutter	303

Assists

Bernie Federko	721
Brian Sutter	334
Brett Hull	284

Points

Bernie Federko	1,073
Brett Hull	649
Brian Sutter	636

Best Individual Seasons

Goals

Brett Hull	1990-91	86
Brett Hull	1989-90	72
Brett Hull	1991-92	70

Assists

Adam Oates	1990-91	90
Craig Janney	1992-93	82
Adam Oates	1989-90	79

Points

Brett Hull	1990-91	131
Adam Oates	1990-91	115
Brett Hull	1989-90	113

Toronto Maple Leafs

Things went from good to bad in Toronto very quickly. Now, it could get even worse. They may not even make the playoffs this year.

They're an old team with fading stars, they lack character, chemistry, have few young prospects, and little hope for improvement.

The Leafs encountered a number of unforeseen problems last season, most notably, the collapse of Doug Gilmour, and through it all managed to set a team record for excuses.

One of the most common excuses was that with so many players new to the team there just wasn't enough time to get to know each other. What was it they needed to know anyway? Sure, it helps to know what a linemate will do in a given situation, but that shouldn't stop anyone from doing their own job. And Pat Burns never keeps lines together anyway.

Lots of teams changed lots of players last season. The one critical difference may have been that they mixed the right ones.

It's called chemistry.

The chart below shows the number of players in each team's lineup at the end of the season that were not there at the end of the previous season.

A player had to have played 35 games this past season, or less than 10 with their team the previous year. In other words, new regulars in the lineup.

St. Louis	11
Toronto	10
Philadelphia	9
Ottawa	8
Montreal	7
Chicago	6
Dallas	6
Pittsburgh	6
Tampa Bay	6
Anaheim	5
Hartford	5
Los Angeles	5
Quebec	5
Boston	4
Calgary	4
Detroit	4
Edmonton	4
New Jersey	4
NY Rangers	4
Vancouver	4
San Jose	3
Winnipeg	3
Florida	2
NY Islanders	2
Washington	2
Buffalo	1

St. Louis, which made the most changes, had the second best record in the Western Conference. Philadelphia, which made one less change than Toronto, was third in the Eastern Conference.

Since both teams improved over their previous season, the changes were for the better.

I guess lots of changes are good, if the team improves. If they don't, well, then it's a convenient excuse.

To be fair, the Leafs did say ahead of time, that the team would take some time to gel. If it had been a full season, the target date was Christmas.

Most everything Cliff Fletcher has done since coming to the Leafs has turned into gold. The Gilmour trade in itself would be a career deal for most general managers.

But last year Fletcher went into a bit of a slump. Since he had already spoiled the Toronto fans, a slump for him meant not everything worked out perfectly.

The good deals last year included getting Randy Wood on waivers from Buffalo; getting Mike Ridley for Rob Pearson and an exchange of draft picks; and getting anything at all for Nikolai Borschevsky (a sixth round pick in 1996).

Larry Murphy for Dimitri Mironov is a steal, but it was also a gift from Pittsburgh trying to unload salaries.

A bad one, but not a big deal was trading Eric Lacroix, Chris Snell and a 4th round pick to Los Angeles for Dixon Ward, Guy Leveque, Shayne Toporowski and Kelly Fairchild. Lacroix, as a rookie, was a regular with the Kings last year and Snell was a semi-regular.

Another questionable move was obtaining Benoit Hogue and a third round pick for goaltender Eric Fichaud and a sixth round selection. Hogue never did show up in Toronto (although he still dressed for the games) while many predict stardom for Fichaud. Trading Fichaud doesn't hurt much because they already have young goalies, and Hogue, with his goal scoring past, was worth the risk. He could still turn out okay.

Getting Tie Domi from Winnipeg for Eastwood hasn't worked out too well so far. Domi didn't do anything in Toronto, while the Leafs missed Eastwood's valuable faceoff skills and some of the other little things he did so well. One of those, incidentally, was usually centering the best line of the night, even though it was supposed to be the third or fourth. But, Domi could be better this season and that, too, could work out.

Signing free agent Mike Craig didn't work and probably never will. He didn't score and only played well for maybe a two or three game stretch near the end of the season.

Questions are being brought up too, about trading Mike Ridley, one of their most consistent performers last year, for Sergio Momesso, who is anything but consistent.

Are we forgetting anything? Oh, yeah, the Sundin, Clark deal. The Leafs missed Lefebvre in that deal most of all, but I bet they would make it again. Sundin played extremely well for Toronto and should be around for a long time. The two prospects they'd probably like to leave out, however. Landon Wilson looks like he's going to be an excellent power forward for the Avalanche, maybe this year. Todd Warriner was terrible and will likely never play another game in the NHL.

TEAM PREVIEW

GOAL: The best you can say about the Toronto goaltending is that they're solid. That's about the worst you can say, too, because it's supposed to be better than that. Felix Potvin finished 27th out of 47 qualifying goalies. He's expected to be in the top 10 at the very least.

Instead, it reached the point where you'd expect one bad goal a game from Potvin. Whether that has to do with concentration or technique is unclear, but you could almost tell when Potvin was losing it because he'd start backing into the net.

There's no question that he's the number-one goaltender for as long as he's in Toronto, and there's no question that he's an outstanding netminder. He just has to be more consistent.

Damian Rhodes is consistent, when he gets the opportunity to play. Burns even started him over a rested Potvin during one stretch last season. His save percentage of .915 was fifth best in the league

	GP	MIN	GA	AVG	W	L	T	SO
Rhodes	13	760	34	2.68	6	6	1	0
Potvin	36	2144	104	2.91	15	13	7	0

DEFENCE: Even with the addition of Larry Murphy, this is a very weak defence. Oh...for the good old days of Sylvain Lefebvre and Bob Rouse. The team just never recovered from their loss.

Garth Butcher didn't start to play well until the playoffs; Jamie Macoun wasn't effective without his old defence partner, Lefebvre; and Dave Ellett, considered by some to be a solid, consistent defenceman, wasn't solid or consistent.

Dimitri Mironov won't be missed. He had a good shot, and a knack for moving in from the point and getting open, but man, did he make bonehead plays. Whatever he gave them offensively wasn't offset by his mental lapses.

Todd Gill was the guy who came through for the Leafs last season. He picked up the slack caused by the lack of a quarterback on the point, and quietly moved into the top 10 scorers among defencemen. Gill still suffers through his giveaway modes, and the mistakes he makes always seem to hurt him, but last year he was still their best defenceman.

Gill has been maligned much over the years and traded in the press even more often. A change of scenery might have done him more good than anybody, getting away from the pressures of playing in Toronto, but he's hung in there. The following list shows those players who have been with their current teams the longest, assuming none of those below are moved before the start of the season.

Bourque	Bos.	15
Daneyko	N.J.	11
Driver	N.J.	11 *
MacLean	N.J.	11
Flatley	NYI	11
Yzerman	Det.	11
GILL	TOR.	10
Roy	Mtl.	10
Lemieux,M	Pit.	10

* still a free agent at press time

Larry Murphy, even at 34 years old, gives the Leafs their first quarterback on the point since Borje Salming in the late seventies. The team record for points by a defenceman is held by Ian Turnbull, with 79 in 1976-77. Murphy has scored more points than that twice during his career, and has earned at least 60 in ten different seasons.

Kenny Jonsson is entering his second year and might be a little more comfortable. He was not very good his rookie season, although he still made the all-rookie team. Maybe by default. The thing with Jonsson is that every once in a while he showed what he could be capable of doing in the future. That future would appear to be far brighter than his play of last year.

The Leafs also picked up Rob Zettler in the off-season, a stay-at-home type who was Philadelphia's seventh or eighth defenceman.

There wasn't much forechecking in the NHL last year, but those teams that did it against Toronto, found surprisingly easy pickings. They'd cough up the puck easily and often.

As well, most of the time they had a free pass to the area in front of the net, and if they held onto the puck they could go wide and beat most of Toronto's rear guards one-on-one.

They don't have a dominant physical type, such as a Scott Stevens, and they need one. Soon.

FORWARD: Doug Gilmour, Doug Gilmour, Doug Gilmour. What's wrong with Doug Gilmour? That was the big news last year, and since it's already been analyzed more ways than the Kennedy assasination, we'll let it go.

The real question is can he rebound. Injuries apparently played a part in his poor season, so assuming he's recovered, will that be good enough?

It's not unusual for players to have off-years. Happens all the time. When they're young it's called a slump. When they're 32 years old, it's looked at differently.

We'll see.

Mats Sundin took over as the team's number one player and did an excellent job. He might have slowed down some towards the end of the year, but for most of the season he was the best player on the ice for Toronto.

Mike Ridley was traded for Sergio Momesso in order to free up the ice time at center for Sundin and Gilmour, according to Fletcher. If that was the real reason, why didn't they just move Ridley to wing? They could use some scoring there.

In fact, they're weak at every position. On the left-side is an aging Dave Andreychuk, who still managed to score 22 goals despite long absences, and general poor play. One of these times, he's going to go in a slump and never come out.

Momesso joins Andreychuk on the left side. He has a reputation of coming to play only every so often. That won't be a problem in Toronto, at least for the first while, because he'll be out to make an impression. If he plays like he can, that deal may not look so bad for long.

Bill Berg was a valuable pickup in 1992-93 for Toronto. For two seasons he hit everything in sight. Good, solid, bone-jarring hits. Last year, he slowed that part of his game down. Some nights he didn't hit anyone. If he doesn't get back to that part of the game, he won't be playing at all.

Kent Manderville had one point last season. One. Unless he at least doubles his output to two, his days may be numbered. Fortunately for him, there's no one else to put there anyway.

Behind Gilmour and Sundin are Hogue and DiPietro. Both were disappointments last year. If we didn't know Hogue had three 30-goal seasons, we'd wonder just what the heck he was doing out there.

DiPietro didn't do much either.

On the right side are Mike Gartner, Randy Wood, Mike Craig and Tie Domi.

Watch Gartner and you'd wonder how he ever became one of the all-time top goal scorers. His problem is age, of course, although he can still skate.

Nobody knows what Mike Craig's problem is.

And if you have a problem, Tie Domi will fix it for you.

Wood was the only consistent one in the bunch.

The Leafs also have three enforcers in Ken Baumgartner, Warren Rychel and Domi. That's two to many, so look for a couple to exit.

The only prospect of note is Brandon Convery.

This is just a terribly weak forward unit, lacking in so many ways. The only way for them to turn out okay is if every one of them has the best season of their career.

Since we know that's not going to happen,

it doesn't look good at all. And since Fletcher doesn't want to make wholesale changes again, it will be a long year.

SPECIAL TEAMS: The Toronto power play was weak for most of last season, but they're going to get considerably better. Larry Murphy is one of the best in the business on the point. That in itself will settle down what was a disorganized mess. And Pat Burns won't have to ban the media from watching what they're attempting to do in practise.

Power Play	G	ATT	PCT
Overall	37	218	17.0% (15th NHL)
Home	20	104	19.2% (12th NHL)
Road	17	114	14.9% (18th NHL)

5 SHORT HANDED GOALS ALLOWED (T-11th NHL)

Penalty Killing	G	TSH	PCT
Overall	28	185	84.9% (5th NHL)
Home	12	80	85.0% (6th NHL)
Road	16	105	84.8% (6th NHL)

5 SHORT HANDED GOALS SCORED (T-13th NHL)

Penalties	GP	MIN	AVG
MAPLE LEAFS	48	744	15.5 (3rd NHL)

MAPLE LEAFS SPECIAL TEAMS TOP SCORERS

Power play	G	A	PTS
SUNDIN	9	10	19
GILMOUR	3	12	15
ANDREYCHUK	8	6	14
GILL	3	9	12
MIRONOV	2	8	10
ELLETT	3	6	9
RIDLEY	2	7	9
JONSSON	0	5	5

Short handed	G	A	PTS
RIDLEY	2	2	4
WOOD	1	2	3

COACHING AND MANAGEMENT: Cliff Fletcher enjoyed special status in his first couple seasons in Toronto but, for the first time, the grumbling started. Anybody can make mistakes, if in fact they were mistakes, but in Fletcher's case he's capable of fixing things that get broke.

One thing I don't understand, though, is his penchant for giving long-term big contracts to old players who have little chance of being effective over the term of the contract. Names like Mike Foligno, Mike Krushelnyski, Mike Gartner and Dave Andreychuk come to mind.

Players get old. Fletcher either has a difficult time believing that or he just wants to make everybody happy. You never hear about contract squabbles in Toronto. But, when he starts talking about staying within a budget and not signing big free agents, well I guess we know why.

Coach Pat Burns has always had an ability to motivate his players. Didn't work last season. The team rarely played with any enthusiasm, and even when they did it wasn't for long.

Even if his act has worn thin, don't expect him to go down with the ship. It doesn't matter who it is, he'll throw them overboard, and not even toss a lifejacket.

In other words expect him to get extremely tough if things don't go well. He's a talented enough coach that he'll be able to get the best out of this group. His worry is if their best isn't good enough.

One more thing about the Toronto front office, which includes Fletcher and Assistant GM Bill Watters. These are not dumb people. They have justification for every single thing they do, and it's all in the interest of making this a better hockey team.

They built this club up from nothing to something. If it falls back down, they'll just build it up again.

DRAFT

1995 DRAFT SELECTIONS

Round	Sel.	Player	Pos	Amateur Team
1	15	Jeff Ware	D	Oshawa (OHL)
3	54	Brian Pepperall	RW	Kitchener (OHL)
6	139	Doug Bonner	G	Seattle (WHL)
6	145	Yanick Tremblay	D	Beauport (QMJHL)
7	171	Marik Melenovsky	C	Czechoslovakia
8	197	Mark Murphy	LW	Stratford (MOJHL)
9	223	Danill Markov	D	Russia

Jeff Ware is a big (6-4, 214) defensive defenceman, the value of which the Leafs learned last season when they were without Lefebvre and Rouse.

The only Toronto first round choice who finished off the season with them last year was Kenny Jonsson, their top pick in the 1993 draft. Interestingly, however, ten of their other first rounders were playing with other clubs. All their first round picks between 1983 and 1990 are on the list below.

Pick	Year	Overall	Current Team
R.Courtnall	1983	7	Vancouver
A.Iafrate	1984	4	Boston
W.Clark	1985	1	Colorado
V.Damphousse	1986	6	Montreal
L.Richardson	1987	7	Edmonton
S.Pearson	1988	6	Buffalo
S.Thornton	1989	3	Edmonton
R.Pearson	1989	12	Washington
D. Berehowsky	1990	10	Pittsburgh

PROGNOSIS: This is not a good team as it stands. They're weak everywhere but in net. It's going to be a battle just to make the play-offs.

As bad as they look for the upcoming season you have to remember they weren't very good last year and still managed to stay around the .500 mark.

Fletcher doesn't want to make wholesale changes and will allow the players to get to know one another. They just might be better off not knowing each other. By the end of the year don't be surprised if there's another airlift.

PREDICTION:
Central Division: 5th
Western Conference: 8th
Overall: 15th

STAT SECTION

Team Rankings 1994/95

		Conference Rank	League Rank
Record	21-19-8	5	12
Home	15-7-2	4	11
Away	6-12-6	9	18
Team Plus\Minus	-20	9	22
Goals For	135	10	17
Goals Against	146	6	16

PLAYERS	OVERALL				Project Over 84 Games		
	GP	G	A	PTS	G	A	PTS
M.SUNDIN	47	23	24	47	41	43	84
D.ANDREYCHUK	48	22	16	38	38	28	66
M.RIDLEY	48	10	27	37	17	47	64
D.GILMOUR	44	10	23	33	19	44	63
T.GILL	47	7	25	32	13	45	58
R.WOOD	48	13	11	24	23	19	42
M.GARTNER	38	12	8	20	27	18	45
D.MIRONOV	33	5	12	17	13	31	44
B.HOGUE	45	9	7	16	17	13	30
D.ELLETT	33	5	10	15	13	25	38
P.DIPIETRO	34	5	6	11	12	15	27
M.CRAIG	37	5	5	10	11	11	22
J.MACOUN	46	2	8	10	4	15	19
T.DOMI	40	4	5	9	8	11	19
*K.JONSSON	39	2	7	9	4	15	19
G.BUTCHER	45	1	7	8	2	13	15
W.RYCHEL	33	1	6	7	3	15	18
B.BERG	32	5	1	6	13	3	16
G.JENNINGS	35	0	6	6	0	14	14
T.YAKE	19	3	2	5	13	9	22
D.WARD	22	0	3	3	0	11	11
R.SUTTER	37	0	3	3	0	7	7
*D.HENDRICKSON	8	0	1	1	0	11	11
K.MANDERVILLE	36	0	1	1	0	2	2
*D.HARLOCK	1	0	0	0	0	0	0
*Z.NEDVED	1	0	0	0	0	0	0
K.BAUMGARTNER	2	0	0	0	0	0	0
*K.BELANGER	3	0	0	0	0	0	0
*T.WARRINER	5	0	0	0	0	0	0
*M.MARTIN	15	0	0	0	0	0	0

MISCELLANEOUS STATS

One Goal Games	12-3
Times outshooting opponent	21
Times outshot	24
Even shots	3
Average Shots For	31.6
Average Shots Against	31.9
Overtime	0-0-8
Longest Winning streak	2
Longest Undefeated streak	4
Longest Losing streak	3
Longest winless streak	4
Versus Teams Over .500	9-9-4
Versus Teams Under .500	12-10-4
First Half Record	11-10-3
Second Half Record	10-9-5

PLAYOFFS

Results: Lost to Chicago in Conference quarter-finals, 4-3.
Record: 3-4
Home: 1-2
Away: 2-2
Goals For: 20 (2.9/gm)
Goals Against: 22 (3.1/gm)
Overtime:
Power play: 19.4% (6th)
Penalty Killing: 92.6% (1st)

PLAYER	GP	G	A	PTS
M.SUNDIN	7	5	4	9
D.GILMOUR	7	0	6	6
D.ANDREYCHUK	7	3	2	5
M.RIDLEY	7	3	1	4
M.GARTNER	5	2	2	4
D.MIRONOV	6	2	1	3
J. MACOUN	7	1	2	3
T.GILL	7	0	3	3
R.WOOD	7	2	0	2
P.DIPIETRO	7	1	1	2
D.ELLETT	7	0	2	2

T.DOMI	7	1	0	1
M.CRAIG	2	0	1	1
B.BERG	7	0	1	1
W.RYCHEL	3	0	0	0
G.JENNINGS	4	0	0	0
R.SUTTER	4	0	0	0
K.JONSSON	4	0	0	0
B.HOGUE	7	0	0	0
G.BUTCHER	7	0	0	0
K.MANDERVILLE	7	0	0	0
F.POTVIN	7	0	0	0

All-Time Rankings - INDIVIDUAL

Goals
Darryl Sittler	389
Dave Keon	365
Ron Ellis	332

Assists
Borje Salming	620
Darryl Sittler	527
Dave Keon	493

Points
Darryl Sittler	916
Dave Keon	858
Borje Salming	768

Best Individual Seasons

Goals
Rick Vaive	1981-82	54
Dave Andreychuk	1993-94	53
Rick Vaive	1983-84	52

Assists
Doug Gilmour	1992-93	95
Doug Gilmour	1993-94	84
Darryl Sittler	1977-78	72

Points
Doug Gilmour	1992-93	127
Darryl Sittler	1977-78	117
Doug Gilmour	1993-94	111

Vancouver Canucks

When the Canucks obtained Alexander Mogilny from Buffalo they not only became an instant Stanley Cup contender but also the most entertaining team in the league.

Bure and Mogilny, together again, should be quite a show.

Mogilny has a career high of 76 goals, Bure has had two 60 goal seasons. Both are coming off uninspired seasons, but now can't wait to get back on the ice.

How high can they go? What's the limit? Which one will score more often? Who gets to be their centerman?

The last question might be the most intriguing. Who wouldn't want that job? It's a license to steal, is what it is. All they have to do is give the puck to one or the other linemate and watch their point production zoom.

Probably, though the two Russians are going to be looking for each other more than their center, and won't involve him as much.

Let's look at the options for the ideal centerman.

A. Big guy. A protector, corner digger, distraction in front of the net, and perhaps most important, someone to play some defence because you know Bure and Mogilny aren't going to play any. As Mogilny said when talking about the stifling Buffalo system: "How can I score when I have to worry about my own end." Uh, yeah, we'll leave that up to someone else, there, Alex. And the nominee is: Trevor Linden.

B. Playmaker. Someone who isn't going to score much themself but can dish off to a couple guys who will. Also, should at least be able to keep up with them. You can forget about the toughness to protect the superstars, but maybe a defenceman can help out in that department. And the nominees are: Mike Ridley and Cliff Ronning.

C: European. Another European between them may make them all feel more comfortable with the playing style. Bure and Mogilny would prefer their old junior linemate, Sergei Fedorov, but then who wouldn't. The nominee is: Josef Beranek.

D. Throwaway. Maybe it doesn't matter who's between them. Put a guy out there who can win the faceoff for them, get back into his own end when the other team gets the puck, and basically just stay out of their way. Also, it frees up some legitimate scoring for the second line, so that opposing teams can't key on the one line. And the nominee is: John McIntyre.

I think the best answer is A - Trevor Linden. Teams are going to have to do something to try and stop these two and won't be adverse to roughing them up a big. Linden could discourage that line of thinking.

Here is a collection of items from the Canucks season:

* At the end of the year, the Canucks announced a drop in ticket prices. They were still outlandish after a huge increase at the start of the season, and they only knocked a buck off, but a reduction is still a reduction.

* Assistant GM George McPhee had some nasty things to say about Mike Keenan and suggested he'd like to "drop him." McPhee was also accused by Trevor Linden's agent, Don Meehan, of breaking a confidentiality agreement when he went on a radio talk show and revealed discussions concerning Linden's contract negotiations. Pat Quinn responded to a tirade by Don Cherry in Coach's Corner against Pavel Bure, and reportedly said he'd like to punch him in the head. This is feisty management.

* The Canucks had a 14-4-6 mark versus the Pacific Divison and were only 4-14-6 versus the Central.

* The Canucks went from having just three ties, the fewest in 1993-94, to 12 last year, which was the most in the league.

* Vancouver was 8-8-8 in the first half of the season and 10-10-4 in the second half. They were the only team in the league to finish with a .500 record.

* The Canucks won 5 and lost 13 against teams over .500, and won 13 and lost five against teams under .500.

* Of those who played with the Canucks last year and were also drafted by the Canucks, they had more from the fifth round than the first. 1st round: 2 - Linden, Stojanov; 2nd round: 2 - Cullimore and Peca (since traded to Buffalo); 3rd round: 1 -Jackson; 4th round: none; 5th round: 3 - Aucoin, Odjick, Walker; 6th round: 2 - Bure, Namestnikov; 10th round - Wotten.

TEAM PREVIEW

GOAL: Kirk McLean's exploits are well-documented although he didn't have quite the same magic in the playoffs last year as he did the season before. But then neither did the team.

Backup Kay Whitmore had a tough season. He had a terrible save percentage, a terrible GAA, and couldn't even manage to win a game.

The Canucks obtained Canadian National team sensation, Corey Hirsch, from the Rangers for Nathan Lafayette, so Whitmore's days may be numbered.

Hirsch, considered one of the top prospects in the league, has just had a tough time finding regular NHL work. In New York, they were already strong at that position, and in Vancouver they aren't in dire need of a goalie either.

Vancouver also has another prospect in Mike Fountain, who played last season in Syracuse. In fact, he was considered their top prospect, so why the Canucks got Hirsch isn't clear.

	GP	MIN	GA	AVG	W	L	T	SO
McLean	40	2374	109	2.75	18	12	10	1
Whitmore	11	558	37	3.98	0	6	2	0

DEFENCE: Jeff Brown was probably the happiest Canuck, besides Bure, when the team obtained Alexander Mogilny. His point totals are going to go way up on the power play.

Defence regulars, besides Brown, should be Dana Murzyn, Jyrki Lumme, Jassen Cullimore, Bret Hedican, and Dave Babych.

Contenders are Yevgeny Namestnikov, Adrian Aucoin, Mark Wotten, Artur Oktyabrev and Scott Walker, all of whom were called up for varying degrees of time.

The number one prospect in the system is Swede, Mattias Ohlund.

Brown and Lumme are the only offensive threats of note among the regulars, while Murzyn is the most physical. They do have plenty of size, however, including rookie Jassen Cullimore (6-5, 225) who made the big club after two years in the AHL.

Speaking of physical, Scott Walker earned 334 penalty minutes in Syracuse and 33 in just 11 games with the Canucks. The interesting thing about Walker is that he's just 5-9. Besides all the penalty minutes, he led Syracuse in defenceman scoring (he's also listed as a winger) with 52 points.

The Canucks auditioned much of their young talent on defence, mostly because of injuries to regulars. Five rookies got playing time and some valuable NHL experience. That's unusual in the NHL today, where if someone needs a defenceman they just trade for him.

It was a very dry year for rookie defencemen, which may have something to do with the shortened season. Defence is the toughest position to learn, so perhaps with the increased importance of each game last season, teams didn't have the patience.

Among those who did play, there was little offensive production. Chris Therien had the most points, with only 13. Therien made the all-rookie team along with Kenny Jonsson of Toronto.

Most games by Rookie Defencemen - 1994-95

Player	Team	Games
Stanislav Neckar	Ott.	48
Chris Therien	Phi.	48
Eric Charron	T.B.	45
Cory Cross	T.B.	43
Kenny Jonsson	Tor.	39
Oleg Tverdovsky	Ana.	36
Chris Tamer	Pit.	36
Jassen Cullimore	Van.	34

FORWARD: Now that they have two of the most explosive forwards in the league don't look for much in the way of defensive play from the Canucks this year.

Mogilny and Bure aren't the only offence-first minded forwards, they have plenty. And since they can put together a good first scoring line, a good second scoring line, and a good third scoring line, don't look for them too often in their own end. Scores of 7-5 and 6-4 could be commonplace in Vancouver this year.

Often that means trouble once you get to the playoffs, but during the regular season the Canucks should be one of the highest scoring teams in the league.

If they don't put Linden between Mogilny and Bure, maybe they'll move him back to the wing where many feel he's better suited. They have decent scoring centers in Ronning, Ridley and Beranek.

They may be a little thin on the wing, however, with Sergio Momesso traded to Toronto. Russ Courtnall, Martin Gelinas and Roman Oksuita can provide the scoring. Gino Odjick can provide the toughness.

Geoff Courtnall left as a free agent to St. Louis despite having the opportunity to fulfill a dream by playing with his brother. They did for a month, however, after Russ was obtained from Dallas for Greg Adams and Dan Kesa.

Geoff wasn't happy with the way his contract negotiations went, especially when they offered Momesso more money than him. He told a St. Louis newspaper that the team increased the offer and then just before the trade deadline told him that if he signed they'd trade for his brother. He didn't, but they made the trade anyway, and Geoff never talked contract with them again.

Ridley was a nice pickup. He was the second most consistent forward in Toronto last year, behind Mats Sundin, and all the Canucks had to give up was Momesso, who gave them headaches anyway with his on-again-off-again style.

If you figure Mogilny and Bure are going to be in the top 10 in scoring, someone else isn't going to be far behind - the guy who plays between them. But, the second line is going to score a lot too, because with all the attention on the top line, they won't have to play against the checkers.

One other factor that enters into the equation; the players, not just fans, are tired of the defensive system used by more and more teams. Once they free themselves of it, they have a lot more fun and play better. Or so they say. Losing isn't much fun either, so we'll have to see how it works out.

SPECIAL TEAMS: The Canucks power play was good last year, and during one two-game span scored eight goals with the man advantage. Mind you, they were both against Los Angeles, but they also went through another eight-game stretch of scoring at least one goal on the power play.

The oddity was that Bure, who led the league in power play goals the previous season, was only fourth in point scoring, and only had six goals, less than Linden and Geoff Courtnall, and the same as Momesso.

That won't happen this year. Bure and Mogilny will score a bundle, and the big beneficiary will be Jeff Brown on the point. Brown's career point high is 78, when he was with St. Louis. He could beat that mark this year.

While down a man, the Canucks like to go on the offensive. Bure tied for the league lead with six shorthanded points.

Power Play	G	ATT	PCT
Overall	47	238	19.7% (7th NHL)
Home	25	121	20.7% (10th NHL)
Road	22	117	18.8% (9th NHL)

10 SHORT HANDED GOALS ALLOWED (25th NHL)

Penalty Killing	G	TSH	PCT
Overall	39	236	83.5% (11th NHL)
Home	7	103	83.5% (12th NHL)
Road	22	133	83.5% (9th NHL)

7 SHORT HANDED GOALS SCORED (T-6th NHL)

Penalties	GP	MIN	AVG
CANUCKS	48	1093	22.8 (20th NHL)

CANUCKS SPECIAL TEAMS TOP SCORERS

Powerplay	G	A	PTS
LINDEN	9	14	23
BROWN	3	18	21
COURTNALL	7	9	16
BURE	6	7	13
RONNING	3	9	12
COURTNALL	2	10	12
BERANEK	3	6	9
OKSIUTA	6	0	6
MOMESSO	6	0	6
LUMME	3	3	6
BABYCH	1	5	6

Shorthanded	G	A	PTS
BURE	2	4	6
COURTNALL	2	1	3
LUMME	0	2	2
HEDICAN	0	2	2
GELINAS	0	1	1
CULLIMORE	0	1	1

COACHING AND MANAGEMENT: Some coaches take over a team and change it to their style. Some coaches take over a team and go with the best style suited to the talent. Rick Ley would probably prefer to be more defensive-oriented, as would most coaches who want to win, but he'll settle for shoot-the-lights-out offence. He doesn't have much choice.

Pat Quinn has established himself as one of the better traders in the league and one of the better undervalued talent recognizers. He's picked up players on waivers who have turned out to be more talented and useful than others would have thought, and he seems to always get more than full value in his trades.

DRAFT

1995 DRAFT SELECTIONS

Round	Sel.	Player	Pos	Amateur Team
2	40	Chris McAllister	D	Saskatoon (WHL)
3	61	Larry Courville	LW	Oshawa (OHL) *PD
3	66	Peter Schaefer	LW	Brandon (WHL)
4	92	Lloyd Shaw	D	Seattle (WHL)
5	120	Todd Norman	LW	Guelph (OHL)
6	144	Brent Sopel	D	Swift Current (WHL)
7	170	Stewart Bodtker	C	Colorado (WCHA)
8	196	Tyler Willis	RW	Swift Current (WHL)
9	222	Jason Cugnet	G	Kelowna (WHL)

The Canucks didn't have a first round choice because they traded it to Buffalo in the Mogilny deal.

Their second round choice, Chris McAllister is a gigantic 6-6, 238.

Vancouver was the only team in the league that didn't draft at least one European.

The notation beside Larry Courville's name means, previously drafted. He was selected 119th by Winnipeg in 1993, but was never signed. His stock has risen considerably since then.

PROGNOSIS: The Canucks had to improve with the Quebec franchise moving to Colorado and into their division. Games between those two should be among the most entertaining in the league. The Avalanche appear to have a more solid lineup from top to bottom than Vancouver. And if they could score against the defensive-minded Eastern Conference teams, imagine what they'll do in the Western Conference.

But, the Canucks are a legitimate Stanley Cup contender now, which means Quinn will pull out all the stops to ensure any problems they have are fixed through the trade route.

They'll be playing for this year, not the future.

PREDICTION
Pacific Division: 2nd
Western Conference: 4th
Overall: 6th

STAT SECTION

Team Rankings 1994/95

		Conference Rank	League Rank
Record	18-18-12	6	13
Home	10-8-6	6	15
Away	8-10-6	5	11
Team Plus\Minus	-3	5	13
Goals For	153	6	8
Goals Against	148	6	17

PLAYERS	1994-95 OVERALL				Projected over 84 games		
	GP	G	A	PTS	G	A	PTS
P.BURE	44	20	23	43	38	44	82
T.LINDEN	48	18	22	40	32	38	70
R.COURTNALL	45	11	24	35	21	45	66
G.COURTNALL	45	16	18	34	30	34	64
J.BERANEK	51	13	18	31	21	30	51
J.BROWN	33	8	23	31	20	59	79
S.MOMESSO	48	10	15	25	17	26	43
C.RONNING	41	6	19	25	12	39	51
M.GELINAS	46	13	10	23	24	18	42
R.OKSIUTA	38	16	4	20	35	9	44
C.RUUTTU	45	7	11	18	13	21	34
J.LUMME	36	5	12	17	12	28	40
D.BABYCH	40	3	11	14	6	23	29
B.HEDICAN	45	2	11	13	4	21	25
M.PECA	33	6	6	12	15	15	30
G.ODJICK	23	4	5	9	15	18	33
D.MURZYN	40	0	8	8	0	17	17
T.HUNTER	34	3	2	5	7	5	12
J.MCINTYRE	28	0	4	4	0	12	12
J.CULLIMORE	34	1	2	3	2	5	7
Y.NAMESTNIKOV	16	0	3	3	0	16	16
G.LEEMAN	10	2	0	2	17	0	17
A.AUCOIN	1	1	0	1	84	0	84
J.CHARBONNEAU	3	1	0	1	28	0	28
D.JACKSON	3	1	0	1	28	0	28
S.WALKER	11	0	1	1	0	8	8
M.WOTTON	1	0	0	0	0	0	0
A.STOJANOV	4	0	0	0	0	0	0

MISCELLANEOUS STATS

One Goal Games	1-3
Times outshooting opponent	34
Times outshot	14
Even shots	0
Overtime	0-1-12
Average Shots For	32.8
Average Shots Against	29.6
Longest Winning streak	3
Longest Undefeated streak	4
Longest Losing streak	3
Longest winless streak	4
Versus Teams Over .500	5-13-3
Versus Teams Under .500	13-5-5
First Half Record	8-8-8
Second Half Record	10-10-4

PLAYOFFS

Results: defeated St. Louis 4-3 in conference quarter-finals lost to Vancouver 4-0 in conference semi-finals
Record: 4-7 Home: 1-4 Away: 3-3
Goals For: 33 (3.0/gm)
Goals Against: 38 (3.5/gm)
Overtime: 1-3
Power play: 21.1% (5th)
Penalty Killing: 87.9% (4th)

PLAYER	GP	G	A	PTS
P.BURE	11	7	6	13
R.COURTNALL	11	4	8	12
C.RONNING	11	3	5	8
J.LUMME	11	2	6	8
T.LINDEN	11	2	6	8
G.COURTNALL	11	4	2	6
R.OKSIUTA	10	2	3	5
S.MOMESSO	11	3	1	4
D.BABYCH	11	2	2	4
J.BROWN	5	1	3	4
C.RUUTTU	9	1	1	2
J.BERANEK	11	1	1	2
B.HEDICAN	11	0	2	2
A.AUCOIN	4	1	0	1
M.GELINAS	3	0	1	1
M.PECA	5	0	1	1
D.MURZYN	8	0	1	1
K.MCLEAN	11	0	1	1
K.WHITMORE	1	0	0	0
Y.NAMESTNIKOV	1	0	0	0
G.ODJICK	5	0	0	0
A.STOJANOV	5	0	0	0
M.WOTTON	5	0	0	0
D.JACKSON	6	0	0	0
T.HUNTER	11	0	0	0
J.CULLIMORE	11	0	0	0

All-Time Rankings - INDIVIDUAL

Goals
Stan Smyl	262
Tony Tanti	250
Trevor Linden	198

Assists
Stan Smyl	411
Thomas Gradin	353
Dennis Kearns	290

Points
Stan Smyl	673
Thomas Gradin	550
Tony Tanti	470

Best Individual Seasons

Goals
Pavel Bure	1993-94	60
Pavel Bure	1992-93	60
Darcy Rota	1983-83	42

Assists
Andre Boudrias	1974-75	62
Andre Boudrias	1973-74	59
Thomas Gradin	1983-84	57

Points
Pavel Bure	1992-93	110
Pavel Bure	1993-94	107
Patrik Sundstrom	1983-84	91

Winnipeg Jets

If this is Tuesday, the Jets must still be in Winnipeg. If it's Wednesday, they're in Minnesota. If it's Thursday, they're back in Winnipeg.

The on-again-off-again move and on-again-off-again tear ducts, still hadn't been closed at press time.

In contrast to the off-ice activities, nothing much was happening on the ice for the Jets.

They had another poor season, but at least they had a couple of all-stars. Both were second team selections for Keith Tkachuk and Alexei Zhamnov, but still almost matched all the Jets who had been named to all-star teams previously.

Interestingly, all except Hawerchuk were non-Canadians, and none has ever been selected twice, while with the Jets.

Winnipeg All-Stars

1994-95	2nd team: C Alexei Zhamnov, LW Keith Tkachuk
1992-93	1st team: RW Teemu Selanne
1991-92	2nd team: D Phil Housley
1984-85	2nd team: C Dale Hawerchuk

In other news, Thomas Steen retired at the end of the season and had his jersey retired. He's the first European to be bestowed with such an honour. Steen was a rarity in that he played his entire career in one city. He was in Winnipeg for 14 years. The only other active player with a longer streak is Ray Bourque, who had played 15 year for Boston before the upcoming season.

A curious thing about the Jets' season was their ability to play well against the good teams. In fact, they fared better against the top teams than the bottom ones.

Against clubs that were .500 or better, they had a record of 11-13-4. Against those under .500 they were 5-12-3.

When a poor team does so well against the top competition it usually means they're a more talented team than their overall record illustrates. It's not unusual to play to the level of competition, but it's not often it's one of the lower standing teams in the league is doing it.

If when they play their best, the Jets can beat the good clubs, it also means they're not playing their best against the weak ones. At that point you have to figure out why not.

Best Records against teams .500 or better.

	W	L	T	%
Detroit	14	7	1	.659
Quebec	14	7	3	.646
Philadelphia	11	8	2	.571
St. Louis	11	8	3	.568
Pittsburgh	11	8	3	.568
Calgary	9	8	4	.524
Toronto	9	9	4	.500
Chicago	8	9	5	.477
Winnipeg	11	13	4	.464

Boston	9	11	3	.457
NY Rangers	11	15	0	.423
Buffalo	7	11	3	.405
New Jersey	7	11	3	.404
Washington	7	12	4	.391
Los Angeles	7	13	5	.380
Hartford	8	15	3	.365
Florida	8	15	2	.360
Dallas	7	15	6	.357
Montreal	7	15	4	.356
NY Islanders	7	16	3	.327
San Jose	7	16	2	.320
Vancouver	5	13	3	.310
Edmonton	7	18	1	.288
Tampa Bay	6	17	2	.280
Anaheim	5	18	3	.250
Ottawa	3	17	4	.200

TEAM PREVIEW

GOAL: Turns out Tim Cheveldae's problem wasn't so much playing in Detroit, but rather playing net. Then again, it's so difficult to tell on a weak defensive team. You can't use goals against average as a judge, unless you're comparing him to a teammate.

To that end, Nikolai Khabibulin was better.

While it might appear to be, goaltending isn't that much of a problem. The best goalie in the league would have had a similar goals against average. It's better to wait until the team becomes competitive and then look again at the goaltender situation.

	GP	MIN	GA	AVG	W	L	T	SO
Khabibulin	26	1339	76	3.41	8	9	4	0
Cheveldae	30	1571	97	3.70	8	16	3	0

DEFENCE: The Jets have an excellent prospect on defence who could give them the quarterback they need, and even challenge for rookie of the year.

His name is Deron Quint and he's an offensive dynamo. Last year, for Seattle in the WHL he scored 89 points from the blueline.

He's about the only prospect of note in the entire Winnipeg Jets organization. They squandered away many of their draft picks on Europeans and are in a recovery stage.

Quint will get an opportunity because they have very little in offence from the defence.

Stephane Quintal was the top point-getter from the blueline, but he was traded to Montreal for a second-round pick. Quintal was a first round pick for Boston in 1987.

Dave Manson is still a valuable commodity on the blueline, and a guy that keeps opposing teams honest.

Also on the blueline is Darryl Shannon, Neil Wilkinson, Greg Brown, Oleg Mikulchik, and Brent Thompson. Jeff Finley was signed as a free agent in the off-season as was Stewart Malgunus who had a regular job in Philadelphia before Bob Clarke came along and upgraded the position.

Thompson, incidentally, had the distinction of playing the most games by a defenceman last season without scoring a single point. He had the second most overall.

Most games without a point - 1993-94

Shawn Antoski	Phi.	32
Brent Thompson	Wpg.	29
Denis Tsygurov	L.A.	25
Todd Ewen	Ana.	24
Yanick Dupre	Phi.	22
Ryan McGill	Edm.	20
Pierre Sevigny	Mtl	19

Shannon's brother, Darrin, is a forward on the team, and since both of their last names are the same and they have the same first initial, it was necessary for the Jets to distinguish between the two on their jerseys. One stayed as just Shannon, while for the other (I forget which was which) they put a D in front of the Shannon. Hmm...that ought to clear it up.

The Jets are among the weakest defensive teams in the league so it's difficult to say much that's good about this group.

FORWARD: If free agent Teemu Selanne returns to Winnipeg, the Jets can put out one of the best first lines in the league. Keith Tkachuk is a second team all-star left winger (and also a restricted free agent) and Alexei Zhamnov is a second team all-star center. Selanne, of course, scored 76 goals in a season not too long ago.

Nelson Emerson, rumored in many trades, is also a pretty good scorer. That's about where it stops.

The most anybody else on the team managed to score was eight, which translated over an 84 game season is only 14.

If they lose Selanne and Tkachuk, the Jets fans might not care too much of the team leaves town.

There are other quality players, if not scorers, however. Kris King (another restricted free agent) is one of the great character players around. Randy Gilhen is a good defensive center who is excellent on faceoffs. And Mike Eastwood is a quality player who does lots of little things well.

You have to watch Eastwood a lot to appreciate what he does. When he was with Toronto, I got that opportunity.

I do some game statistics for the Toronto Sun, and included in that package is faceoffs. In five years of doing them, no one could even approach his numbers in terms of winning the draw. Ironically, when I was talking to him about that a couple weeks before he was traded to Winnipeg, and he mentioned Keith Tkachuk as someone who was very dif-

ficult to beat. Tkachuk, of course, is a left-winger, but he takes lots of faceoffs.

In Winnipeg, with two good draw guys already in Tkachuk and Gilhen, his top skill wasn't needed so much.

Another thing Eastwood does, with almost uncanny ability, is come up with the puck when it's along the boards. And use the boards to carry the puck in the offensive zone. He's not a physical player by any means, but if Eastwood is near the boards and the puck is close by, the end result has Eastwood with the puck on his stick.

Finally, Eastwood has another ability. In Toronto, things weren't going well with the top scorers. Eastwood would center some of the leftovers on the third or fourth lines, and the majority of the nights, his line would be the best during the game.

You won't find Eastwood on any all-star teams, but you'll find him on mine. Hey, it's the in-thing these days. I'll call it the All-Townsend Team. Just guys I like, mostly with an undervalued skill, but not necessarily. Something about their play, or even their statistics, that have stuck out with me.

LW	Jeff Freisen, San Jose
C	Mike Eastwood, Winnipeg
RW	Mark Recchi, Montreal
D	Dave Manson, Winnipeg
D	Bryan Marchment, Edmonton
G	Chris Osgood, Detroit

SPECIAL TEAMS: Winnipeg has some excellent power play components including snipers and playmakers. What they lacked, they may have found in Deron Quint. A legitimate power play quarterback is going to make the rest of them even better.

Power Play	G	ATT	PCT
Overall	42	219	19.2% (9th NHL)
Home	16	102	15.7% (T-20th NHL)
Road	26	117	22.2% (4th NHL)

6 SHORT HANDED GOALS ALLOWED (T-14th NHL)

Penalty Killing	G	TSH	PCT
Overall	40	235	83.0% (13th NHL)
Home	19	114	83.3% (13th NHL)
Road	21	121	82.6% (11th NHL)

7 SHORT HANDED GOALS SCORED (T-6th NHL)

Penalties	GP	MIN	AVG
JETS	48	1141	23.8 (T-23rd NHL)

Top Scorers
JETS SPECIAL TEAMS TOP SCORERS

Power play	G	A	PTS
ZHAMNOV	9	16	25
SELANNE	8	10	18
TKACHUK	7	10	17
EMERSON	4	10	14
QUINTAL	3	6	9
NUMMINEN	2	6	8
MANSON	2	6	8
OLCZYK	2	4	6
KOROLEV	1	4	5

Short handed	G	A	PTS
TKACHUK	2	3	5
EMERSON	1	2	3
SELANNE	2	0	2
SHANNON	1	1	2

COACHING AND MANAGEMENT: Terry Simpson coached the Jets near the end of last year, but only became the team's coach over the summer. Huh?

Last year he was just an "interim" coach. GM John Paddock was apparently not wanted by the potential new owners, but tired of waiting to see what would happen, hired Simpson for the upcoming year, anyway.

After Paddock fired himself as coach last season, Simpson took the team to a 7-7-1 record the rest of the way.

Paddock is in an impossible situation in Winnipeg, and has been from the start when he took over a mess from Mike Smith. The talent within the organization is weak and the ownership uncertainties restrict his options for change.

1995 DRAFT SELECTIONS

Round	Sel.	Player	Pos	Amateur Team
1	7	Shane Doan	RW	Kamloops (WHL)
2	32	Marc Chouinard	C	Beauport (QMJHL)
2	34	Jason Doig	D	Laval (QMJHL)
3	67	Brad Isbister	RW	Portland (WHL)
4	84	Justin Kurtz	D	Brandon (WHL)
5	121	Brian Elder	G	Brandon (WHL)
6	136	Sylvain Daigle	G	Shawinigan (QMJHL)
7	162	Paul Traynor	D	Kitchener (OHL)
8	188	Jaroslav Obsut	D	N. Battleford (SJHL)
8	189	Frederik Loven	C	Sweden
9	214	Rob Decaintis	C	Kitchener (OHL)

That was Shane Doan's name you heard the crowd chanting when it was Edmonton's turn to pick at the draft. The popular Albertan went one pick later. He's considered a prototypical power forward type. He's big, strong, tough, and can score.

The Jets took all North Americans in this draft, except one, in contrast to some of their other recent drafts when they tried unsuccessfuly to build with Europeans. The chart below shows a dramatic change in draft strategy.

The following is a breakdown of choices by country. All players taken from the former Soviet Union are under the heading of "Rus." That's not quite politically correct, but it saves space, and we all know what it means. Slovakia and the Czech Republic are also listed as one (Cz). The chart only suggests where they were drafted from, not their place of birth.

	Fin.	Cz.	Rus.	U.S.	Can.	Swe.	Swit.
1995	-	-	-	-	10	1	-
1994	-	-	1	1	8	1	-
1993	-	1	5	-	5	1	1
1992	-	-	9	1	2	-	-
1991	1	-	4	2	3	-	-
1990	2	1	1	5	2	2	-
1989	1	-	2	9	3	-	-
1988	2	-	1	3	7	1	-
1987	1	-	-	7	1	2	-
1986	3	-	-	4	3	1	-

PROGNOSIS: The Jets can throw some pretty good talent out on the ice, but even with it last year, they couldn't do much. Since there's nothing new that's going to improve things much, there's nowhere up to go.

Maybe, once the ownership issue is settled they can concentrate on hockey again, and build the organization back up.

It is possible to win with just one good scoring line - other teams, such as Philadelphia, have done it. Assuming it's intact, Selanne, Tkachuk and Zhamnov would be one of the best lines in the league and can take care of the scoring if the other guys play more defensive roles.

If that happens, it helps the defencemen and the goalies, and gives the team a better shot at winning.

PREDICTION
Central Division: 6th
Western Conference: 10th
Overall: 19th

STAT SECTION

Team Rankings 1994/95

		Conference Rank	League Rank
Record	16-25-7	10	21
Home	10-10-4	8	18
Away	6-15-3	10	21
Team Plus\Minus	-22	10	23
Goals For	157	4	6
Goals Against	177	11	25

MISCELLANEOUS STATS

One Goal Games	6-11
Times outshooting opponent	18
Times outshot	29
Even shots	1
Overtime	0-2-7
Average Shots For	29.7
Average Shots Against	32.1
Longest Winning streak	3
Longest Undefeated streak	3
Longest Losing streak	4
Longest winless streak	10
Versus Teams Over .500	11-13-4
Versus Teams Under .500	5-12-3
First Half Record	9-12-3
Second Half Record	7-13-4

PLAYERS	OVERALL				Projected over 84 Games		
	GP	G	A	PTS	G	A	PTS
A.ZHAMNOV	48	30	35	65	53	61	114
K.TKACHUK	48	22	29	51	38	51	89
T.SELANNE	45	22	26	48	41	49	90
N.EMERSON	48	14	23	37	24	40	64
I.KOROLEV	45	8	22	30	15	41	56
D.DRAKE	43	8	18	26	16	35	51
S.QUINTAL	43	6	17	23	12	33	45
T.NUMMINEN	42	5	16	21	10	32	42
M.EASTWOOD	49	8	11	19	14	19	33
D.MANSON	44	3	15	18	6	29	35
T.STEEN	31	5	10	15	14	27	41
D.SHANNON	40	5	9	14	11	19	30
E.OLCZYK	33	4	9	13	10	23	33
R.GILHEN	44	5	6	11	10	11	21
D.SHANNON	19	5	3	8	22	13	35
K.KING	48	4	2	6	7	3	10
N.WILKINSON	40	1	4	5	2	8	10
M.GROSEK	24	2	2	4	7	7	14
G.BROWN	9	0	3	3	0	28	28
R.MURRAY	10	0	2	2	0	17	17
O.MIKULCHIK	25	0	2	2	0	7	7
C.MARTIN	20	0	1	1	0	4	4
T.HANSEN	1	0	0	0	0	0	0
J.LEBLANC	2	0	0	0	0	0	0
L.BORSATO	4	0	0	0	0	0	0
R.ROMANIUK	6	0	0	0	0	0	0
B.THOMPSON	29	0	0	0	0	0	0

All-Time Rankings - INDIVIDUAL

Goals
Dale Hawerchuk	379
Thomas Steen	259
Paul MacLean	248

Assists
Dale Hawerchuk	550
Thomas Steen	543
Paul MacLean	270

Points
Dale Hawerchuk	929
Thomas Steen	802
Paul MacLean	518

Best Individual Seasons

Goals
Teemu Selanne	1992-93	76
Dale Hawerchuk	1984-85	53
Dale Hawerchuk	1986-87	47

Assists
Phil Housley	1992-93	79
Dale Hawerchuk	1987-88	77
Dale Hawerchuk	1984-85	77

Points
Teemu Selanne	1992-93	132
Dale Hawerchuk	1984-85	130
Dale Hawerchuk	1987-88	121

EASTERN
CONFERENCE

Boston Bruins

Depending on your point of view, the Boston Garden was a shrine, oozing with memories and character, or it was a dilapidated old relic, oozing with memories and rats.

That's up for debate, but last season's playoff collapse isn't. That was just plain ugly. The Bruins were shut out three times in their five-game first round loss to New Jersey, including the first two at home.

That gave everyone the opportunity to play the *Blame Game*. Harry Sinden pointed at the forwards and said they quit, didn't work hard enough and weren't physical enough. Cam Neely said the playoff collapse shouldn't have been a surprise because they weren't good enough. Coach Brian Sutter, after he was fired, said the team played better than should be expected considering the talent.

Translation of the latter two: Sinden's fault for not getting better players.

Sinden didn't get around to blaming Sutter until after the playoffs when he fired him. The players had already beaten him to the punch, around mid-season suggesting nobody liked him, and that most of the players on the farm team didn't either.

Sinden took care of that problem when he hired Kasper, the Friendly Coach. More on him in the coaching section.

The team now moves into the FleetCentre, which logically means they no longer have the advantage of playing in Boston Garden.

It's been 28 years to be exact since they last had a losing season at home, or a losing season of any kind.

Twenty-eight consecutive seasons in the playoffs is an NHL record. Twenty-eight winning seasons is equally impressive, but it's not an NHL record.

Consecutive Winning Seasons

	From	Through	Years
Montreal	1948-49	1982-83	35
Boston	1967-69	1994-95	28*
Chicago	1960-61	1975-76	16
Philadelphia	1972-73	1987-88	16
NY Islanders	1974-75	1987-88	14
Buffalo	1974-75	1984-85	11

* streak is current

Sinden has been the general manager for 23 of the 28 years. A man without a losing season. Ten times the Bruins have finished first in their division and 12 times they've had more than 100 points. Pretty impressive, huh?

That's if you're looking at the water bottle as half full. If you look at as half-empty then you'd notice that they've never won a Stanley Cup during that stretch and on eight occasions were knocked out in the first round of the playoffs.

Perhaps Sinden builds teams that are meant to perform well during the regular season and doesn't take into consideration the playoffs.

Let's just assume that's true, us being negative types and all. Let's examine some theories of how the Bruins could perform so well during the regular season and then fall short in the playoffs.

Theory #1 - Boston Garden

There's always been a huge advantage in playing in Boston Garden – the small ice-surface, the closeness of the fans, the intimidation. Sinden had the luxury of building a team based on the arena.

Maybe that stuff all works fine during the regular season but isn't as big a factor during the playoffs when teams are more intense and less likely to be distracted.

And maybe it only works against the weak and mediocre. I went back and checked how the Bruins have done at home versus the top three teams from each of the past 10 seasons, excluding last year.

Versus the top three teams, between 1984-95 and 1993-94, the Bruins had a home record of 19-27-10 for a winning percentage of only .429. Against everyone else they had a mark of 213-93-42 for a .672 percentage.

Good teams apparently weren't intimidated by playing in the Bruins Garden – during the regular season or the playoffs. Perhaps the more talented teams could adapt easier to the smaller ice surface, or possibly they even enjoyed playing on it.

Theory #2 - Intense Coaches

An intense coach demands the most from his players all the time. It's a long season, and by the playoffs maybe that type of team doesn't have anything extra to give. They've already been playing playoff hockey and that's as good as they get.

We can't go back and judge all the coaches. We know Brian Sutter is intense, but what about the other nine coaches Sinden has employed besides himself. How do we judge them?

Oh, I know. Let's see how many of them also were with the Bruins when they played. That way, we know they learned the Bruin way.

Surprise. Seven of the 10 played in the NHL with the Boston Bruins.

Steve Kasper, next in line, also played with Boston.

Theory #3 - Late call-ups

It's a Sinden tradition to bring guys in near the end of the year. They play a couple games and then get full billing in the playoffs. It happens almost every season.

I went through the list last year in *The Hockey Annual*, so I won't do it again. But, trust me it happens. This year the latecomers were Sandy Moger and Fred Knipscheer.

These late additions often make a substantial contribution, no doubt about it, but the problem is they weren't sweating it out in the trenches with the team all season. Some of those who were, end up sitting in the press box, and you just know they're not smiling very much.

But, we don't want to get too stupid about this. Sinden has had a winning team for 23 years and few would argue that he's one of the smartest hockey people in the game.

Perhaps we're just nit-picking.

(Or perhaps we're not.)

TEAM PREVIEW

GOAL: The biggest question mark before last season began was who was going to play goal. Blaine Lacher, a fiery, competitive free agent signee out of Lake Superior University, answered that question early. He had a sensational start and quickly entrenched himself as the number one goalie. Later in the season he slowed down somewhat, but he's a sure bet to be number one again.

The word on Lacher is that he's not technically sound, but there's a long list of successful NHL goalies who couldn't spell technical. What it probably means in Lacher's case is that he'll have his ups and downs and end up splitting the chores more evenly when there's someone else worthy enough to split them.

Vincent Riendeau didn't work out and was put on waivers late in the season. He quit the team rather than be sent to the minors, but then reconsidered, and then left again after one game in Providence. His future with the Bruins is as bright as mud.

John Blue doesn't seem to be an integral part of it either, especially after the Bruins acquired Craig Billington from Ottawa at the trade deadline. Billington's stats weren't impressive (3.06 GAA, .864 save percentage) but he won five of six decisions. He also became an unrestricted free agent at the end of the season.

Evgeny Ryabchikov, a first round draft pick in 1994 was supposed to challenge Lacher for a spot on the Bruins but he didn't even challenge in Providence. The Bruins called him up during the lockout so they wouldn't have to pay his salary, a curious move considering Ryabchikov needs to become acclimatized to the North American game if he is to have a future with the Bruins.

Oddly enough, the number one goalie prospect now appears to be Scott Bailey, who bounced around the lowly East Coast League before getting a full time shot with Providence last year. He excelled there, was up among the league goaltending leaders and may earn a shot this season with the big club.

1994/95	GP	MIN	GA	AVG	W	L	T	SO
Lacher	35	1965	79	2.41	19	11	2	4
Riendeau	11	565	27	2.87	3	6	1	0
Billington	8	373	19	3.06	5	1	0	0

DEFENCE: If not for Ray Bourque this would be a fairly lousy defence. If not for Bourque and Don Sweeney this would be a terrible defence. If not for Al Iafrate, everybody wouldn't be scratching their heads all the time.

Let's start with Bourque. It's gets kind of boring just saying how good the guy is all the time. But, he'll be 35 this season, so we only have to say it for, what, 10 more years? Bourque has been a first or second all-star selection each of his 16 years in the league and has now tied for most first-team selections. This is how the list looks.

Most first-team all-star selections

Ray Bourque	12
Gordie Howe	12
Doug Harvey	10
Bobby Hull	10
Bobby Orr	8
Ted Lindsay	8
Maurice Richard	8
Wayne Gretzky	8
Eddie Shore	7
Glenn Hall	7

New coach Kasper said Bourque won't be getting as much ice-time this season so he can save him some wear and tear. That's what he said when he was first hired, but wait until he's behind the bench deciding which defencemen to put out next. He's going to have an awful hard time not patting Bourque on the shoulder.

Don Sweeney wasn't supposed to be as good as he's turned out – small (5-10, 188 lbs.) and selected 166th overall in the 1984 draft. This will be his eighth season in the NHL and he's proven his critics wrong. Last season he was called on to play more often and he came through. After the season he was rewarded with a nice five year contract.

Al Iafrate missed all of last year with knee problems. He also accused the Bruins of trying to rush him back into the lineup when he wasn't ready, and not telling him the damage he was doing to his knee in the previous playoffs. Everybody denies everything, but the bottom line is the Bruins sure could use him.

I like Iafrate for personal reasons. It was maybe 10 years ago at Maple Leaf Gardens and I was assigned to do a feature story on him. It was my first interview with a player and I was a bit apprehensive, especially considering it was a tight deadline. In those days, with Harold Ballard around, the media was banned from the dressing room. At practise, I approached Iafrate before he went into the room to get ready and asked him for an interview afterwards. He nodded his head and went by. I was positive he would forget, and that I would be quickly out of a job.

After practise, he came off the ice, looked around for me, and then motioned me down from the stands to the players' bench where he gave me a lengthy in-depth and pleasant interview.

I was always grateful for that, being my first time, and always wished him well. Most of us know the rest of the story. A guy with maybe the most talent in the league, who has had his personal problems, and just never has been able to put it all together consistently. A truly awesome specimen when he does, however.

The rest of the defense is nothing special, especially after they traded Glen Wesley to Hartford. Not that they could resist. New Whaler GM Jim Rutherford handed over three first round draft picks. Sinden must have thought it was Christmas.

David Shaw, Alexei Kasatonov, Jamie Huscroft, Jon Rohloff and John Gruden round out last year's defense corps.

Huscroft is a journeyman tough guy; Kasatonov will be 36 this year; Gruden is a mobile, speedy defenceman who hasn't shown his offensive talent yet; and Rohloff is best known so far for having the puck knocked off his stick in overtime in last year's playoffs, allowing New Jersey to score.

Down on the farm is Jeff Serowik, an offensive defenceman of some note who has spent five years in the minors.

Not much depth on this defence and not much on the way up, which makes this a problem area. If Iafrate is back, however, it's certainly not a bad defence, and one that won't be hurt by the larger ice surface in the new arena.

FORWARD: It's a Bruin tradition to have a whole bunch of guys scoring a mediocre amount of goals. That seems to have worked just fine in the past, and as long as Neely and Oates are around, that's pretty much all it takes.

But, if Neely doesn't score in the playoffs, and nobody else does either, than it becomes a trouble area. And when minor league call-up Guy Larose is the most aggressive forward in the post-season, that spells trouble as well.

There are few better goal scorers around than Neely when he's healthy, and hey, he's not a bad actor either (*Dumb and Dumber*).

Neely led the league last year in power play goals, and if you project his total over an 84 game schedule, it gives him 32, just two shy of the 34, the all-time record set by Tim Kerr in Philadelphia.

Most Power Play Goals - 1994-95 Season

Cam Neely	Bos.	16
Donald Audette	Buf.	13
Owen Nolan	Que.	13
Alexander Mogilny	Buf.	12
Peter Bondra	Wsh.	12

Much of last season was spent auditioning left wingers for Neely and Oates. That's when Sutter didn't experiment with playing them apart. Playing with those two guys, you'd think your mother could pile up the points, but just about everyone failed. Marius Czerkawski had a couple shots at it, Mikko Makela, Ted Donato, Glen Murray, and the list goes on.

Now they have somebody they KNOW will fit in. During the summer, the Bruins traded Bryan Smolinski and Glen Murray to Pittsburgh for Kevin Stevens and Shawn McEachern.

Stevens, who is from the area, has two 50 goal seasons, and two in the forties, plus (and this is a big plus) he has a history of being outstanding in the playoffs.

The trade gives them one of the best lines in the league, and takes some pressure off the other under-achieving forwards. McEachern almost replaces Smolinski's production, and with the free agent signing of Todd Elik, they suddenly are pretty decent at center.

The danger with this trade, of course, is that Smolinski might not have reached his full potential, and Murray hasn't reached any potential. Smolinski scored 30 goals in his rookie season and 18 last year (projected to 34 over 84 games) and he's only 23 years old. Murray, who is 22, has been a big disappointment to the Bruins. Just a big guy with small numbers.

The thing about the bigger players is that it often takes them longer to develop. But, when they do, they can be dominant. Even Neely took four years to develop into a good goal scorer.

Stevens, who has had some tough luck with injuries recently, is 30 years old, and McEachern, who also hails from Massachusetts, is 26.

I told you last year about Sinden's penchant for old Europeans, despite his lack of success in that area. The latest flop was Makela, who hadn't played in the NHL the previous three years, for good reason. Undaunted, Sinden signed Mats Naslund, four years removed from the NHL.

Naslund got off to a slow start, but turned out okay, if not especially good. In the second half of the season he was fourth in team scoring. It was just a one time deal, however and he won't be back this season.

Marius Czercawski, an extremely rare Polish product, had a decent rookie season, finishing fifth in scoring.

Most of the remaining Bruin forwards are on-again, off-again types, who show something for a spell, and then go into hiding. Otherwise, the idea, it seems, is to get as many Massachusetts-born players or old Europeans into the lineup as possible. Stevens, McEachern, Steve Heinze, Ted Donato and Stephen Leach all hail from Massachusetts.

SPECIAL TEAMS: Opposing teams are going to try very hard to stay out of the penalty box when they play the Bruins this year. Neely, Oates, Stevens, Bourque and Iafrate are a formidable extra-man force and should challenge for the best overall.

Mind you, last year in the playoffs it all fell apart. The power play went from 23.1% to 10.0%, and penalty killing fell from first in the league to 15th out of 16 teams.

The nature of power plays is that they can get hot and go on a roll for a while, or can get cold and roll over. It happens to every team, up and down during the season, so the play-off collapse really isn't anything to worry about.

The penalty killing percentage was first overall for the second year in a row. They have lots of talent in that area and have probably been helped by their arena. With everything so close, it was easier to crowd the opponents and get on them fast. Buffalo, which also has a small ice surface, finished second two years ago, and third last season.

It will be interesting to see if the bigger ice surface has much affect on the penalty killing. But, they were third overall on the road last year, so maybe not.

Power Play	G	ATT	PCT	
Overall	46	211	21.8%	(4th NHL)
Home	25	120	20.8%	(9th NHL)
Road	21	91	23.1%	(3rd NHL)

4 SHORT HANDED GOALS ALLOWED (T-9th NHL)

Penalty Killing	G	TSH	PCT	
Overall	24	183	86.9%	(1st NHL)
Home	12	96	87.5%	(2nd NHL)
Road	12	87	86.2%	(3rd NHL)

3 SHORT HANDED GOALS SCORED (T-20th NHL)

Penalties	GP	MIN	AVG	
BRUINS	48	793	16.5	(9th NHL)

BRUINS SPECIAL TEAMS SCORING

Power play	G	A	PTS
BOURQUE	9	20	29
OATES	4	19	23
NEELY	16	3	19
NASLUND	2	9	11
CZERKAWSKI	1	7	8
SMOLINSKI	6	3	9
SWEENEY	1	6	7
KASATONOV	0	7	7

Short handed	G	A	PTS
OATES	1	0	1
KASATONOV	1	0	1
HEINZE	1	0	1
DONATO	0	1	1

COACHING AND MANAGEMENT: If you didn't develop a higher respect for Harry Sinden during the lockout then you're probably a player.

Of course, Sinden didn't need any more respect because he already had plenty with his managing of the Bruins. Oh, he takes some heat on occasion (see Bruins introduction), and would probably tell you himself that he isn't perfect. But, his incidence of error is among the lowest.

Sinden is supposed to step down soon and hand the reins over to Assistant GM Mike O'Connell.

As for the hiring of Steve Kasper, that too was not without controversy. Assistant coach Tommy McVie thought the Bruin head coaching job was his, and even went so far as to suggest Kasper needed more time in the minors.

Sinden didn't tell McVie in person that he would be fired instead of promoted, and took some heat for it. He had his reasons, he said. Fair enough. Maybe there was something personal between the two.

Kasper is only 33 years old (McVie was 59) and coached the Bruin farm team in Providence last year. In fact, he's even younger than Bourque, a friend and former teammate. The reports on Kasper are glowing, just as they are with the hiring of every new coach. The players in Providence liked him and he's supposed to be a good communicator.

Whatever the case, he has a short life expectancy in Boston as long as Sinden is still running the show. Two years, maybe, if they win, less if they lose. If the Bruins have a poor start, he won't last the year.

DRAFT

1995 DRAFT SELECTIONS

Round	Sel.	Player	Pos	Amateur Team
1	9	Kyle McLaren	D	Kelowna (WHL)
1	21	Sean Brown	D	Belleville (OHL)
2	47	Paxton Schafer	G	Medicine Hat (WHL)
3	73	Bill McCauley	C	Detroit (OHL)
4	99	Cameron Mann	RW	Peterborough (OHL)
6	151	Yevgeny Shaldybin	D	Russia
7	177	Per Johan Axelsson	RW	Sweden
8	203	Sergei Zhukov	D	Russia
9	229	Jonathan Murphy	D	Peterborough (OHL)

Kyle McLaren is big at 6-4, 210 lbs. He's compared (they're all compared to someone) to Larry Robinson, except that he's supposed to be more physical. He is also supposed to be a great skater, but doesn't have great offensive numbers in junior. He was 13-19-32 last year in Tacoma in 47 games. And judging by his penalty minute totals (68 minutes in 47 games) isn't all that aggressive or mean for a big guy.

Sean Brown is a big (6-2, 196) stay-at-home defenseman. Last year in Belleville he was 2-16-18, with 200 penalty minutes. That sounds a lot more mean and aggressive.

PROGNOSIS: The core Bruin players are getting on in years so the team has to take a run at it now. They can get by during the regular season on the strength of the power play alone. Plus, they've got a great first line, the potential for a decent second line, and now the role players can play their roles without feeling so much responsibility to score. In other words, they can score a moderate amount and still make a big contribution.

Before the Stevens trade, I might have suggested the Bruins would hover dangerously close to the .500 level, but now they have a chance to be a very good team.

Once it becomes clear they have a shot at it, Sinden will make some adjustments – he can't help it. Those adjustments will probably come in the form of an old European or bringing up young guys just before the playoffs.

Here's some free advice. DON'T DO IT.

Get your team set by the trading deadline and run with them.

PREDICTION:
Northeast Division: 1st
Eastern Conference: 3rd
Overall: 7th

STAT SECTION

	Conference Rank	League Rank
Record 27-18-3	4	6
Home 15-7-2	7	9
Away 12-11-1	2	5
Team Plus\Minus +1	6	10
Goals For 150	3	9
Goals Against 127	4	6

PLAYER	1994-95 OVERALL				PROJECTED 84 GAME TOTALS		
	GP	G	A	PTS	G	A	PTS
A.OATES	48	12	41	53	21	72	93
R.BOURQUE	46	12	31	43	22	57	79
C.NEELY	42	27	14	41	54	28	82
B.SMOLINSKI	44	18	13	31	34	25	59
M.CZERKAWSKI	47	12	14	26	21	25	46
M.NASLUND	34	8	14	22	20	35	55
D.SWEENEY	47	3	19	22	5	34	39
T.DONATO	47	10	10	20	18	18	36
J.STUMPEL	44	5	13	18	10	25	35
S.HEINZE	36	7	9	16	16	21	37
A.KASATONOV	44	2	14	16	4	27	31
B.HUGHES	44	6	6	12	11	11	22
S.LEACH	35	5	6	11	12	14	26
J.ROHLOFF	34	3	8	11	7	20	27
D.REID	38	5	5	10	11	11	22
S.MOGER	18	2	6	8	9	28	37
G.MURRAY	35	5	2	7	12	5	17
D.SHAW	44	3	4	7	6	8	14
J.HUSCROFT	34	0	6	6	0	15	15
J.GRUDEN	38	0	6	6	0	13	13
F.KNIPSCHEER	16	3	1	4	16	5	21
M.MAKELA	11	1	2	3	8	15	23
B.HARKINS	1	0	1	1	0	84	84
M.POTVIN	6	0	1	1	0	14	14
B.LACHER	35	0	1	1	0	2	2
J.SEROWIK	1	0	0	0	0	0	0
G.PANTELEEV	1	0	0	0	0	0	0
C.STEWART	5	0	0	0	0	0	0
V.RIENDEAU	11	0	0	0	0	0	0
C.BILLINGTON	17	0	0	0	0	0	0

MISCELLANEOUS STATS

One Goal Games	15-9
Times outshooting opponent	43
Times outshot	5
Even shots	0
Average Shots For	34.3
Average Shots Against	24.3
Overtime	2-3-3
Longest Winning streak	4
Longest Undefeated streak	4
Longest Losing streak	3
Longest winless streak	3
Versus Teams Over .500	9-11-3
Versus Teams Under .500	18-7-0
First Half Record	12-10-2
Second Half Record	15-8-1

PLAYOFFS

Results:	Lost to New Jersey in opening round 4-1.
Record: 1-4	Home: 0-3 Away: 1-1
Goals For:	5 (1.0/gm)
Goals Against:	14 (2.8/gm)
Overtime:	0-1
Power play:	10.0% (15th)
Penalty Killing:	70.6% (15th)

BOSTON BRUINS

	GP	G	A	PTS	+/-	PIM
RAY BOURQUE	5	0	3	3	5-	0
CAM NEELY	5	2	0	2	4-	2
MATS NASLUND	5	1	0	1	3-	0
ADAM OATES	5	1	0	1	6-	2
MARIUSZ CZERKAWSKI	5	1	0	1	0	0
DAVID SHAW	5	0	1	1	2-	4
BRYAN SMOLINSKI	5	0	1	1	2-	4
CRAIG BILLINGTON	1	0	0	0	0	0
GLEN MURRAY	2	0	0	0	1-	2
GUY LAROSE	4	0	0	0	0	0
FRED KNIPSCHEER	4	0	0	0	0	0
BRENT HUGHES	5	0	0	0	2-	4
JAMIE HUSCROFT	5	0	0	0	0	11
ALEXEI KASATONOV	5	0	0	0	0	2
DAVE REID	5	0	0	0	1	0
DON SWEENEY	5	0	0	0	4-	4
TED DONATO	5	0	0	0	0	4
STEVE HEINZE	5	0	0	0	0	0
JON ROHLOFF	5	0	0	0	1-	6
JOZEF STUMPEL	5	0	0	0	1-	0
BLAINE LACHER	5	0	0	0	0	0

All-Time Rankings - INDIVIDUAL

Goals

John Bucyk	545
Phil Esposito	459
Rick Middleton	402

Assists

Ray Bourque	908
John Bucyk	794
Bobby Orr	624

Points

John Bucyk	1,339
Ray Bourque	1,231
Phil Esposito	1,012

Best Individual Seasons

Goals

Phil Esposito	70/71	76
Phil Esposito	73/74	68
Phil Esposito	71/72	66

Assists

Bobby Orr	70/71	102
Adam Oates	92/93	97
Bobby Orr	73/74	90

Points

Phil Esposito	70/71	152
Phil Esposito	73/74	145
Adam Oates	92/93	142

Buffalo Sabres

The Sabres' silver season was anything but golden.

All the signs were there for Buffalo to come up big in their 25th NHL year. After a successful 1993/94 campaign, despite injuries to their stars, everything was in place for a run to the top.

They had a good defensive system, an excellent coach, maybe the best goaltending, big scorers returning in Pat LaFontaine and Alexander Mogilny, a good mix of youth and veterans, and a solid if unspectacular defence.

So what did all those ingredients add up to? Chopped ice. They were also-rans and then performed their usual belly flop in the playoffs.

A mediocre regular season is acceptable – just ask the New Jersey Devils who finished with one more point than the Sabres – if a team can play well in the playoffs.

But Buffalo refuses to do that. Even when they have a good regular season.

Five games against Philadelphia and the Sabres were once again assured their vacation time wouldn't be cut short.

No team in the league has been as unsuccessful as the Sabres recently at getting past the first round. Consider the following chart.

First Round Record
(last 10 times in the playoffs)

Buffalo	1-9
Hartford	1-7 *
Calgary	2-8
Winnipeg	2-8
Boston	4-6
Chicago	4-6
Detroit	4-6
Toronto	4-6
Dallas	5-5
Los Angeles	5-5
New Jersey	3-5 *
NY Rangers	5-5
Philadelphia	5-5
Quebec	4-5 *
Vancouver	5-5
Washington	5-5
NY Islanders	6-4
Pittsburgh	6-4
St. Louis	6-4
Montreal	8-2
Edmonton	9-1
San Jose	2-0 *

* Less than 10 playoff appearances.

Terrible. The only thing that can be said in their defence is that they had to face tougher teams than most. Seven of the nine defeats came at the hands of either Montreal or Boston.

In any event, another first round loss means another housecleaning. Out as coach is genius John Muckler. Former genius, that is. It's amazing the number of brain cells coaches can lose in one year.

He stays on as GM, and we're told, made the decision himself to step back from the bench. A little tough to believe that one, however.

A story came out of Buffalo that he had lost control of the team and the respect of the players. What is it with that stuff all the time? Run a tight ship and try to instill some discipline and the players prepare to mutiny?

Doesn't bother Mike Keenan any. It's his way or the highway. He doesn't go around handing out candy.

Things got so bad for Muckler that he got into an altercation with a heckler who turned out to be an assistant district attorney. Stories vary depending on the source, but one says he struck the heckler. No charges were laid, however, but he and assistant John Tortorelli were suspended by the league for three games.

Charges were laid against Dominik Hasek, however, when he was caught driving while intoxicated.

The Sabres will do their best to forget last season, and many of the players. The enigmatic Alexander Mogilny was traded to Vancouver, Dale Hawerchuk and Wayne Presley were lost to free agency, and new coach Ted Nolan takes over behind the bench.

It will be a rebuilding year in Buffalo, but with some nice building materials.

TEAM PREVIEW

GOAL: Dominik Hasek proved his first year in Buffalo was no fluke. For the second season in a row he took home the Vezina Trophy as the league's top goaltender.

Hasek had the best goals against average for the second year in a row at 2.11, posted the highest save percentage at .930 and tied Ed Belfour for the most shutouts with five.

In a late season edition of *The Hockey News* he was named number one in their list of top 40 players in the game.

The closest thing you can find to a negative about Hasek is that he will be 30 years old this season, surprising considering he's only been the number one man for two of them. Not to worry, while other players are starting to get old at that age, 30 is still prime time for a netminder.

Oh, one other negative. He was picked up last season and charged with drunk driving, and was in a car accident on a separate occasion where alcohol was involved.

Grant Fuhr was the backup to Hasek and was kept around as trade bait. He was washed up. Some people knew it, and some didn't. Sam McMaster apparently didn't, so Fuhr was eventually sent to Los Angeles and Robb Stauber became the new backup man.

Stauber can handle the role as long as he doesn't play too often, and down on the farm are Markus Ketterer and Steve Shields, neither of whom would make him fear for his job. Free agent Eric Raymond came on and played better than both of them. And just to make sure, free agent Andrei Trefilov was signed away from Calgary in the off-season. And just to make doubly, triply, sure, the Sabres also drafted goalie Martin Biron in the first round.

Lowest Goals Against Average Leaders - Last 20 Years

DOMINIK HASEK	BUF.	1993-94	1.95
Ken Dryden	Mtl.	1974-75	2.03
Ken Dryden	Mtl.	1977-78	2.05
Bunny Larocque	Mtl.	1976-77	2.09
DOMINIK HASEK	BUF.	1994-95	2.11
Ken Dryden	Mtl.	1978-79	2.30

1994/95	GP	MIN	GA	AVG	W	L	T	SO
Hasek	41	2416	85	2.11	19	14	7	5
Stauber	6	317	20	3.79	2	3	0	0
Fuhr	3	180	12	4.00	1	2	0	0

DEFENCE: There are a lot of the puzzle pieces on the Sabres that go into making a successful defence. They have a young hot-shot quarterback in Alexei Zhitnik; other offensive types in Garry Galley and Doug Bodger; a solid defensive type in Craig Muni; promise in Richard Smehlik, Mark Astley, and Mike Wilson, a huge defenseman obtained from Vanvouver in the Mogilny deal; and experience in Charlie Huddy (unrestricted free agent) and Doug Houda.

But, they're missing a corner piece – toughness, size, meanness, somebody who scares the opposing forwards. Someone like Brian Marchment or Scott Stevens or Chris Chelios or Kevin Hatcher.

Not that it will matter much anyway this year. For now, they need to build a defense that will still be around in a couple years.

The Sabre defense made a transformation of sorts last season. Two years ago when they had a successful regular season they had more defensive defensemen in the lineup. But, then it was determined they needed more offense out of their defence. Bodger was their only serious offensive threat and he wasn't much of one at that. So, Muckler went out and got Garry Galley and Alexei Zhitnik.

Maybe that's one too many offensive types, which frees one of them up, probably Bodger, for a trade.

The Sabres want to get their young guys into the lineup, but they still are going to need their veterans, especially with so many youngsters on the forward line.

FORWARD: I don't know why this was considered a problem area for the Sabres. They had everything – superstar scorers, secondary scorers, toughness, good checkers, good young players, experienced veterans, and plenty of top prospects ready to give it a go.

Oh, wait a minute. I know why.

It's because they didn't score. Eighteenth in the league last year, but we don't know if that was a product of the system, injuries, bad karma or what.

Scoring will be more difficult this year without Mogilny and Hawerchuk.

LaFontaine is still there but he has been slowed by injuries over the last two years, and has only played 38 games during that stretch. His projected point total from last season put him over 100 points.

Now, to the secondary scorers. Okay, uh, scorer. Right winger Donald Audette turned into somewhat of a sniper last season. He's a little guy (5-8, 175) and not an all-star defensively, but he put in 24 goals, 13 of them on the power play for the second most in the league. But, he's an upsy-downsy type of guy and can't be depended on to do the same year after year.

Yuri Khymylev is also a mid-range secondary scorer, but is 31 years old and can't be expected to improve much.

Craig Simpson can also score, but only played 24 games last year and is always iffy with a bad back.

Mike Peca, obtained from Vancouver in the Mogilny deal, was a prolific minor league scorer, but had his ups and downs with the Canucks last year in his rookie season.

One guy who was supposed to be a secondary scorer but ended up being a secondary player was Derek Plante. He scored a miniscule three goals in 47 games and had lost his job by playoff time. It seems, according to the chart below, he was getting the shots, they just weren't going in.

LOWEST SHOOTING PERCENTAGE
(forwards, 80 or more shots)

		Shots	Goals	Shooting %
Derek Plante	Buf.	94	3	3.2
Claude Lemieux	N.J.	117	6	5.1
Cliff Ronning	Van.	93	6	6.5
Doug Weight	Edm.	104	7	6.7
Brian Bellows	Mtl.	110	8	7.3
Brian Rolston	N.J.	92	7	7.6
Wayne Gretzky	L.A.	142	11	7.7
Chris Gratton	T.B.	91	7	7.7

The toughness comes from Rob Ray and Brad May. Ray is one of the premier roughniks in the league, and tied for fourth in league penalty minutes with 173. He also surpassed Mike Foligno as the all-time penalty king in Buffalo with 1,459 penalty minutes.

May is a power forward waiting to happen. Waiting a little too long perhaps. Just three goals is a major step back for him after improving each of his first three years. But, it's not usual for a big (in size) goal scorer to wait three or four years to develop. This will be his fifth so time to put up.

Matthew Barnaby also fills the tough-guy role when he's in the lineup. Including time spent with Rochester he had 390 penalty minutes last season.

The checkers, and some of the veterans, can be found in Dave Hannan, Scott Pearson, and Bob Sweeney. Presley is gone, signed as a free agent by the Rangers. He was a valuable guy because he was a checker who could score. Presley's 14 goals were third on the team, and he and Hannan were among the league leaders in short-handed goals.

Now for the youth, all of whom will get a chance to play with the Sabres this year.

Jason Dawe has split the last two seasons between Buffalo and Rochester. He had 27 goals in Rochester last year, second behind Viktor Gordiouk, despite only playing 44 games. With Buffalo he had seven goals in 42 games but dressed for each playoff game.

Center Brian Holzinger joined the Sabres after finishing his college career at Bowling Green by winning the Hobey Baker award as the most valuable college player in the United States. He's considered by some to be a Pat LaFontaine type of player. In four regular season games he earned three assists, and in five playoff contests he earned another three points.

Two other prospects got into late season games after their teams were knocked out of the junior playoffs. Both of them scored a goal in their first and only NHL games. Wayne Primeau (6-3, 193), brother of Keith, was 34-62-96 with Owen Sound in the OHL. Curtis Brown was 51-53-104 for Moose Jaw in the WHL.

There's not much point getting into who will play what position for the Sabres. People are going to have to move around with the departures of right-wingers Mogilny and Presley.

Heck, there's not too much point in going into who will play and who won't. But, as long as the Sabres fans keep their expectations low, this could be an exciting season waiting and watching which of the youngsters come through for them.

SPECIAL TEAMS: The Sabres special teams are often near the top of the league, especially penalty killing where they've finished no worse than third the last three years. One of the reasons is the small ice surface which doesn't allow opposing players the time to set up in the offensive zone. Interestingly, both Buffalo and Boston who have been playing on small rinks, are often among the league leaders in penalty killing.

Another Sabre plus last season was their expertise at scoring short-handed goals. They had 13 to tie Washington for the league lead. The year before they had 21 for second place.

Wayne Presley and Dave Hannan led the way. Presley, with five goals and one assist, was tied for the league lead with six points. Presley, however, is now with the Rangers.

The power play won't be any better with Mogilny gone. They should be okay from the points, with Zhitnik, Galley and Bodger, but up front there's only LaFontaine and Audette with any proven scoring ability. Audette's 13 power play markers were the second most in the league, behind Cam Neeley's 16.

Power Play	G	ATT	PCT
Overall	45	242	18.6% (11th NHL)
Home	26	118	22.0% (8th NHL)
Road	19	124	15.3% (T-16th NHL)

7 SHORT HANDED GOALS ALLOWED (T-18th NHL)

Penalty Killing	G	TSH	PCT
Overall	32	220	85.5% (3rd NHL)
Home	14	105	86.7% (4th NHL)
Road	18	115	84.3% (8th NHL)

13 SHORT HANDED GOALS SCORED (T-1st NHL)

Penalties	GP	MIN	AVG
SABRES	48	1022	21.3 (16th NHL)

TOP SPECIAL TEAM SCORERS

Power play	G	A	PTS
MOGILNY	12	14	26
AUDETTE	13	10	23
GALLEY	2	15	17
LAFONTAINE	6	10	16
BODGER	2	10	12
PLANTE	2	8	10
HAWERCHUK	2	8	10
ZHITNIK	3	5	8

Short handed	G	A	PTS
PRESLEY	5	1	6
HANNAN	2	3	5
SWEENEY	2	1	3
BODGER	0	3	3

COACHING AND MANAGEMENT: John Muckler won't be coaching this season but he'll still be around to handle the general manager chores. In my opinion, he was one of the best at both, but in just the GM role he's still one of the smartest. He's able to determine the needs and then go out and fill them.

Needed more offensive defensemen – got Alexei Zhitnik and Garry Galley. Needed a bigger tougher winger – got Scott Pearson. Needed another veteran on defense – got Charlie Huddy. He did the same thing the year before.

Ted Nolan is the new coach, a surprise to many, considering the prospective coaches available, and considering Nolan has no NHL coaching experience.

Nolan did coach Sault Ste. Marie to the Memorial Cup, and has been an assistant at the NHL level.

He's not in a bad situation in Buffalo, because the Sabres aren't expected to win much. All he has to do is bring along the young players and show improvement.

DRAFT

1995 DRAFT SELECTIONS

Round	Sel.	Player	Pos	Amateur Team
1	14	Jay McKee	D	Niagara Falls (OHL)
1	16	Martin Biron	G	Beauport (QMJHL)
2	42	Mark Dutiaume	LW	Brandon (WHL)
3	66	Mathieu Sunderland	RW	Drummond-ville(QMJHL)
4	94	Matt Davidson	RW	Portland (WHL)
5	111	Marian Menhart	D	Czechoslo-vakia
5	119	Kevin Popp	D	Seattle (WHL)
5	123	Daniel Bienvenue	LW	Val d'Or (QMJHL)
7	172	Brian Scott	LW	Kitchener (OHL)
8	198	Mike Zanutto	C	Oshawa (OHL)
9	224	Rod Skriac	LW	Kamloops (WHL)

In the mid-season Central Scouting Bureau rankings, Jay McKee was ranked 24th among North American skaters, so his stock improved as the year went on. He's tall at almost 6-3, but not very heavy at only 175 pounds. He's considered an all-round type defenseman, but as for offense it will be interesting to see how much his numbers improve from 9-19-28, not very high junior totals.

The other Sabre first round pick comes from the goaltender factory in the Quebec Major Junior Hockey League. He was named the outstanding junior goaltender in Canada last year while setting a Quebec League goals against record of 2.48 and was second in the playoffs with a 2.47 mark. The Quebec League also named him their best professional prospect.

PROGNOSIS: At least Sabre fans won't have to hear the same old excuses this year when the team gets knocked out of the playoffs in the first round. That's because they're not going to make the playoffs.

They're going to take their lumps and like many young teams will have some excellent nights to go along with that.

They're not good enough to make the playoffs this year, although with Quebec shifting divisions they could battle for the last spot.

In any event, the Sabres have some nice young talent, and within a year or two could be ready to start challenging again.

PREDICTION:
Northeast Division: 5th
Eastern Conference: 9th
Overall: 18th

STAT SECTION

		Conference Rank	League Rank
Record	22-19-7	7	11
Home	15-8-1	8	12
Away	7-11-6	7	14
Team Plus\Minus	-2	8	12
Goals For	130	8	18
Goals Against	119	1	3

PLAYERS	1994-95 OVERALL					PROJECTED 84 GAME TOTALS			
	GP	G	A	PTS	PIM	G	A	PTS	PIM
ALEXANDER MOGILNY	44	19	28	47	36	36	53	89	69
DONALD AUDETTE	46	24	13	37	27	44	24	68	49
GARRY GALLEY	47	3	29	32	30	5	52	57	54
PAT LAFONTAINE	22	12	15	27	4	46	57	103	15
YURI KHMYLEV	48	8	17	25	14	14	30	44	24
DEREK PLANTE	47	3	19	22	12	5	34	39	21
DOUG BODGER	44	3	17	20	47	6	32	38	90
WAYNE PRESLEY	46	14	5	19	41	26	9	35	75
DALE HAWERCHUK	23	5	11	16	2	18	40	58	7
DAVE HANNAN	42	4	12	16	32	8	24	32	64
ALEXEI ZHITNIK	32	4	10	14	61	11	26	37	160
JASON DAWE	42	7	4	11	19	14	8	22	38
CRAIG SIMPSON	24	4	7	11	26	14	24	38	91
RICHARD SMEHLIK	39	4	7	11	46	9	15	24	99
BOB SWEENEY	45	5	4	9	18	9	7	16	34
SCOTT PEARSON	42	3	5	8	74	6	10	16	148
CHARLIE HUDDY	41	2	5	7	42	4	10	14	86
BRAD MAY	33	3	3	6	87	8	8	16	221
CRAIG MUNI	40	0	6	6	36	0	13	13	76
MARK ASTLEY	14	2	1	3	12	12	6	18	72
DOUG HOUDA	28	1	2	3	68	3	6	9	204
BRIAN HOLZINGER	4	0	3	3	0	0	63	63	0
ROB RAY	47	0	3	3	173	0	5	5	309
CURTIS BROWN	1	1	1	2	2	84	84	168	168
MATTHEW BARNABY	23	1	1	2	116	4	4	8	423
VIKTOR GORDIOUK	10	0	2	2	0	0	17	17	0
WAYNE PRIMEAU	1	1	0	1	0	84	0	84	0
PETER AMBROZIAK	12	0	1	1	0	0	7	7	0
DOUG MACDONALD	2	0	0	0	0	0	0	0	0
DEAN MELANSON	5	0	0	0	4	0	0	0	67
ROBB STAUBER	7	0	0	0	0	0	0	0	0
DOMINIK HASEK	41	0	0	0	2	0	0	0	4

MISCELLANEOUS STATS

One Goal Games	8-8
Times outshooting opponent	15
Times outshot	32
Even shots	1
Average Shots For	26.5
Average Shots Against	30.3
Overtime	1-1-7
Longest Winning streak	4
Longest Undefeated streak	5
Longest Losing streak	4
Longest winless streak	5
Versus Teams Over .500	7-11-3
Versus Teams Under .500	15-8-4
First Half Record	11-8-5
Second Half Record	11-11-2

PLAYOFFS

Results: Lost conference quarter-finals to Philadelphia
Record: 1-4 Home: 1-1 Away: 0-3
Goals For: 13 (2.6/gm)
Goals Against: 18 (3.6/gm)
Overtime:
Power play: 11.5% (13th)
Penalty Killing: 88.5% (3rd)

PLAYER	GP	G	A	PTS
ALEXANDER MOGILNY	5	3	2	5
WAYNE PRESLEY	5	3	1	4
PAT LAFONTAINE	5	2	2	4
DOUG BODGER	5	0	4	4
BRIAN HOLZINGER	4	2	1	3
JASON DAWE	5	2	1	3
GARRY GALLEY	5	0	3	3
DONALD AUDETTE	5	1	1	2
DAVE HANNAN	5	0	2	2
CRAIG MUNI	5	0	1	1
ALEXEI ZHITNIK	5	0	1	1
YURI KHMYLEV	5	0	1	1
DALE HAWERCHUK	2	0	0	0

MARK ASTLEY	2	0	0	0
CHARLIE HUDDY	3	0	0	0
BRAD MAY	4	0	0	0
DOMINIK HASEK	5	0	0	0
SCOTT PEARSON	5	0	0	0
ROB RAY	5	0	0	0
BOB SWEENEY	5	0	0	0
RICHARD SMEHLIK	5	0	0	0

All-Time Rankings

Goals
Gil Perreault	512
Rick Martin	382
Dave Andreychuk	348

Assists
Gil Perreault	814
Dave Andreychuk	423
Craig Ramsay	420

Points
Gil Perreault	1,326
Dave Andreychuk	771
Rick Martin	695

Shutouts
Don Edwards	14
Tom Barrasso	13
Dominik Hasek	12

Best Seasons

Goals
Alexander Mogilny	92-93	76
Danny Gare	79-80	56
Pat LaFontaine	92-93	53

Assists
Pat LaFontaine	92-93	95
Dale Hawerchuk	92-93	80
Dale Hawerchuk	91-92	75

Points
Pat LaFontaine	92-93	148
Alexander Mogilny	92-93	127
Gil Perreault	75-76	113

Florida Panthers

What's the reward for leading an expansion team to the best first two seasons in NHL history?

Roger Neilson figured it was a contract extension. Instead it was the old heave-ho, despite missing the playoffs by only a point in the franchise's first two seasons.

Neilson's shortcoming was that he only knows how to coach to win. Apparently, he's not a nuturer of young talent. Although with Florida that's a hard conclusion to reach because they didn't have much of it.

In fact, it's a stupid conclusion. On other teams Neilson has coached, rookies have had lots of playing time, and have responded.

I went back and checked some of his other clubs. He never seemed to have a problem playing them when he had them. His most successful season, with the Rangers in 1991-92, featured Tony Amonte and Doug Weight in leading roles as rookies, and a number of other young players.

Neilson's other major problem is that he likes to play a defensive style. Gee, that's awfully unusual in today's NHL. All that style does is...what? Make you better than your talent?

You'd have a hard time coming up with another coach, in the history of the game, who coaxed more out of less. For the Florida Panthers to be so close to the .500 mark in their first two NHL seasons shows his genius.

When the Panthers sink to the depth of the standings, that's when they'll appreciate what he's done for them.

Neilson has been fired plenty of times. He's been behind the bench for six different NHL teams, seven if you count his co-coach title with the Blackhawks for two years.

Beginning with Toronto in the late seventies, Neilson somehow got two winning seasons out of the team in a terrible environment. After he was fired, the Maple Leafs wouldn't have another winning season for 14 years.

In two seasons in Buffalo in the early eighties, Neilson led them to two first place finishes in their division. They haven't had another one since.

In Vancouver he took a weak team to the Stanley Cup finals, and then in his only full season with the club, led them to the most points they'd earn for 10 more years.

With the Rangers he earned that team's best record in almost 20 years and then was fired halfway through the next season.

Gee, no wonder everybody keeps firing him.

The one drawback with Neilson is that because he's able to get the most out of the least, he builds expectations that the team can do even better. But, overachieving isn't something that can always continue. Eventually, they have to return to the level of their talent.

General Manager Bryan Murray, whose coaching legacy is outstanding regular seasons followed by an early playoff exit, hired his buddy Doug MacLean. They worked together in Detroit and Washington, although MacLean's role was always a supporting one.

It will be a supporting role in Florida, too. Murray will have control and for MacLean to earn a niche as his own man will be awfully difficult in that situation.

Expansion Team Records
First two seasons

FLORIDA	53-56-23	.489
Atlanta	55-72-29	.446
Anaheim	49-73-10	.409
Tampa Bay	53-97-18	.369
Buffalo	40-82-34	.365
Vancouver	44-96-16	.333
NY Islanders	31-101-24	.277
Kansas City	27-110-23	.241
San Jose	28-129-7	.192
Ottawa	24-131-13	.182
Washington	19-126-15	.166

TEAM PREVIEW

GOAL: So maybe John Vanbiesbrouck didn't set the league on fire like he did the previous season when he was a viable candidate for both the Vezina and the Hart Trophy. He was still in the upper echelon of NHL goaltenders.

Backup to Vanbiesbrouck is Mark Fitzpatrick, who pushed aside personal problems and did his job well.

Roger Neilson, who knows motivation, did a smart thing with Vanbiesbrouck and Fitzpatrick. They both played every minute in games against their former teams.

Vanbiesbrouck posted a 1-2-1 record against the Rangers, playing especially well against the defending Stanley Cup champs in New York, where there was a 0-0 tie, and a 4-3 Panther win.

Fitzpatrick also performed well against the Islanders, especially on Long Island where there was a 2-2 tie and a 2-1 Islander win.

In Cincinnati last season were Frederic Chabot (25-12-7, 2.93) and Danny Lorenz (24-10-3, 3.40). Both are well travelled and can fill in at the NHL level if someone gets injured.

In six pro seasons, Chabot has played with nine different teams, including five in one year.

The duo combined to finish fourth in the IHL in goals against average.

	GP	MIN	GA	AVG	W	L	T	SO
Vanbiesbrouck	37	2087	86	2.47	14	15	4	4
Fitzpatrick	15	819	36	2.64	6	7	2	2

DEFENCE: Only two Panther defensemen last year were full-timers – Gord Murphy and Geoff Smith. That means it's going to be a battle for jobs this year.

1994 first overall pick Ed Jovanovski should have one of them. After going back to junior last year with Windsor in the OHL, he proved to be dominant at times. He had 23 goals and 42 assists in 50 games and used his size to bully opponents.

He did, however, have his problems off the ice where he faced criminal assault charges along with a couple of his teammates in Windsor.

It's not very likely he'll be a dominant player in the NHL for the first couple years. But, the Panthers have already indicated they will make a bigger committment to youth, so Jovanovski should be there game in and game out. His opportunity to play on the power play seems fairly decent as well.

Gord Murphy has been playing one point regularly, but Swede Magnus Svensson and journeyman Jason Wooley both also hung out there after joining the team. Svensson, 27 years old, had been playing in Davos,

Switzerland, and is a member of the 1994 Swedish team that won the Olympic gold medal. In fact, he was one of the players who scored against Canada in the sudden-death shootout.

It will be interesting to see how many points Jovanovski earns this season. The following chart lists most of the top proven offensive defensemen in the game today and how they performed in their first year. The first one shows those who didn't have overwhelming numbers. The second shows those who had outstanding point totals as rookies.

Rookie Point Totals of Active Proven Offensive Defensemen

The Lower End

Player	Team	G	A	Pts
Kevin Hatcher	Wsh	9	10	19
Al Iafrate	Tor	5	16	21
Scott Stevens	Wsh	9	16	25
Sergei Zubov	NYR	8	23	31
Paul Coffey	Edm	9	23	32
Bruce Driver	NJ	9	23	32
Fredrik Olausson	Wpg	7	29	36
James Patrick	NYR	8	28	36
Steve Duchesne	LA	13	25	38
Dave Ellett	Wpg	11	26	38
Garry Galley	LA	8	30	38
Al MacInnis	Cgy	11	34	45
Rob Blake	LA	12	34	46

The Higher End

Player	Team	G	A	Pts
Larry Murphy	LA	16	60	76 * NHL record
Brian Leetch	NYR	23	48	71
Gary Suter	Cgy	18	50	68
Phil Housley	Buf	19	47	66
Ray Bourque	Bos	17	48	65
Chris Chelios	Mtl	9	55	64
Niklas Lidstrom	Det	11	49	60
Jeff Brown	Que	16	36	52

There's not a lot of big, physical, all-round defensemen on these lists, but interestingly three of the biggest and toughest had three of the worst offensive rookie seasons. Kevin Hatcher, Al Iafrate and Scott Stevens all fit the mold and all had their problems in their first year.

This is because those offensive defensemen who also want to excel defensively need time to learn the defensive side of the game at the NHL level. The defensive responsibilities can be overwhelming at first, but after that, they can develop their own style of game (with good coaching).

Jovanovski would appear to be in the Stevens, Hatcher mold, so it won't be surprising if he doesn't pile up a lot of points this year. But, down the road, that's a different story.

After Jovanovski, Smith and Murphy, it will be a dogfight for playing time. Svensson, Wooley, Robert Svehla will have an opportunity, along with tough guy Paul Laus, who had 427 PIM in the IHL a couple years ago. Dallas Eakins, a career minor-leaguer got the call last year in 17 games with Florida.

Oldsters like Brian Benning, Randy Moller and Joe Cirella had limited playing time last year and should expect more of the same. However, you don't want to rule out all of them, especially if the team moves more towards youth.

Chris Armstrong was 17-55-72 at Moose Jaw, good enough to be the third highest scoring defenseman in the WHL last season. He joins Rhett Warrener as the top defense prospects after Jovanovski.

FORWARD: If the Panthers want to change from a defensive-oriented team to one that's younger and more offensive, then they are going to have to make a lot of changes. Last year's forward units were geared to playing their own end of the ice first.

But, you never know, if they're turned loose they could improve their point totals considerably. Still, there's no legitimate big-time scorer.

The best thing would be to play defensive hockey until they get some scorers on board. Ooops they don't want to do that.

Okay, then, what we have left is… a mess. Let's start with those who are proven scorers.

Okay, scrap that, let's start with the best scorers they have.

Scott Mellanby scored 60 points in the Panthers first season to set the team record. Bob Kudelski has scored the most points of any current Panther when he had 70 combined with Ottawa and Florida.

Jesse Belanger and Stu Barnes are two others who can reach the 50 point range. They tied for the team lead last season with 29 points, the lowest for a team leader in the NHL last season. Johan Garpenlov has had some decent numbers with San Jose.

It's a safe bet that none of the Florida forwards would be on the top offensive line of almost any team in the league. But, a lot of their forwards could make the checking line of many teams.

That's what makes it all so confusing. What the heck are they going to do? Wholesale trades?

Maybe. They have good defensive players that would interest other teams.

Down the middle, if they don't jumble things up, are Barnes, Belanger, Niedermayer and Skrudland. Niedermayer, however, moved to right wing late last season and seemed to be more at home there.

Skrudland is one of the better defensive centers around, although he's getting on at 32 years of age.

Big things are predicted for Niedermayer, although he's not nearly as aggressive as predicted. He scores in spurts, including points in four of the Panther's first five games, which accounted for 40 percent of his production on the year. Another point streak a week later accounted for another 30 percent of his total on the year. The thing is, one of these times Nidermayer's going to go on a binge and it won't stop. Maybe this year, maybe next year.

Scott Mellanby is the prize on the wings. He's big, strong, tough, and can score as well. Jody Hull, Dave Lowry, Mike Hough, and Tom Fitzgerald are low scoring defensive types. Gaetan Duchesne, another in that mold, was not offered a contract for this season.

Bill Lindsay, the only Panther to play every game in their history, was a 151 point scorer in junior, but has a season high of only 19 in the NHL. Andrei Lomakin, who was offered a termination contract, spent a lot of last season in the press box, along with Bob Kudelski, who had a 40 goal season two years ago. Since, apparently, the Panthers aren't going to be as worried about their defensive game, Kudelski could get back in the lineup on a regular basis and maybe make a dent as a power play sniper.

Czech Radek Dvorak, selected 10th overall in last year's draft, is a desperately needed scorer and could make the jump immediately. Junior Steve Washburn had 106 points for Ottawa in the OHL. Alexei Kudashov was signed as a free agent away from Toronto, who were no longer interested in a guy who skates nice, has good moves, but does nothing. In 25 games with the Maple Leafs he had one point. He did, however, lead their farm team in St. John's last year with 79 points.

Expect some trades before the season is too far underway or even before it's underway. With the emphasis on defense around the league, it gives the Florida players value they might not otherwise have.

SPECIAL TEAMS: The power play rank is right about where it should be and will be again this year. Perhaps a little improvement might be in order considering they're going to be more offensive. But, somebody has to score the goals and they don't have goal scorers.

Penalty killing was once again decent and should remain that way considering the personnel.

Power Play	G	ATT	PCT
Overall	29	222	13.1% (24th NHL)
Home	17	126	13.5% (22nd NHL)
Road	12	96	12.5% (21st NHL)

6 SHORT HANDED GOALS ALLOWED (T-14th NHL)

Penalty Killing	G	TSH	PCT
Overall	32	191	83.2% (12th NHL)
Home	18	93	80.6% (T-21st NHL)
Road	14	98	85.7% (4th NHL)

1 SHORT HANDED GOALS SCORED (T-24th NHL)

Penalties	GP	MIN	AVG
PANTHERS	48	770	16.0 (T-5th NHL)

PANTHERS SPECIAL TEAMS SCORING

Power play	G	A	PTS
BELANGER	6	8	14
MURPHY	5	6	11
MELLANBY	4	6	10
LOWRY	2	5	7
WOOLLEY	1	6	7
BARNES	1	5	6

Short handed	G	A	PTS
DUCHESNE	0	2	2
LINDSAY	1	0	1
EAKINS	0	1	1
BARNES	0	1	1

COACHING AND MANAGEMENT: I wouldn't want to be the coach following Roger Neilson. It's a no-win situation because Neilson always gets more out his players than their normal talent level. It will be a long year for new skipper Doug MacLean. Or maybe a short one.

DRAFT

1995 DRAFT SELECTIONS

Round	Sel.	Player	Pos	Amateur Team
1	10	Radek Dvorak	LW	Czechoslovakia
2	36	Aaron McDonald	G	Swift Current (WHL)
3	62	Mike O'Grady	D	Saskatoon (WHL)
4	80	Dave Duerden	LW	Peterborough (OHL)
4	86	Daniel Tjarnquist	D	Sweden
5	114	Francois Cloutier	LW	Hull (QMJHL)
7	166	Peter Worrell	LW	Hull (QMJHL)
8	192	Flip Kuba	D	Czechoslovakia
9	218	David Lemanowicz	G	Spokane (WHL)

Radek Dvorak has a chance to step right into the Florida lineup. It's not as if they don't want some scoring power. He's a big guy, but like most young Czechs and Russians, it's unlikely he'll make a big impact in his first North American season.

Second round choice Aaron McDonald is a big goalie at 6-1, and is held in high esteem by goalie coach Billy Smith.

PROGNOSIS: Panther fans have become used to being competitive. Now, they're going to have to get used to losing. Oh, it will be explained to them that it's all in the interest of winning in the future, and it will be up to them whether or not they buy it.

Attendance has been excellent so far. Last year they played to 97% capacity in front of an average crowd of 14,192. Half of their home games were sellouts.

They may, however, enjoy the games even more if the team is able to produce a few more goals. Alas, it will be in a losing cause. The Panthers will battle for the worst record in the NHL.

PREDICTION:
Atlantic Division: 7th
Eastern Conference: 12th
Overall: 25th

STAT SECTION

Team Rankings 1994/95

		Conference Rank	League Rank
Record	20-22-6	9	15
Home	9-12-3	12	23
Away	11-10-3	3	6
Team Plus\Minus	-9	8	16
Goals For	115	12	26
Goals Against	127	4	7
Average Shots For	24.8		
Average Shots Against	28.4		

MISCELLANEOUS STATS

One Goal Games	8-8
Times outshooting opponent	16
Times outshot	31
Even shots	1
Average Shots For	24.8
Average Shots Against	28.4
Overtime	0-3-6
Longest Winning streak	3
Longest Undefeated streak	3
Longest Losing streak	4

Longest winless streak	5
Versus Teams Over .500	8-15-2
Versus Teams Under .500	12-7-4
First Half Record	9-12-3
Second Half Record	11-10-3

All-Time Rankings - INDIVIDUAL
Goals
Scott Mellanby	43
Jese Belanger	32
Stu Barnes	28
Assists
Jesse Belanger	47
Gord Murphy	45
Scott Mellanby	42
Points
Scott Mellanby	85
Jesse Belanger	79
Stu Barnes	67

BEST INDIVIDUAL SEASONS

Goals
Scott Mellanby	1993-94	30
Andrei Lomakin	1993-94	19
Stu Barnes	1993-94	18
Tom Fitzgerald	1993-94	18
Assists
Jesse Belanger	1993-94	33
Scott Mellanby	1993-94	30
Gord Murphy	1993-94	29
Points
Scott Mellanby	1993-94	60
Jesse Belanger	1993-94	50
Andrei Lomakin	1993-94	47

	1994-95 OVERALL				PROJECTED 84 GAME TOTAL		
	GP	G	A	PTS	G	A	PTS
J.BELANGER	47	15	14	29	27	25	52
S.BARNES	41	10	19	29	20	39	59
S.MELLANBY	48	13	12	25	23	21	44
G.MURPHY	46	6	16	22	11	29	40
D.LOWRY	45	10	10	20	19	19	38
J.HULL	46	11	8	19	20	15	35
B.LINDSAY	48	10	9	19	17	16	32
T.FITZGERALD	48	3	13	16	5	23	28
B.SKRUDLAND	47	5	9	14	9	16	25
J.GARPENLOV	40	4	10	14	8	21	29
M.HOUGH	48	6	7	13	11	12	23
J.WOOLLEY	34	4	9	13	10	22	32
G.DUCHESNE	46	3	9	12	5	16	21
R.NIEDERMAYER	48	4	6	10	7	11	18
B.KUDELSKI	26	6	3	9	19	10	29
B.BENNING	24	1	7	8	3	24	27
M.SVENSSON	19	2	5	7	9	22	31
A.LOMAKIN	31	1	6	7	3	16	19
P.LAUS	37	0	7	7	0	16	16
G.SMITH	47	2	4	6	4	7	11
R.MOLLER	17	0	3	3	0	15	15
*R.SVEHLA	5	1	1	2	17	17	34
D.EAKINS	17	0	1	1	0	5	5
J.CIRELLA	20	0	1	1	0	4	4
S.RICHER	1	0	0	0	0	0	0
J.DANIELS	3	0	0	0	0	0	0
*J.LINDEN	4	0	0	0	0	0	0
D.TOMLINSON	5	0	0	0	0	0	0
K.BROWN	13	0	0	0	0	0	0

Hartford Whalers

It was early morning, the sun was just starting to peak over the horizon, and I had just finished writing the Hartford section of this book. I had dissed them badly all the way through, with little good to say about anyone except Sean Burke, rookie of the year candidate Jeff O'Neill, and their team statistician Frank Polnaszek.

And then before heading off to bed I went and checked the wire services to see if there were any new developments anywhere.

WHALERS GET SHANAHAN said the headline.

Shoot! Shoot! Shoot! The Whalers had done something right. All that work down the drain. Up all night for nothing. I would have to rewrite the whole section.

Brendan Shanahan is an impact player in the biggest way. Strange that Mike Keenan didn't like him, but just about every other team in the league would be ecstatic to get him.

Shanahan gives Hartford their only legitimate star who's not a goalie. Giving up possible future star, Chris Pronger, for a current one that's only 26 years old is a great deal for the Whalers. In fact, they got him fairly cheap.

If this is the type of thing Whaler fans can expect in the future from management, then the future is considerably brighter than might have been thought previously.

It all started with one of the worst deals in the history of the modern age. Glen Wesley for three first round draft picks? GM Jim Rutherford tried all year to justify it, but he can't because it's impossible.

That's not the only silliness that went on in the new Hartford regime last year. How about signing stiff free agent Jimmy Carson, a player nobody wanted, to a three year contract. How about losing valuable defenseman Bryan Marchment (who it could be argued is even more valuable than Wesley) for Steven Rice in a free agent compensation deal. How about their problems handling the Jeff O'Neill contract negotiations last season. How about majority owner, Peter Karmanos predicting a 90 point season. How about General Manager (and part owner) Jim Rutherford suggesting Alexander Godynyuk (a.k.a. the Human Pylon) was one of the big four that would be the mainstay of the Whaler defense for many years.

It's obvious these folks weren't shy and wanted to jump in head-first, but it looks like they hit their head on the bottom. They're just now coming up for air.

They've run an extremely successful operation at the Junior level, and Rutherford has indicated that stability will be a key in Hartford. And with many things they did early, it was obvious they had that goal in mind.

Mind you, a lot of things they've done since suggest they've wisely scrapped the stability mode until they have a decent team with which to be stable.

Whichever route they choose, they're not going to get much help from the draft. Rutherford doesn't think the draft is that crucial anyway, especially with picks in the last half of the first round.

He's assuming the picks he gave to Boston will be later in the first round, but that's hardly a certainty. Last year's gift to the Bruins was ninth overall.

Let's assume the picks Hartford gave up were in the second half of the draft, say 10th pick and later. That's when Rutherford said it wasn't all that important.

The following chart studies from 10th pick to 21st pick (22 selections in 1991) over a 10 year period. The draft years run from 1982 to 1991. Anything more recent and too many of the players haven't had a shot at the NHL yet. As it is, some in 1991 are still trying to make their mark or will play in the NHL but haven't yet. Those selected from that year are still only 22-years-old.

For each of the draft slots, the chart shows the number of NHL regulars and the number who played at least one game in the NHL. There are ten players selected at draft slot, except for the 22nd position. Some of the "NHL regular" decisions were discretionary, but the general guideline was that they played at least one full season in the NHL.

Draft Success - Last half of the first round.

Pick	NHL Regular	NHL Games	Top Players
10	9	10	Teemu Selanne
11	9	10	Trevor Kidd, Dave Manson
12	5	10	Gary Roberts, Dave Gagner
13	6	8	Craig Janney, Derek King, Dan Quinn
14	10	10	Calle Johansson, Stephane Quintal
15	7	9	Joe Sakic, Alexei Kovalev
16	6	7	Dave Andreychuk, Bryan Marchment
17	5	6	Kevin Hatcher, Murray Craven, Andrew Cassels
18	7	10	Ken Daneyko
19	6	7	Keith Tkachuk, Jeff Beukeboom
20	5	9	Martin Brodeur
21	4	8	Pat Flatley
22	1	1	(only one player drafted in that position)

The chart shows that 80 of 121 players, drafted 10th or later in the first round, played regularly in the NHL. That's 66 percent, or two-thirds. Eighty-seven percent of the draft selections played at least one game.

As well, the numbers of both of the above will increase as a few more late-bloomers get a shot at the NHL.

In any event, Rutherford was dead wrong in his assessment of the first round.

In any event, part II, he's dead right in trading for Shanahan.

GOAL: Not only did Sean Burke have his best NHL season, but he had the best season of any Hartford Whaler. He was voted the team's MVP by the players and had a huge lead in their three-star voting.

The three star award voting shows just how much better he was than his teammates last year. In Hartford, five points are awarded for a first star, three for second, and one for third.

	1	2	3	Total
Sean Burke	6	8	3	57
Geoff Sanderson	3	1	3	21
Steven Rice	2	2	0	21
Andrei Nikolishin	1	2	2	13
Jeff Reese	1	2	1	12
Andrew Cassels	1	1	2	10
Darren Turcotte	1	1	2	10
Robert Kron	1	0	4	9
Jocelyn Lemieux	1	1	1	9
Adam Burt	1	0	1	6
Jimmy Carson	1	0	1	6
Paul Ranheim	0	2	0	6
Igor Chiberev	1	0	0	5
Chris Pronger	0	1	2	5
Glen Wesley	0	1	1	4
Frantisek Kucera	0	1	0	3

With Burke getting most of the playing time, Jeff Reese is suitable for the backup role. Down on the farm is Manny Legace, and with their first round pick this year they selected Jean-Sebastien Giguere from the Quebec League goalie factory.

	GP	MIN	GA	AVG	W	L	T	SO
Burke	42	2418	108	2.68	17	19	4	0
Reese	11	477	26	3.27	2	5	1	0

DEFENCE: The Whalers aren't particularly strong at this position, but they won't miss Pronger. The second pick overall in the 1993 draft could be an outstanding player eventually, but he hadn't shown much in Hartford.

He might have had too much responsibility thrust on him at such a young age. Once he adds some maturity and experience he could break out and play up to expectations. It usually takes longer for defensemen to make their mark in the NHL because it's a much more difficult position to learn. In St. Louis, he won't have the burden of carrying the franchise on his back.

Glen Wesley has to bear the burden of knowing he was traded for three first round draft picks. He can't live up to that, of course, and it's certainly not his fault the team made a dumb trade. He plays the Hartford power play point where he has learned it's a heck of lot harder to get on the scoresheet when Ray Bourque isn't on the other point.

Frantisek Kucera, acquired from Chicago two years ago, for somewhat less than three first rounders, won the team's most valuable defenseman award. He played every game and led the defensemen with 20 points.

Adam Burt isn't exactly a household name, but he's played more games than any active Whaler with 350. Befitting a player who's not a household name but is a decent player, he won the team's Unsung Hero award.

Brian Glynn, Glen Featherstone and Brad McCrimmon are other quality veterans, although McCrimmon is 36 years old. Free agent Gerald Diduck, a stay-at-home defenceman was also signed. He was with Vancouver and Chicago last season. Alexander Godynyuk came on board last year, his fourth team in four years. He didn't play much and won't this year unless everyone else gets the flu.

Some youngsters with promise, and their Springfield totals, are giant Marek Malik (11-30-41), Jason McBain (16-28-44) and Michael Stewart (6-24-30).

FORWARD: Before the trade I had written here that the Whalers had a lot of useful forwards - if they were filling a role for other teams. Together, I said, they didn't add up to match.

Getting perhaps the top power forward in the league changes a lot of things. Now, with Shanahan there, those same players can fill useful roles on Hartford.

Shanahan has two fifty goal seasons to his credit and Geoff Sanderson has two 40 goal seasons. That gives them sniper power.

Andrew Cassels is a playmaker at center and all of a sudden he has a chance to regain his scoring touch of a few years ago when he got 85 points.

With possible rookie of the year candidate Jeff O'Neill on board at centre the Whalers have a good first and a second line center/left wing combination. O'Neill, the fifth overall selection in the 1994 draft was 43-81-124 with Guelph in the OHL last year. He's been compared to a lot of players, including Steve Yzerman. He can skate, he can shoot, he can score, he can be a playmaker and he's good on faceoffs.

The rest of the forwards are going to have to shuffle positions because there aren't two natural right wingers to play on the two top scoring lines.

Darren Turcotte, with 17 goals and 35 points, had a nice comeback year, moving back to the range he belongs – 30 goals, 60 points. But, he's a left winger or a center, and more suited to second line duty than third.

The Whalers can put some speedy guys on the right side. Robert Kron, a small unagressive guy with a mediocre scoring touch would benefit with two good linemates. Same with speedster Andrei Nikolishin who showed plenty last year in his rookie season. Paul Ranheim is another speedy left wing/center who showed some scoring potential early in his career in Calgary before getting stuck with a defensive role.

Steven Rice is a natural right winger, who doesn't belong on the first line, where he was used sometimes last year. He's a sturdy guy who needs to use the body to be useful. He had some decent offensive production last year, partly because he got power play time, but he's never going to be a big scorer. That's

not his game and that's not where his value lies.

Mark Janssens is a fourth line center, and teams could do a lot worse than him. He doesn't score, and doesn't need to. He's a big guy who uses that size.

Kelly Chase is the designated hit-man and Jocelyn Lemieux is a checking forward, a sort of poor man's Claude Lemieux.

The Whalers will tell you differently, but signing free agent Jimmy Carson to a fairly hefty three year contract was a mistake. Something about being friends of the family? He has no trading value because nobody wants him, and he'll prove to have little value to the team. His best position is Left Out.

The Whalers indicated they were not going to re-sign disappointment Jim Sandlak, or selfish troublemaker Igor Chiberev, or Jim Storm despite the fact he has a great name for hockey.

Others hanging around trying to make their way are Ted Drury, Scott Daniels, Kevin Smyth and Robert Petrovicky. Petrovicky, a former first round pick, led Springfield in scoring in the AHL, but has shown little at the NHL level.

Before Shanahan, this group had little to get excited about. After Shanahan, many of them all of a sudden have a purpose.

What a great acquisition.

SPECIAL TEAMS: Shanahan makes an average power play a very good one. Maybe even one of the top six in the league. They don't have any great pointmen, however, so that could be a problem.

The penalty-killing was weak last year, but hey, guess what, Shanahan makes that much better as well.

Speaking of great pointmen, Whalers' statistician Frank Polnaszek is the best in the business. There's no comparison. Just tons and tons of great stuff on Hartford and the whole NHL. Even regular stats we take for granted he finds a way to make interesting.

One of his stats, my favorite, shows how successful teams are when they pull their goalie for a sixth attacker. I had no idea how often pulling the goalie works. Now, I do, and so do you.

His calculations for the last four years in the NHL are presented below.

Pulling the Goalie

	Times Pulled	Goals Scored	Success %	Success Frequency
1991-92	392	29	7.4	13.52
1992-93	457	46	10.1	9.93
1993-94	512	46	9.0	11.13
1994-95	366	36	9.8	10.17
4 Yr Ave.	432	39	9.1	11.00

* Success frequency shows the number of attempts for each success. For example, the four year average of 11.00 means pulling the goalie has worked once in every 11 attempts.

The flip side to scoring with the goalie pulled is giving up an empty net goal.

Empty Net Goals

	Times Pulled	ENG	ENG %	ENG Frequency
1991-92	392	125	31.9	3.14
1992-93	457	137	30.0	3.34
1993-94	512	153	29.9	3.35
1994-95	366	96	26.2	3.81
4 Yr Ave.	432	128	29.6	3.38

Power Play	G	ATT	PCT
Overall	30	174	17.2% (14th NHL)
Home	20	89	22.5% (6th NHL)
Road	10	85	11.8% (23rd NHL)

6 SHORT HANDED GOALS ALLOWED (T-14th NHL)

Penalty Killing	G	TSH	PCT
Overall	37	185	80.0% (22nd NHL)
Home	18	87	79.3% (24th NHL)
Road	19	98	80.6% (16th NHL)

3 SHORT HANDED GOALS SCORED (T-20th NHL)

Penalties	GP	MIN	AVG
WHALERS	48	915	19.1 (13th NHL)

TOP WHALERS SPECIAL TEAMS SCORING

Power play	G	A	PTS
WESLEY	1	10	11
TURCOTTE	3	7	10
SANDERSON	4	5	9
CASSELS	1	8	9
RICE	4	4	8
BURT	3	4	7
CARSON	4	2	6
KRON	3	3	6
PRONGER	3	2	5

Short handed	G	A	PTS
KRON	1	1	2
TURCOTTE	1	0	1
NIKOLISHIN	1	0	1
LEMIEUX	0	1	1

COACHING AND MANAGEMENT: Rutherford went from making one of the worst deals in recent memory to one of the best.

Perhaps the new regime got in there and wanted to accomplish too much too soon.

Okay, the rookie season is finished with, and, okay, the Whalers made more than their share of rookie mistakes. Heck, even the most experienced GM's in the business make errors.

The turnaround started with the Pat Verbeek deal last season, sending him to the Rangers for Glen Featherstone, Michael Stewart, a first rounder in 1995 and a fourth rounder in 1996. In fact, that's an outstanding deal, except for the first rounder, which isn't worth all that much according to Rutherford.

Okay, listen, one mistake, great job otherwise.

I concede.

Paul Holmgren did a decent job as coach considering he got booted out of the front office when the new owners came aboard. This, after he had indicated previously that he had tired of coaching. So, we'll give him the Comeback Coach of the Year award.

DRAFT

1995 DRAFT SELECTIONS

Round	Sel.	Player	Pos	Amateur Team
1	13	Jean-Sebastien Giguere	G	Halifax (QMJHL)
2	35	Sergei Fedotov	D	Russia
4	85	Ian MacNeil	C	Oshawa (OHL)
4	87	Sami Kapanen	LW	Finland
5	113	Hugh Hamilton	D	Spokane (WHL)
7	165	Byron Ritcher	C	Lethbridge (WHL)
8	191	Milan Kostolny	RW	Detroit (OHL)
9	217	Mike Rucinski	D	Detroit (OHL)

Credit Patrick Roy for the Whalers first round selection. Giguere patterns himself after Roy, like so many of the goalies being mined from the Quebec motherlode. Gigeure was the first goalie selected in the draft, just three picks ahead of Martin Biron, rated number one by the Central Scouting Bureau.

PROGNOSIS: The Whalers weren't going to make the playoffs until they got Brendan Shanahan. Now, they will. They're certainly

not a Stanley Cup contender yet, but they're at least out of the driveway and on the road.

They'll probably hover above the .500 mark this year, where they haven't been for five years, and where they've only been three times in their history.

PREDICTION:
Northeast Division: 3rd
Eastern Conference: 7th
Overall: 14th

STAT SECTION

Team Rankings 1994/95

		Conference Rank	League Rank
Record	19-24-5	10	16
Home	12-10-2	9	13
Away	7-14-3	10	13
Team Plus\Minus	-7	7	15
Goals For	127	9	20
Goals Against	141	9	14

MISCELLANEOUS STATS

One Goal Games	10-10
Times outshooting opponent	21
Times outshot	25
Even shots	2
Average Shots For	29.7
Average Shots Against	30.7
Overtime	4-0-5
Longest Winning streak	3
Longest Undefeated streak	4
Longest Losing streak	5
Longest winless streak	6
Versus Teams Over .500	8-15-3
Versus Teams Under .500	11-9-2
First Half Record	9-12-3
Second Half Record	10-12-2

PLAYERS	1994-95 OVERALL				84 GAME PROJECTION		
	GP	G	A	PTS	G	A	PTS
A.CASSELS	46	7	30	37	13	55	68
D.TURCOTTE	47	17	18	35	30	32	62
G.SANDERSON	46	18	14	32	33	26	59
S.RICE	40	11	10	21	23	21	44
P.RANHEIM	47	6	14	20	11	25	36
F.KUCERA	48	3	17	20	5	30	35
J.CARSON	38	9	10	19	20	22	42
R.KRON	37	10	8	18	23	18	41
A.NIKOLISHIN	39	8	10	18	17	22	39
A.BURT	46	7	11	18	13	20	33
G.WESLEY	48	2	14	16	3	24	27
C.PRONGER	43	5	9	14	10	18	28
J.LEMIEUX	41	6	5	11	12	10	22
T.DRURY	34	3	6	9	7	15	22
M.JANSSENS	46	2	5	7	4	9	13
B.GLYNN	43	1	6	7	2	12	14
K.SMYTH	16	1	5	6	5	26	31
I.CHIBIREV	8	3	1	4	31	11	42
K.CHASE	28	0	4	4	0	12	12
G.FEATHERSTONE	19	2	1	3	9	4	13
J.STORM	6	0	3	3	0	42	42
S.DANIELS	12	0	2	2	0	14	14
M.MALIK	1	0	1	1	0	84	84
B.MCCRIMMON	33	0	1	1	0	3	3
R.PETROVICKY	2	0	0	0	0	0	0
J.SANDLAK	13	0	0	0	0	0	0
A.GODYNYUK	14	0	0	0	0	0	0

All-Time Rankings - INDIVIDUAL

Goals
Ron Francis   264
Blaine Stoughton   219
Kevin Dineen   214

Assists
Ron Francis   557
Kevin Dineen   232
Pat Verbeek   211

Points
Ron Francis   821
Kevin Dineen   446
Pat Verbeek   403

Best Seasons

Goals
Blaine Stoughton   1979-80   56
Blaine Stoughton   1981-82   52
Geoff Sanderson   1992-93   46

Assists
Ron Francis   1989-90   69
Mike Rogers   1980-81   65
Andrew Cassels   1992-93   65

Points
Mike Rogers   1979-80   105
Mike Rogers   1980-81   105
Ron Francis   1989-90   101

Montreal Canadiens

Don't blame the rest of the hockey world for enjoying themselves so much last year when the Canadiens didn't make the playoffs. It doesn't happen very often.

The last time was in 1970, and the time before was in 1948. Twice in 46 years.

The following chart shows the most consecutive seasons in the playoffs in NHL history.

Most Consecutive Seasons in the Playoffs

Team	Years	Seasons
Boston Bruins	1968 - 1995	28 *
Chicago Blackhawks	1970 - 1995	26 *
MONTREAL CANADIENS	1971 - 1994	24
MONTREAL CANADIENS	1949 - 1969	21
Detroit Red Wings	1939 - 1958	20
Philadelphia Flyers	1973 - 1989	17
Atlanta-Calgary Flames	1976 - 1991	16
St. Louis Blues	1980 - 1994	16 *

* streak is current

It will be difficult for the Canadiens to miss the playoffs again, not only because Quebec has moved to Denver and the other conference, but also because they couldn't possibly be as bad as they were last season on the road.

Montreal's 3-18-3 mark on the road was the poorest in the league, and their 47 road goals scored were the fewest, an average of just two per game.

The road record was the second worst in Montreal history. Way back in the 1932-33 season, also in a 48 game schedule, they had a 3-20-1 mark.

The following chart lists the worst league road records in seasons with at least 70 games.

Fewest Road Wins (min. 70 game schedule)

Team	Year	Record
Ottawa (includes one neutral site loss)	1992-93	1-41-0
Washington	1974-75	1-39-0
California	1973-74	2-37-0
NY Islanders	1972-73	2-35-2
Winnipeg	1980-81	2-32-6
Boston	1960-61	2-25-8
Los Angeles	1969-70	2-30-6
Quebec	1991-92	2-29-9
Colorado	1977-78	2-26-12

The interesting thing about the above teams is that they were just crummy hockey clubs. Montreal is a little different in that they were just mediocre and had one of the best home records in the league.

So, how do you figure their road failure? One reason might be their size. They're a puny little team, with puny guys on the way up. Even most of their big guys play puny.

Otherwise it may just get to be a psychological thing. You can bet they heard a lot about their road record and perhaps after a while they started to believe they couldn't win on the road.

Another explanation might be that with just one line that could score, home teams – with the last change – could easily get their checkers out against them and shut their offence down completely.

The Canadiens made some major trades last season. They had to because they weren't going anywhere with the people they had and it was obvious a change was in order.

The first was Eric Desjardins, John LeClair and Gilbert Dionne for Mark Recchi. It didn't turn out too good, at least for last season.

LeClair ended up as the first team all-star left winger. Like, who knew? It's not as if he had done much of anything in Montreal and it's a good bet he would have continued along the same path had he stayed there. A change of scenery obviously did him good, and having Lindros as your center would help anyone.

It's very common for a player traded during the season to set a hot pace with their new team. In many cases, they revert to their original level, but as long as LeClair keeps playing with Lindros that isn't likely to happen.

That's the good thing about Recchi. He's an outstanding scorer in his own right, even though he's mostly played with superstars during his career. The stats have proven in the past that his scoring power didn't go down when the superstars were out with injury. He's had three 100 point season and one with 97 in just five full NHL seasons.

Another added dimension to Recchi is that he's not just a scorer and not just a playmaker, he does both, which isn't all that common.

Desjardins played extremely well for the Flyers, but nobody ever thought he wasn't a good defensman. A change of scenery was good for him too.

Didn't do much for Dionne, however. He scored zero goals in Montreal, and equaled that total in Philly.

The next major deal sent captain Kirk Muller, Mathieu Schneider and prospect Craig Darby to the Islanders for Pierre Turgeon and Vladimir Malakhov.

Nobody would dispute Muller's heart, but the Habs needed scoring and he wasn't providing it. Turgeon isn't in the same league in the character department, but he can score 100 points plus which is something Montreal wasn't going to get from Muller.

Schneider wasn't missed by the other Montreal players. They accused him of being selfish and distant, and it was even reported he got into a between period fistfight with Patrick Roy.

Malakhov is bigger than Schneider and has about the same point potential.

During the off-season Brian Bellows was traded to Tampa Bay for Marc Bureau. Bureau gives them some size, which they are so sorely lacking, and Bellows had become pretty much a non-entity anyway.

Montreal fans were up in arms at the start of last season because they thought Savard was going to make some big deals. It took him longer than expected, but he's made them. Most trades are a risk, and while some may not work out so well to start with, you have to give them time.

TEAM PREVIEW

GOAL: Last year's edition of the Canadiens proved how much a team is responsible for a netminder's goals against average. Roy's GAA of 2.97 was one of the worst of his career, in a year when goal scoring was way down.

The strange part was that Roy didn't play badly at all. In fact, often he was the only thing that kept his team in the game.

Backup Ron Tugnutt is a free agent but it's unlikely the Canadiens will sign him. He wants some good money and with Roy around in Montreal, he wouldn't play enough to be worth it.

That means Montreal can either go out and find one of the dime-a-dozen veteran goalies (Red Light Racicot?) or bring up Martin Brochu or Patrick Labrecque from Fredericton.

Brochu was considered the better prospect before last season, but Labrecque compiled the better regular season GAA and played all but one of Fredericton's playoff games. He had a playoff GAA of 2.48, second best in the AHL, as Fredericton went to the finals, losing 4-0 to Albany.

The goalie of the future might be Jose Theodore, who was selected in the second round of the 1994 draft. He played with Hull in the Quebec League last season and was voted MVP of the playoffs.

	GP	MIN	GA	AVG	W	L	T	SO
Roy	43	2566	127	2.97	17	20	6	1
Tugnutt	7	346	18	3.12	1	3	1	0

DEFENCE: In terms of numbers, the Habs have plenty on defence. In terms of quality, the numbers aren't as high.

With the exception of Lyle Odelein and perhaps Stephane Quintal, who was picked up in the off-season from Winnipeg, you have a bunch of guys in a race for the defenseman Lady Byng trophy.

Fewest Penalty minutes
– defensemen with at least 30 games played

Niklas Lidstrom	Det	6
PETER POPOVIC	MTL	8
Bobby Dollas	Ana	12
Shawn Chambers	TB/NJ	12
Doug Lidster	StL	12
Oleg Tverdovsky	Ana	14
James Patrick	Cgy	14
Eric Desjardins	Mtl/Phi	14

Others low PIM totals on Montreal:

Patrice Brisebois	26
J.J. Daigneault	40
Yves Racine	42
Vladimir	46

Vladimir Malakhov will be the offensive force from the blueline and the power play quarterback.

Those responsibilities are something you might have heard associated with Patrice Brisebois' name as well, but he hasn't delivered yet. He's only 24-years-old though, so maybe this year.

The Habs obtained a proven performer in Yves Racine last year to help out in that area, but he didn't. He had just 11 points which pro-rates to 20 for 84 games. This, a season after earning 52 with Philadelphia.

Bryan Fogarty appeared to be coming around and getting his life in order, but showed other irresponsibility not associated with his drinking problem, and won't be back.

Stephane Quintal can help out offensively as well, but Montreal likes him for his size and physical presence, something in short supply on this team.

Peter Popovic is a big guy at 6-5, for all it's worth. He had eight penalty minutes in 33 games, an almost unheard of low total for a defenseman, missing out by two penalty minutes of winning the Defenceman Lady Byng unofficial award.

J.J. Daigneault is small for a defenseman, listed at 5-11, but strikes more fear into opposing forwards than Popovic.

That leaves the prospects. David Wilkie is supposed to have one of the better shots in hockey. In his last year of junior he had 38 goals and 39 assists, an unbelievable ratio for a defenceman. With Fredericton last year he had 10 goals and 40 assists.

Brent Bilodeau, at 6-4, 215, is a big guy who could help out and Brad Brown, 6-3, 218, a first round choice in 1994 who had 172 penalty minutes with North Bay in the OHL last season, is also ready for action.

Finn Marko Kiprusoff, another offensive threat, could get a shot.

FORWARD: They have a line that could be the best in hockey, they have a legitimate rookie of the year candidate, they have a budding star or two, and best of all, they're not tired out from having to play in the playoffs last year.

Pierre Turgeon between Vincent Damphousse and Mark Recchi combines two 50 goal scorers and 100 point men, along with one that's come close.

The first two are prone to slumps, but still, the only line that might be better is, uh, LeClair, Lindros and Renberg in Philadelphia.

After the big three, there are some low scoring veterans and potential.

It's the potential that has them excited. Saku Koivu has been called the best player not in the NHL, the same handle Peter Forsberg wore before last season. The Finn is small, at only 5-9, 165 pounds, but he's considered a feisty sort, at least against other Finnish players.

There are only so many fearless small guys, such as Theoren Fleury and Doug Gilmour, and whether a Finn can fit in with those guys is something we'll just have to see. There aren't a lot of doubts about Koivu's scoring ability, however. He's expected to light up the scoreboard.

Valeri Bure, Pavel's brother, was expected to do the same thing last year, but he earned just four points in 24 games. He's a little guy as well, 5-11 164 pounds, but like Koivu, stardom has been predicted for him.

Brian Savage showed something in his rookie season with 12 goals (pro-rated to 27) in 37 games as a center, and with Koivu there along with Turgeon, a weak position could become a strength.

Mike Keane, who took over the captaincy when Muller was traded, is also a center, but will likely be moved to the wing.

Defensive centermen, Mark Lamb and Marc Bureau are also on board.

Turner Stevenson provides some rare toughness for the Habs. He's on right wing along with Recchi and Bure. Keane may also play the right side. Ed Ronan is a free agent and probably won't be back.

At left wing, behind Damphousse, are Benoit Brunet and Pierre Sevigny and whichever tough guy they decide to use. Could be Mario Roberge or Donald Brashear, although the latter fell out of favor last year. But they do need an enforcer there. Somebody's got to protect all the little fellas.

The Montreal forwards are still too soft and too small, and there's little proven scoring after the big three. Potential is nice to have, but it's even better when you don't have to use the word potential with a player's name. There's no guarantee it's going to come through for them this year.

It's still a lineup that other teams don't mind facing. They can key on the scoring line, and have lots of fun pushing them around.

SPECIAL TEAMS: The power play should be better this year with Turgeon, Damphousse and Recchi around from day one. Malakhov should handle one power play point and there's plenty of guys who can take care of the other. If Koivu and Bure come through, there's even more potential power play scoring.

Power Play	G	ATT	PCT
Overall	28	172	16.3% (17th NHL)
Home	14	89	15.7% (T-20th NHL)
Road	14	83	16.9% (T-10th NHL)

3 SHORT HANDED GOALS ALLOWED (T-3rd NHL)

Penalty Killing	G	TSH	PCT
Overall	37	191	80.6% (19th NHL)
Home	16	92	82.6% (T-16th NHL)
Road	21	99	78.8% (20th NHL)

1 SHORT HANDED GOALS SCORED (T-24th NHL)

Top Scorers

Power play	G	A	PTS
TURGEON	5	12	17
RECCHI	9	7	16
DAMPHOUSSE	4	10	14
MALAKHOV	1	10	11
BELLOWS	1	4	5
RACINE	2	2	4

Short handed	G	A	PTS
TURGEON	2	0	2
BRUNET	1	0	1
DAIGNEAULT	0	1	1

COACHING AND MANAGEMENT: With Montreal not making the playoffs you would have thought Jacques Demers and Serge Savard would be run out of town.

But, it wasn't too long ago that the two of them combined to give Montreal a Stanley Cup victory.

Savard has two in his tenure with the Habs, beginning in 1983.

The bottom line is they can do the job. They've already proven it.

Last year was a difficult season, of course. They had a team with no chemistry, lots of whiners and troublemakers.

Demers is always rumored to be on his way out the door, but he's been around the second longest of all current coaches.

Current Coaches Longevity

Coach	Team	Seasons Coached
Bob Gainey	Dal	5
Jacques Demers	Mtl	3
Rick Bowness	Ott	3
Terry Crisp	TB	3
Pat Burns	Tor	3
Paul Holmgren	Hfd	3 *
Kevin Constantine	SJ	2
Jacques Lemaire	NJ	2
Ron Wilson	Ana	2
Ed Johnston	Pit	2
Scotty Bowman	Det	2
Jim Schoenfeld	Wsh	2*
Colin Campbell	NYR	1
Terry Murray	Phi	1
Marc Crawford	Col	1
Mike Keenan	St.L.	1
Rick Ley	Van	1
Terry Simpson	Wpg	1*
Ron Low	Edm	1*
Steve Kasper	Bos	-
Ted Nolan	Buf	-
Pierre Page	Cgy	-
Craig Hartsburg	Chi	-
Doug McLean	Fla	-
Larry Robinson	LLA	-
Mike Milbury	NYI	-

* includes partial season

DRAFT

1995 DRAFT SELECTIONS

Round	Sel.	Player	Pos	Amateur Team
1	8	Terry Ryan	LW	Tri-City (WHL)
3	60	Miroslav Guren	D	Czechoslovakia
3	74	M. Hohenberger	LW	Prince George (WHL)
4	86	Xavier DeLisle	C	Granby (QMJHL)

5	112	Niklas Anger	RW	Sweden
6	138	Boyd Olson	C	Tri-City (WHL)
7	164	Stephane Robidas	D	Shawinigan (QMJHL)
8	190	Greg Hart	RW	Kamloops (WHL)
9	216	Eric Houde	C	Halifax (QMJHL)

There's some question about Terry Ryan's skating ability, but not much about everything else. He's big (6-1, 207), tough (207 PIM last season), can score goals (50) and gets a lot of points (110).

Ryan played on a line with Daymond Langkow, who was selected fifth in the draft by Tampa Bay. Langkow had 67 goals and 140 points, which means Ryan was helped considerably by playing with him. Nobody seems to think it's a problem in this case, but often the stats of a player are distorted when he's on a line with a superior scorer, and he doesn't turn out to be as good as expected.

PROGNOSIS: Montreal fans are going to have to lower their standards considerably. While in the past a Stanley Cup was their expectation, this year getting into the playoffs will be the goal.

That shouldn't be too difficult. Not many teams can boast a first line like theirs, or a goaltender like Patrick Roy. It's everywhere else that they have problems.

They need more than one line scoring for them, which means their young players are going to have to come through for them. They also need to beef up on the blueline and on the forward line.

PREDICTION:
Northeast Division: 4th
Eastern Conference: 8th
Overall: 17th

STAT SECTION

Team Rankings 1994/95

	Conference Rank (14)	League Rank
Record	18-23-7	11	17
Home	15-5-4	3	5
Away	3-18-3	14	26
Team Plus\Minus	-14	11	17
Goals For	125	11	22
Goals Against	148	11	17

MISCELLANEOUS STATS

One Goal Games	6-8
Times outshooting opponent	19
Times outshot	27
Even shots	2
Average Shots For	28.6
Average Shots Against	31.9
Overtime	1-2-7
Longest Winning streak	3
Longest Undefeated streak	4
Longest Losing streak	5
Longest winless streak	6
Versus Teams Over .500	7-15-4
Versus Teams Under .500	11-8-3
First Half Record	8-11-5
Second Half Record	10-12-2

PLAYERS	1994-95 OVERALL				PROJECTED 84 GAMES		
	GP	G	A	PTS	G	A	PTS
M.RECCHI	49	16	32	48	27	55	82
P.TURGEON	49	24	23	47	41	39	80
V.DAMPHOUSSE	48	10	30	40	17	53	70
B.BRUNET	45	7	18	25	13	34	47
V.MALAKHOV	40	4	17	21	8	36	44
M.KEANE	48	10	10	20	17	17	34
*B.SAVAGE	37	12	7	19	27	16	43
B.BELLOWS	41	8	8	16	16	16	32
P.BRISEBOIS	35	4	8	12	10	19	29
Y.RACINE	47	4	7	11	7	13	20
L.ODELEIN	48	3	7	10	5	12	17
J.DAIGNEAULT	45	3	5	8	6	9	15
*T.STEVENSON	41	6	1	7	12	2	14
B.FOGARTY	21	5	2	7	20	8	28
O.PETROV	12	2	3	5	14	21	35
E.RONAN	30	1	4	5	3	11	14
P.POPOVIC	33	0	5	5	0	13	13
*V.BURE	24	3	1	4	11	4	15
M.LAMB	47	1	2	3	2	4	6
*D.BRASHEAR	20	1	1	2	4	4	8
*C.CONROY	6	1	0	1	14	0	14
*C.RIVET	5	0	1	1	0	17	17
*Y.SARAULT	8	0	1	1	0	11	11
*C.FERGUSON	1	0	0	0	0	0	0
*D.WILKIE	1	0	0	0	0	0	0
C.MURRAY	3	0	0	0	0	0	0
G.FLEMING	6	0	0	0	0	0	0
M.ROBERGE	9	0	0	0	0	0	0
P.SEVIGNY	19	0	0	0	0	0	0

All-Time Rankings - INDIVIDUAL (3)

Goals
Maurice Richard	544
Guy Lafleur	518
Jean Beliveau	507

Assists
Guy Lafleur	728
Jean Beliveau	712
Henri Richard	688

Points
Guy Lafleur	1,246
Jean Beliveau	1,219
Henri Richard	1,046

Best Individual Seasons

Goals
Steve Shutt	1976-77	60
Guy Lafleur	1977-78	60
Guy Lafleur	1976-77	56
Guy Lafleur	1975-76	56

Assists
Peter Mahovlich	1974-75	82
Guy Lafleur	1976-77	80
Guy Lafleur	1978-79	77

Points
Guy Lafleur	1976-77	136
Guy Lafleur	1977-78	132
Guy Lafleur	1978-79	129

New Jersey Devils

When baseball teams win with pitching, nobody complains; when football teams win with defence, nobody complains; when hockey teams win with defense, it's a travesty and it's time to change the rules.

That's all you heard about the Devils in the finals last year – boring, boring, boring. They're killing the game.

Actually, they were winning the game. But, because they didn't do it "nicely" it's as if they cheated and weren't worthy of being crowned champions.

Lots of teams play the neutral zone trap and they don't have a Stanley Cup. Those teams don't have the same talent, and more importantly, the same determination and discipline.

I think that makes New Jersey worthy winners.

If it took a team this long to perfect such a defensive system, why expect somebody to solve it overnight? Defence wins baseball, defence wins football, and right now defense wins hockey.

Not so long ago, it was offence that won hockey. Great teams in Edmonton, Pittsburgh and Montreal. And it will happen again. There haven't been that many strictly defensive teams that have won the Stanley Cup, anyway.

So, let's not get all aflutter and change all the rules. Okay, so maybe try to cut down on some of the interference and holding in the neutral zone. But, a parade of penalties isn't going to make things any more exciting.

The idea is that if they start calling everything early, the players will learn and won't do it any more. Maybe, but the last time they tried it, it was a major pain.

Back to the Devils. It's hard to imagine now, but they were only six points away from not making the playoffs at all. They were only fifth in the conference.

But, their playoff run was nothing short of incredible. Consider:

* They defeated Boston, Pittsburgh, Philadelphia and Detroit, four of the top six teams in the overall standings.

* They were 10-1 on the road, an NHL record. The most wins previously won on the road in a playoff year was eight.

* They were 16-4 overall during the playoffs, with three of the losses coming by one goal, and the other by two.

* They outshot their opponents in 17 of the 20 games.

* They had twice as many goals as their opponents - 67 to 34.

* They were tied six times after two periods, and went on to win five of them.

So, how does a mediocre regular season do so well in the playoffs? Obviously, they weren't as mediocre as their record indicated. Don't forget, the year before New Jersey came within an overtime seventh game loss of defeating the Rangers and going to the finals against Vancouver.

So, maybe they did coast a bit. That's often a trait of a Stanley Cup champion or finalist the following season, when the intensity of the games seems to be so lacking in comparison to what they just went through.

And, of course, the Devils have a couple of legendary regular season coasters in Claude Lemieux and Stephane Richer. In Lemieux's case, the Conn Smythe winner last year, his playoff performances are enough to almost completely ignore what he does during the regular season.

This team knew how to win when it counted. In the final analysis, nothing matters more.

Lowest Regular Season Winning Percentage for Stanley Cup Winners (since expansion In 1967-68)

NEW JERSEY	1994-95	22-18-8	.542
Pittsburgh	1991-92	39-32-9	.544
Montreal	1985-86	40-33-7	.544
Pittsburgh	1990-91	41-33-6	.550
Edmonton	1989-90	38-28-14	.563
NY Islanders	1979-80	39-28-13	.569

Lowest All-Time

Chicago	1937-38	14-25-9	.385
Toronto	1948-49	22-25-13	.467
Toronto	1944-45	24-22-4	.520
Chicago	1933-34	20-17-11	.531
NY Rangers	1927-28	19-16-9	.534
Toronto	1966-67	35-27-11	.536
Chicago	1960-61	29-24-17	.536
Montreal	1952-53	28-23-19	.536
NEW JERSEY	1994-95	22-18-8	.542

The above lists are separated at the time the NHL expanded. Obviously, winning a Stanley Cup in a 26 team league is considerably more difficult than in a six team league. Even so, the Devils still make the all-time top 10.

The regular season has been overated for a while, anyway. Why knock yourself out. Most years, it was almost impossible not to make the playoffs.

With more teams now, and as the expansion entries become more competitive, a wake up call is coming. As long as the league doesn't start adding more playoff positions, the regular season will once again have some meaning.

So, the big question is, can the New Jersey Devils win it again next year?

They won last year on heart, desire, and teamwork. They had talent, of course, but not as much as a lot of other teams. Sometimes, that kind of total effort is difficult to repeat.

They can do it again, but don't judge them after the regular season. Wait for the playoffs, when it counts most.

TEAM PREVIEW

GOAL: Martin Brodeur didn't get a single vote in the all-star balloting and was eighth in Vezina Trophy voting. If the voters could have waited until after the playoffs to cast their votes he would been number one on both, probably unanimously.

Those awards are for the regular season, of course, but where a goalie really establishes himself is in the playoffs. For the second year in a row, Brodeur had the best playoff goals against average. Even though the Devils play a defensive style, they probably wouldn't have won the Stanley Cup without Brodeur's heroics.

Brodeur was a free agent at the end of the season, but not an unrestricted one, and you can be sure the Devils would match any offer.

Even so, New Jersey is overloaded at this position. Not only do they have Chris Terreri, who has proven very capable at the NHL level, but they had Corey Schwab and Mike Dunham in Albany. The pair split the chores there fairly evenly, and even ended up sharing the playoff MVP award when Albany won the AHL championship. During the regular season they finished first in goals against average.

	GP	MIN	GA	AVG	W	L	T	SO
Brodeur	40	2184	89	2.45	19	11	6	3
Terreri	15	734	31	2.53	3	7	2	0

DEFENCE: It is sort of ironic that the signature play from last year's finals was Scott Niedermayer's rink-long rush. That's not something you saw from the Devils very often.

But, what you did see was great defensive play.

Everybody on the Devils had a great playoffs. From Scott Stevens, which was no surprise, to somebody like Shawn Chambers, which was a surprise.

Ken Daneyko was outstanding defensively, Bruce Driver came through offensively, and Tommy Albelin was there as well.

All veterans, with the exception of Niedermayer.

Before last season, Scott Stevens had 911 NHL games to his credit without a Stanley Cup victory. That's not the most, but it was in the top 15 before last year.

Three Devils in total are in the list, along with some former Devils, most notably Bernie Nicholls, who was with the team the previous season.

BEFORE LAST YEAR - Most Games Without a Stanley Cup Victory (active players last season)

Mike Gartner	1,170
Ray Bourque	1,100
Dale Hunter	1,054
Dale Hawerchuk	1,032
Mike Ramsay	988
Gaetan Duchesne	982
Dino Ciccarelli	973
Peter Stastny	971
NEAL BROTEN	955
Dave Babych	930
Thomas Steen	919
SCOTT STEVENS	911
Mark Howe	911
BOB CARPENTER	901
Bernie Nicholls	885

Other top Devils

John MacLean	706
Ken Daneyko	691
Bruce Driver	661
Claude Lemieux	589

As for this year, there will be a few changes on the New Jersey defence. Driver is an unrestricted free agent and likely won't be back. Niedermayer is a restricted free agent, and likely will be back.

There are some youngsters with talent that need playing time. They include Kevin Dean, Chris McAlpine and Jason Smith.

FORWARD: Sometime during the season, frustrated with the way his contract talks were going, Claude Lemieux asked to be traded. Jacques Lemaire's response was that he didn't care much for guys who put themselves before the team, inferring he wouldn't mind if Lemieux got his wish.

Okay, so all is forgiven.

Lemieux had 16 points during the playoffs and won the Conn Smythe trophy as the MVP. His scoring was incidental, even though, incidentally, he only had 19 points during the regular season. It was all the other things he did well, his "team play" if you will.

While it could be argued that the Devils might not have gone all the way without Lemieux, it was still evident that the most valuable entity the Devils have is the team itself, especially with the forwards.

On paper, they don't look like much, but fortunately for them the game is played on ice.

Heck, they don't have a dominant center, they don't have much in the way of scoring, they have too much unproven talent, and too many underachievers.

But, they do have something more important than all of the above. They have a Stanley Cup. Go figure.

Now, the Red Wings, they had a forward lineup that could easily go all the way. So did the Penguins, and the Nordiques, and St. Louis, and maybe even Calgary. But not New Jersey.

Apparently the lack of a superstar scorer helps them rather than hurts them. That keeps everybody on a more or less even playing field and helps ensure that the team is the thing.

Does that mean the parts are interchangable, like a machine? Anybody could step into the lineup and the team would get the same result as long as Lemaire is coaching?

Who knows? But, maybe it takes a while to learn that disciplined style of play, as well as full committment.

There wasn't much turnover from the previous season. All of the changes were in the middle, with softies like Corey Millen and Alexander Semak replaced with Neal Broten and Brian Rolston or Jim Dowd.

Along with Bob Carpenter and Bobby Holik, this group of centers would not be counted among the strongest in the league if you were ranking them. But, Carpenter and Holik went from disappointment to usefulness, and Broten went from oblivion to usefulness. Rolston and Dowd are two pretty good young players.

Holik, of course, centered the Crash Line, probably the best fourth line in the league. Carpenter, a former 50 goal scorer, became a checker, and Broten found the fountain of youth, (or Denis Savard found it and shared it with him).

Lemieux, Richer, McLean, Chorske, Zelepukin, Guerin, McKay, Peluso and company are set to give it another go on the wings.

In the background is Sergei Brylin, Danton Cole and rookie Vadim Sharifijanov. Otherwise, there's not much need for fixing something that ain't broke.

SPECIAL TEAMS: Ho, hum... yet another myth destroyed by the Devils. Can't win without a decent power play? Think again. The Devils were ranked 23rd during the regular season and last on the road.

They did pick it up considerably in the playoffs when they were ranked second. Their 18 power play goals in the post-season were only four shy of their regular season total.

Penalty killing wasn't all that great either, only 16th. In the playoffs it was ranked fifth.

Power Play	G	ATT	PCT
Overall	22	164	13.4% (23rd NHL)
Home	15	84	17.9% (14th NHL)
Road	7	80	8.8% (26th NHL)

3 SHORT HANDED GOALS ALLOWED (T-3rd NHL)

Penalty Killing	G	TSH	PCT
Overall	28	149	81.2% (16th NHL)
Home	13	77	83.1% (14th NHL)
Road	15	72	79.2% (19th NHL)

3 SHORT HANDED GOALS SCORED (T-20th NHL)

Penalties	GP	MIN	AVG
DEVILS	48	787	16.4 (8th NHL)

Top Scorers
DEVILS SPECIAL TEAMS SCORING

Power play	G	A	PTS
DRIVER	1	8	9
NIEDERMAYER	4	4	8
MACLEAN	2	6	8
CHAMBERS	2	5	7
BROTEN	2	5	7
GUERIN	4	2	6
STEVENS	1	5	6

Short handed	G	A	PTS
RICHER	2	0	2

COACHING AND MANAGEMENT: Every coach tries to get his players to play his way. Nobody in recent memory has succeeded like Jacques Lemaire.

He isn't the first to invoke a defensive system. Other coaches have tried, but they run into roadblocks: the star player whines that it's not fun, or the players start a mutiny against the coach and leak reports that nobody likes him, or other assorted things.

The reason Lemaire might have been successful, apart from the fact that he knows what he's doing, is that he didn't have star players. He preached the team concept, and with the group of players he had, they were able to play it.

And, perhaps most importantly, Lemaire commands respect. Second guessers are second-guessed, rather than Lemaire.

Lemaire, of course, was a star player in his days with the Canadiens. That makes his coaching success all the more unusual.

There haven't been many stars who had great coaching careers. That holds true for all sports. Often, it's just too frustrating for them because the things that came easily to them are difficult to teach.

The smartest thing general manager Lou Lamiorello ever did was hire Jacques Lemaire.

But, he does some other smart things. He keeps his players around, more so than most organizations nowadays. He still builds through the draft, but he doesn't panic by making wholesale changes based on a month or two of hockey.

DRAFT

1995 DRAFT SELECTIONS

Round	Sel.	Player	Pos	Amateur Team
1	18	Petr Sykora	C	Detroit Vipers (IHL)
2	44	Nathan Perrot	RW	Oshawa (OHL)
3	70	S. Vyshedkevich	D	Russia
3	78	David Gosselin	RW	Sherbrooke (QMJHL)
4	79	Alyn McCauley	C	Ottawa (OHL)
4	96	Henrik Rehnberg	D	Sweden
5	122	Chris Mason	G	Prince George (WHL)
6	148	Adam Young	D	Windsor (OHL)
7	174	R. Rochefort	C	Sudbury (OHL)
8	200	Frederic Henry	G	Granby (QMJHL)
9	226	Colin O'Hara	D	Winnipeg (MJHL)

At one time, Petr Sykora was projected to be the first pick in this draft. His stock dropped dramatically, however, because of injuries last season, including shoulder surgery, but perhaps more so for another reason.

Sykora chose the same route as fellow Czech Radek Bonk by playing in the IHL as an underager. Bonk put up some big numbers in the IHL but was a total flop in his first NHL season.

Sykora is also a lightweight at 5-11, 167 pounds. The Devils were excited to get him, but 17 other teams passed him by so you have to wonder.

PREDICTION: I don't have a good reason, but I don't think the Devils can do it again. To win the Stanley Cup without a tremendously talent team means everything has to go your way.

That's not the type of thing that happens every year, even though the Devils demolished everything in sight.

Will they contend for the Cup? Sure, why not. But, it's harder now. Teams are thinking already in terms of beating them.

It's a possibility we won't see the real Devils again until the playoffs anyway. They had a poor regular season last year and learned in the process that it doesn't really matter. It's hard to be hungry when your belly is already full.

But, when the playoffs start, you know guys like Lemieux and Stevens and Brodeur will be there.

STAT SECTION

Team Rankings 1994/95

		Conference Rank	League Rank
Record	22-18-8	5	9
Home	14-4-6	4	6
Away	8-14-2	9	17
Team Plus\Minus	+21	3	7
Goals For	136	6	13
Goals Against	121	3	5

MISCELLANEOUS STATS

One Goal Games	7-11
Times outshooting opponent	30
Times outshot	16
Even shots	2
Average Shots For	30.0
Average Shots Against	25.3
Overtime	1-2-8
Longest Winning streak	3
Longest Undefeated streak	7
Longest Losing streak	3
Longest winless streak	4
Versus Teams Over .500	7-11-3
Versus Teams Under .500	15-7-5
First Half Record	9-11-4
Second Half Record	13-7-4

PLAYOFFS

Results: WON STANLEY CUP
Record: 16-4
Home: 6-3
Away: 10-1
Goals For: 67, 3.4/gm
Goals Against: 34, 1.7/gm
Overtime: 2-0
Power play: 25.0 (2nd)
Penalty Killing: 86.5 (5th)

PLAYERS	1994-95 OVERALL				PROJECTED OVER 84 GAMES		
	GP	G	A	PTS	G	A	Pts
S.RICHER	45	23	16	39	43	30	73
N.BROTEN	47	8	24	32	14	43	57
J.MACLEAN	46	17	12	29	31	22	53
B.GUERIN	48	12	13	25	21	23	44
S.STEVENS	48	2	20	22	3	35	38
S.CHAMBERS	45	4	17	21	7	32	39
B.HOLIK	48	10	10	20	17	17	34
C.LEMIEUX	45	6	13	19	11	24	35
S.NIEDERMAYER	48	4	15	19	7	26	33
T.CHORSKE	42	10	8	18	20	16	36
*B.ROLSTON	40	7	11	18	15	23	38
B.CARPENTER	41	5	11	16	10	23	33
B.DRIVER	41	4	12	16	8	25	33
T.ALBELIN	48	5	10	15	9	17	26
*S.BRYLIN	26	6	8	14	19	26	45
R.MCKAY	33	5	7	12	13	18	31
M.PELUSO	46	2	9	11	4	16	20
D.COLE	38	4	5	9	9	11	20
J.DOWD	10	1	4	5	8	34	42
V.ZELEPUKIN	4	1	2	3	21	42	63
K.DANEYKO	25	1	2	3	3	7	10
*C.MCALPINE	24	0	3	3	0	11	11
*D.EMMA	6	0	1	1	0	14	14
*K.DEAN	17	0	1	1	0	5	5
J.SMITH	2	0	0	0	0	0	0
*R.SIMPSON	9	0	0	0	0	0	0
J.MODRY	11	0	0	0	0	0	0

All-Time Rankings - INDIVIDUAL

Goals
John MacLean	312
Kirk Muller	185
Pat Verbeek	170

Assists
Kirk Muller	335
Bruce Driver	328
Aaron Broten	307

Points
John MacLean	617
Kirk Muller	520
Aaron Broten	469

Best Individual Seasons

Goals
Pat Verbeek	1987-88	46
John MacLean	1990-91	45
John MacLean	1988-89	42

Assists
Scott Stevens	1993-94	60
Aaron Broten	1987-88	57
Kirk Muller	1987-88	57

Points
Kirk Muller	1987-88	94
John MacLean	1988-89	87
Kirk Muller	1989-90	86

Playoff Scoring Leaders

	GP	G	A	PTS
STEPHANE RICHER	19	6	15	21
NEAL BROTEN	20	7	12	19
JOHN MACLEAN	20	5	13	18
CLAUDE LEMIEUX	20	13	3	16
RANDY MCKAY	19	8	4	12
SCOTT NIEDERMAYER	20	4	7	11
BILL GUERIN	20	3	8	11
SHAWN CHAMBERS	20	4	5	9
BOBBY HOLIK	20	4	4	8
TOMMY ALBELIN	20	1	7	8
SCOTT STEVENS	20	1	7	8
BRUCE DRIVER	17	1	6	7
TOM CHORSKE	17	1	5	6
BOB CARPENTER	17	1	4	5
BRIAN ROLSTON	6	2	1	3
JIM DOWD	11	2	1	3
SERGEI BRYLIN	12	1	2	3
VALERI ZELEPUKIN	18	1	2	3
MIKE PELUSO	20	1	2	3
KEVIN DEAN	3	0	2	2
KEN DANEYKO	20	1	0	1
MARTIN BRODEUR	20	0	1	1
DANTON COLE	1	0	0	0
CHRIS TERRERI	1	0	0	0

New York Islanders

The most exciting thing about the New York Islanders this season may be their new uniforms. The new logo sports an angry looking fisherman guarding a hockey net while holding a hockey stick.

Oooooh...scary.

You don't find many actual people on sports team logos. The Senators have a trojan looking guy, and the Blackhawks have an Indian. That's it in the NHL.

If it's anything living, it's usually a mean looking animal. That's what sells, according to the marketing people, and what sells is most important these days. The Washington Capitals new logo, for example, features a swooping eagle.

Whether or not people will be thrilled about an unhappy fisherman (what's his problem, anyway, didn't catch any fish?) and will go out and buy the jersey will be determined, but undoubtably the old logo was boring. Filled with tradition, mind you, but boring, and that just doesn't cut it anymore.

By the way, don't fishermen usually want their nets filled? This guy's trying to keep things out. Doesn't make any sense.   Let's take a closer look at the NHL logos. The Colorado logo was unknown at press time.

Six teams feature animals in their logo, and three others have animal parts. Now, the Ducks logo is clearly a duck mask, but whether or not there's a duck behind it, isn't clear.

The panther and the shark, which is biting a hockey stick, are scary looking, as is the new Eagle on the Washington logo. Buffalo's buffalo appears to be charging, so it could also be considered intimidating.

Wisely, Pittsburgh doesn't try to make its penguin look ferocious. On second thought, if a duck can look ferocious, why not a penguin?

Four teams have animal parts in their logos. The Red Wings, of course have a red wing, while St. Louis and Philadelphia also feature wings on their crest. The Hartford Whalers animal part is a fish tail, a whale's you'd think. Just wait until they play the Islanders — do you think the fisherman wants keep a whale out of his net?

None of the animals or people are happy. Besides grouchy Mr. Fisherman, the Ottawa Senator guy is clearly frowning, and the Indian on Chicago's logo may be frowning or may be smiling slightly. Kind of like the Mona Lisa.

Boston, Calgary, Hartford, Montreal and New Jersey stylize their initial or initials; the Oilers and Canucks stylize their nicknames; Los Angeles Kings, the New York Rangers, Toronto Maple Leafs, and Winnipeg Jets stylize their full names.

The Sabres have crossed sabres, the Dallas Stars have a star, the Los Angeles Kings have a crown and the Tampa Bay Lightning have a lightning bolt.

Most teams in the league would like a new logo and new jersey color scheme. It's a money-maker. It's not likely any of the original six would change but now that the Islanders have gone fishing, the rest of them can figure on forgetting tradition.

With the new logo also comes a team makeover for the Islanders. That means they'll have to get the veterans to produce again, the underachievers to achieve, and the youngsters to learn at the NHL level.

Not an easy task, and certainly not one to brighten up that fisherman's day.

Speaking of the Islanders glory days, John Tonelli is eligible for induction into the Hockey Hall of Fame this year.

Apparently, it's not so easy to get into the Hall anymore. Ever since Gil Stein tried to orchestrate his own immortality, there's been a little more attention paid to the qualifications of potential members.

Last year, for example, Bernie Federko didn't make it. He has 1,130 career points, 26th on the all-time point list before last season. Not so long ago, he'd get in automatically.

It's still possible for Federko to gain entry, but with the selection committee being more selective it's not a sure thing. And that's a good thing because some of those that have got in, don't belong in a Hall of Fame.

It shouldn't be an easy thing to get into. It's supposed to be a special place, not a home for retired players. If there's some doubt, the guy's not worthy.

For example, you wouldn't even have to think about some of the stars in the game today. Gretzky, Messier, Coffey, Kurri, Lemieux, Bourque, and Roy are all automatic choices, with a whole other group not far behind.

Federko and Tonelli belong in the Hall based on previous occupancy, but will be hurt by higher standards. That's not fair to them, but it's better in the long run.

I think Tonelli belongs anyway because he was a special player. He was a dominant NHLer for a while and his play during the Canada Cup is almost legendary. As a matter of fact, he's worthy for his Canada Cup exploits alone.

Plus, he comes from Milton, Ontario, a place where I've spent most of my adult years. They named an arena after him there and they don't just do that for anybody.

Incidentally, the Hockey Hall of Fame is a wonderful place to visit, with great interactive stuff and outstanding exhibits. I can't say enough good about it.

Hockey Hall of Fame Chairman, Scotty Morrison, lived near me when I was growing up and I went to school with one of his sons. I could see his personal influence there, in the attic exhibit, where an old Royal York Rangers jersey is hanging up. There was some sentiment attached to that, I'm sure, considering one of his sons who played for that organization was killed on an off-shore drilling rig accident.

Another exhibit that touched me was the family sitting around the living room watching Hockey Night in Canada in the sixties. Few Canadians over 30 can think of that time without it bringing back warm, cozy memories.

TEAM PREVIEW

GOAL: Tommy Salo did just about everything a goaltender can do outside of the NHL last season. In the IHL, he was the Rookie of the Year, Goaltender of the Year and Player of the Year. He finished first in wins, goals against average, shutouts and games played. The Hockey News named him the Minor Pro Prospect of the Year.

He joined the Islanders late in the season and started six games, losing five of them, despite playing Ottawa twice and Tampa Bay once. His only win was against Quebec when he stopped 40 of 42 shots.

Oddly enough, Salo replaced Jamie McLennan in New York, and when McLennan was sent down to Denver, he caught fire as Denver went on to win the Turner Cup. Salo was sent back down too after the Islanders were knocked out of the playoffs.

McLennan had a 2.15 goals against average in the playoffs for Denver (Salo was 3.07) so maybe Salo did so well during the regular season because the team was so powerful. Perhaps it was a team thing more than an individual thing.

In any event, Salo will get a chance to prove himself at the NHL level this year. McLennan was a free agent, with compensation, so the Islanders might let him go.

The other Islander goaltender will be Tommy Soderstrom, giving them an all Swedish goaltending duo. I can't think of any team that's ever had two Europeans sharing the duties.

It's only in recent years that Europeans have come into any prominence in the nets. Dominik Hasek and Arturs Irbe have sort of paved the way in that area after so many unsuccessful attempts.

The different style of play in Europe means often their goaltenders aren't suited to the NHL unless they can get by on their reflexes. One difference is that they don't handle the puck much there because of the larger area behind the net. Their skills in that area are often comical. It's an adventure every time Irbe comes out of his net.

As well, they don't grow up with catching games, such as baseball, so sometimes their gloves aren't as good. And the European style is to move the puck more towards the center of the ice for scoring opportunities as opposed to in North America where they'll blast the puck from any angle.

One particular region that has had no problems in recent years turning out goaltenders is the Quebec League, and the Islanders have a dandy prospect in Eric Fichaud, whom they obtained from Toronto for Benoit Hogue.

	GP	MIN	GA	AVG	W	L	T	SO
Salo	6	358	18	3.02	1	5	0	0
Soderstrom	26	1350	70	3.11	8	12	3	1
McLennan	21	1185	67	3.39	6	11	2	0

DEFENCE: While you wouldn't exactly call the defence a strength for the Islanders, they at least have strength in numbers. And it's probably the strongest position on the team.

Last year they suffered all kinds of injuries, but it allowed some players to get ice time that they wouldn't have had otherwise, giving them the opportunity to prove themselves.

Chris Luongo fits into that category. He's bounced around a bit, and did play a full season in Ottawa a couple years ago, but he seemed ticketed for a career in the minor leagues.

Unfortunately for him, despite playing the most games of the Islander defencemen last season, it won't be so easy to get ice time this year.

Mathieu Schneider, obtained in the Montreal deal, is their top defenceman, and as long as his attitude doesn't get in the way, he'll be their quarterback on the power play and the number one offensive defenceman.

Scott Lachance appeared to be coming into his own offensively as well last season with 13 points in 26 games. And they'll probably have Bob Beers around too, although he was offered a termination contract. A player of his type gets shuffled around from team to team, whoever is looking for a power play boost at the time.

More offence could come from rookie Bryan McCabe. He had 69 points in 62 games for Brandon in the WHL to go along with 153 penalty minutes.

And don't forget the second choice overall in this year's draft, Wade Redden. He's supposed to be an all-round defenceman who can step into the NHL right away.

On the defensive end of things there's Darius Kaspairitus, the NHL's dirtiest player or toughest player, depending on who's doing the judging. Others include Dean Chynoweth, Rich Pilon, Dennis Vaske, Brent Severyn and another youngster in Jason Widmer.

Obviously, they can't all play, but it will give coach Milbury the opportunity to mix or match depending on the opponent. Or the ability to send somebody in from the press box if they're struggling on the ice. And, it opens up more trading options for Maloney.

Depth is never a bad thing, especially with a number of the Islanders defensemen still restricted free agents at press time.

Not a bad group, and one that in a few years could be outstanding.

FORWARD: There's a very serious problem here. In the NHL, the team that scores more goals wins the game. Period. The Islanders are going to have a tough time doing that because they don't have any scorers.

Last year, they only had one, and he's gone to the Rangers as a free agent. Ray Ferraro had 22 goals, but the next highest scorer only had half that.

In a full season those 11 goals projected mean they don't even have a 20-goal scorer. Is that scary, or what?

Oh, they have a couple guys who have scored in the past. Steve Thomas had 42 goals just two years ago, but he was playing with a scoring center at the time, and now he's 32 years old, and the scoring center is in Montreal. Last year, he had just 11 goals.

Derek King has had a 40-goal season and a couple in the thirties, but he's inconsistent, and isn't the type to do it on his own. He needs a center, too. He had just 10 goals last year.

That leaves Kirk Muller as the only other scorer of note with rookie Todd Bertuzzi as the only other potential high point man.

Muller, of course, is a character player, who can't score as much as Pierre Turgeon, but brings more to the party.

But, the Islanders need to score more often at parties.

Bertuzzi might be able to help out there. He was a second team all-star right winger in the OHL and was 54-65-119 for Guelph in the OHL last year

What the Islanders might consider, as long as they have little chance of winning anyway, is trading those veterans, now or at the trading deadline, while they still have some value. There was interest in Thomas last year, which would have been the perfect time to trade him, but no deal could be worked out. Thomas was still a restricted free agent at press time.

At center, behind Muller, is defensive center Travis Green, a potential scorer in Craig Darby and minor league scoring whiz Chris Taylor. It's a position that isn't likely to remain that way, however. They're going to need something more.

At left wing is Derek King and Marty McInnis, both of whom need to get out of whatever funk they were in last season, and start scoring again. Brett Lindros is still developing, and even if he's not scoring, his size and toughness is still worth having him around. Chris Marinucci, a former Hobey Baker award winner, and U.S. Born Rookie of the Year in the IHL last season, made an impression when he was called up, even getting playing time on the top line with Muller and Thomas. He had five points in 12 games and could end up sticking around.

The right side has Thomas, often-injured Pat Flatley, rookie Todd Bertuzzi (listed as left winger, but played right wing with Guelph), Brad Dalgarno and little fella Zigmund Palffy who scored six of his 10 goals and 11 of his 17 points in the team's final 15 games when he finally earned his chance to play regularly. Mick Vukota, the necessary enforcer, also plays the right side.

All in all, the lineup continues to get bigger and stronger, and I don't want to be repetitive but who's gonna score the goals, who's gonna score the goals, who's gonna score the goals...

SPECIAL TEAMS: With 28 goals on the power play last season, the Islanders tied the team's all-time record holder. Mind you, when Mike Bossy set the record in 1980-81, he played 31 more games.

Ahh...Bossy, Trottier and Potvin on the power play. Those were the days.

The Islanders finished 19th last year, and there's no particular reason to think they can move up with only one scoring line, and a questionable one at that.

Schneider on the power play point is a positive. He scored nine points in 13 games after being obtained from Montreal. Bryan McCabe, expected to make the team this year, had 69 points in 62 games for Brandon in the WHL last season, so he could make an impact. And there are others who can play there as well.

Up front, the Islanders need one of their snipers, King or Thomas, to return to form, or someone else to pick up the slack.

Mike Milbury probably won't stand for one of the lowest ranked penalty killing units in the league and will likely invoke some improvement in that area.

Power Play	G	ATT	PCT
Overall	28	178	15.7% (T-19th NHL)
Home	10	83	12.0% (25th NHL)
Road	18	95	18.9% (8th NHL)

11 SHORT HANDED GOALS ALLOWED (26th NHL)

Penalty Killing	G	TSH	PCT
Overall	46	213	78.4% (24th NHL)
Home	19	98	80.6% (T-21st NHL)
Road	27	115	76.5% (T-23rd NHL)

4 SHORT HANDED GOALS SCORED (T-17th NHL)

Penalties	GP	MIN	AVG
ISLANDERS	48	901	18.8 (12th NHL)

Top Scorers
ISLANDERS SPECIAL TEAMS SCORING

Power play	G	A	PTS
SCHNEIDER	3	10	13
KING	7	4	11
THOMAS	3	6	9
MULLER	4	3	7
FERRARO	2	5	7
LACHANCE	3	3	6

Short handed	G	A	PTS
MULLER	1	0	1
DALGARNO	1	0	1
LUONGO	0	1	1

COACHING AND MANAGEMENT: Mike Milbury is the new coach and already is a step ahead of the game because of the respect he's earned in his years with the Bruins. He also has a sense of humor, which he will need with this team.

He's expected to make them better, but as they say, you can't make a silk purse out of a sow's ear.

At least if the Islanders don't play well this year, he's likely to be given more of a chance than Lorne Henning, who was dumped after just one lockout-shortened, injury-plagued season.

Maybe Milbury won't want to stick around long, anyway. Some flightiness has dotted his career. He was supposed to be the heir apparent to Harry Sinden in Boston at one time, and then later he signed on with Boston College only to quit almost immediately.

GM Don Maloney made his first major deal shipping Pierre Turgeon and Vladimir Malakhov to Montreal for Kirk Muller, Mathieu Schneider and Craig Darby. He also dumped off Benoit Hogue and got a top goaltending prospect in Eric Fichaud.

Those deals make it look like he's trying to build a team with some character. But, he also needs to build a team that can play the game, so he's got quite a bit of work to do. He absolutely hates to see his team get pushed around, especially in their own rink, and it seems to be a priority with him to get bigger and stronger, especially up front.

DRAFT

1995 DRAFT SELECTIONS

Round	Sel.	Player	Pos	Amateur Team
1	2	Wade Redden	D	Brandon (WHL)
2	28	Jan Hlavac	LW	Czechoslovakia
2	41	Denis Smith	D	Windsor (OHL)
5	106	Vladimir Orsagh	LW	Slovakia
7	158	Andrew Taylor	LW	Detroit (OHL)
9	210	Dave MacDonald	G	Sudbury (OHL)
9	211	Mike Broda	LW	Moose Jaw (WHL)

The Islanders haven't had a first round pick become a star since Pat LaFontaine in 1983. Most are still playing, but none have excelled.

Redden isn't supposed to be an NHL superstar, either, but he's expected to be very good. No one particular part of his game sets him way above his contemporaries, but when you add up all the pieces he's at or near the top.

PROGNOSIS: It's going to be a long season for the Islanders. But, they do have some things to get excited about, besides the deranged fisherman on the new logo. They have some good young players, a fresh new coach, and a continued committment to building a winner.

It's what they don't have that's going to require patience from their fans. Scoring, for instance, can be a problem when you don't have it. And their goaltending is unproven.

The most they can hope for in the next couple years is steady improvement. Unfortunately, for them, that does not include making the playoffs this year.

PREDICTION:
Atlantic Division: 5th
Eastern Conference: 10th
Overall: 20th

STAT SECTION

Team Rankings 1994/95

		Conference Rank	League Rank
Record	15-28-5	13	25
Home	10-11-3	11	20
Away	5-17-2	12	23
Team Plus\Minus	-14	11	17
Goals For	126	10	21
Goals Against	158	12	19

PLAYERS	1994-95 OVERALL				Projected over 84 games		
	GP	G	A	PTS	G	A	PTS
R.FERRARO	47	22	21	43	39	38	77
M.SCHNEIDER	43	8	21	29	16	41	57
K.MULLER	45	11	16	27	21	30	51
P.FLATLEY	45	7	20	27	13	37	50
S.THOMAS	47	11	15	26	20	27	47
D.KING	43	10	16	26	20	31	51
*Z.PALFFY	33	10	7	17	25	18	43
M.MCINNIS	41	9	7	16	18	14	32
S.LACHANCE	26	6	7	13	18	23	41
T.GREEN	42	5	7	12	10	14	24
D.VASKE	41	1	11	12	2	23	25
B.BEERS	22	2	7	9	8	27	35
B.SEVERYN	28	2	4	6	6	12	18
B.DALGARNO	22	3	2	5	11	8	19
*C.MARINUCCI	12	1	4	5	7	28	35
R.SUTTER	27	1	4	5	3	12	15
*B.LINDROS	33	1	3	4	3	8	11
C.LUONGO	47	1	3	4	2	5	7
P.STANTON	18	0	4	4	0	19	19
*C.TAYLOR	10	0	3	3	0	25	25
*Y.KAMINSKY	2	1	1	2	42	42	84
R.PILON	20	1	1	2	4	4	8
*C.DARBY	13	0	2	2	0	13	13
D.CHYNOWETH	32	0	2	2	0	5	5
M.VUKOTA	40	0	2	2	0	4	4
K.MILLER	8	0	1	1	0	11	11
D.KASPARAITIS	13	0	1	1	0	6	6
*J.WIDMER	1	0	0	0	0	0	0
*M.TICHY	2	0	0	0	0	0	0
*A.VASILJEV	2	0	0	0	0	0	0
G.DINEEN	9	0	0	0	0	0	0
D.CHYZOWSKI	13	0	0	0	0	0	0

MISCELLANEOUS STATS

One Goal Games	8-12
Times outshooting opponent	17
Times outshot	29
Even shots	2
Average Shots For	28.2
Average Shots Against	30.1
Overtime	1-1-5
Longest Winning streak	2
Longest Undefeated streak	3
Longest Losing streak	5
Longest winless streak	6
Versus Teams Over .500	7-16-3
Versus Teams Under .500	8-10-2
First Half Record	9-12-3
Second Half Record	6-14-2

All-Time Rankings — INDIVIDUAL

Goals

Mike Bossy	573
Bryan Trottier	500
Denis Potvin	310

Assists

Bryan Trottier	853
Denis Potvin	742
Mike Bossy	553

Points

Bryan Trottier	1,153
Mike Bossy	1,126
Denis Potvin	1,052

Best Individual Seasons

Goals

Mike Bossy	1978-79	69
Mike Bossy	1980-81	68
Mike Bossy	1981-82	64

Assists

Bryan Trottier	1978-79	87
Mike Bossy	1981-82	83
Bryan Trottier	1981-82	79

Points

Mike Bossy	1981-82	147
Bryan Trottier	1978-79	134
Pierre Turgeon	1992-93	132

New York Rangers

When the Rangers won the Stanley Cup two years ago, it was their first since 1940. Last year they ended another streak of sorts. They became the first team since 1948 to have a losing season the year following a Stanley Cup triumph.

Losing Seasons after Winning Stanley Cup

	Cup Year	Following Season
Toronto	1917-18	5-13-0
Chicago	1937-38	12-28-8
Toronto	1944-45	19-24-7
Toronto	1947-48	22-25-13
NY Rangers	1994-95	22-23-3

The list of teams with that dubious accomplishment is a short one, and each of them, except the Rangers, have extenuating circumstances. The Toronto team in 1917-18 was in a three-team league, the Chicago team in 1937-38 had a losing season the year they won the Cup, the Toronto team in 1944-45 was in the war years, and the Toronto team in 1947-48 still managed to win the Cup despite the losing record.

I suppose you could say that the Rangers extenuating circumstance was the reduced schedule, but it would just be another excuse for a poor season.

It's no secret why the Rangers faltered, although you'd get a lot of argument from some sources. First of all, they were a team built for a one-season run at the Cup. Secondly, and most importantly, they never would have got that far without Mike Keenan.

There's no better coach in the game now than Keenan, and he ranks up there among the best of all time.

That's no knock against coach Colin Campbell, who came in under a no-win situation. He can't do what Keenan can do, but then neither can most others.

Keenan, who has a penchant for retooling with players who have played for him before, has taken Brian Noonan (free agent) and Jay Wells (trade) from the Rangers since the season was over . Can Stephane Matteau be far behind?

You have to wonder how the Wells for Bruce Driver trade ever came off, considering the animosity between Keenan and GM Neil Smith. Apparently, during last season, Keenan inexplicably tried to make a deal through coach Colin Campbell.

At any rate, the Rangers were doomed for failure and things aren't getting any brighter. They have Leetch and Zubov, but most of the rest of their key players are oldtimers or sleepwalkers that only Keenan would be able to succeed in waking up.

The Rangers finished eighth last season, and had to work down the stretch just to make the playoffs. They ended up beating the conference first place finisher, Quebec, which oddly enough wasn't all that much of a surprise.

Teams who have been through recent playoff wars often have a difficult time with the relatively small battle of the regular season. They had the experience and savy to beat Quebec, but not enough talent to go much further.

Heck, they might not even have beaten Quebec if an important goal by Quebec hadn't been disallowed after Kovalev faked an injury.

Michel Bergeron, Quebec media personality and former coach of both the Nords and the Rangers, claimed that it was considerably easier for New York's coaches than Quebec's because the referees liked going to the Big Apple more.

You'd be extremely hard pressed to prove Bergeron's claim. In fact, you could make a better case for the referees favoring Quebec. In 1992, Quebec had a whopping 55 more man-advantages than their opponents at home.

The Rangers appear to get no advantage whatsoever. Except for last year when they were one advantage over, they were below the league average every season, and way below over the five year period.

The reality of the situation is that neither team had any advantage. The difference in penalty calls probably has more to do with the style of play for each team that particular year.

Home teams are going to get more advantages, not because refs like their city or because they're afraid to call penalties, but because visitors are more likely to take penalties. Home teams wins more often, so the visitors are more likely to do more to try and stop them. Plus, visitors are more likely to play a defensive or clutch and grab style because they're not worried about entertaining their own fans.

In fairness to Bergeron's assessment, however, the year he was in New York, 1987-88, the team was plus 50 in home ice advantages.

TEAM PREVIEW

GOAL: Maybe one of these days Glenn Healy is going to get some respect. Don't bet on it. It doesn't matter how well he plays, he's always going to be considered a second banana.

Take the playoffs last year. Mike Richter started the first game against Quebec and lost. Colin Campbell came back with Healey in the second game, and they won.

That started the great goaltender debate. Who would start game three?

Healey had played most of the games down the stretch drive and had a considerably better goals against average over the season, plus he had been sensational for the Islanders in the playoffs two years earlier.

But, Richter was the number one goalie on paper and on the salary scale. And he led the Rangers to the Stanley Cup the year before.

Tough choice, but Campbell went with Healey and they won 4-3. That made the game four choice considerably easier. It was Healey again, but he didn't last long. He was pulled after the first period for letting in just two goals — any excuse to get him out of there.

Richter came on and shut out the Nords the rest of the way, including overtime, with the Rangers winning 3-2.

Richter started the next two, losing one and winning one, as the Rangers eliminated the Nordiques from the playoffs. Then he started the opener in the next round against Philadelphia but faltered as the Rangers lost 5-4. No matter, he was in again for the next game, a 4-3 loss. And he started the next one. But after allowing four goals in the first 30:23 of the game, Healey came on and allowed just one goal the rest of the way in a 5-2 loss.

Healey, of course, started game four, a 4-1 loss, and it was all over.

It will be the same deal for Healey again this year, no matter how well he plays, he'll be Richter's backup regardless of real numbers. If Healey's still around in another year or so, he'll probably lose his job to Dan Cloutier anyway, a young goaltender who sparkled for Canada in their world junior championship victory.

Such is life as an NHL goaltender.

	GP	MIN	GA	AVG	W	L	T	SO
Healy	17	888	35	2.36	8	6	1	1
Richter	35	1993	97	2.92	14	17	2	2

DEFENCE: Brian Leetch and Sergei Zubov rank up among the best two offensive defensemen duos in the league.

Most Points — Top Two Defensemen — 1993-94

Detroit	Coffey, Lidstrom	84
NY Rangers	Leetch, Zubov	77
Chicago	Chelios, Suter	73
Calgary	Housley, Zalapski	71
St.Louis	Duchesne, Norton	68
Boston	Bourque, Sweeney	65

Of course, those two are nowhere near the top two in the league defensively, but neither are many of the other duos in the top six, and all of these teams are successful.

Elsewhere they have veterans Kevin Lowe and Doug Lidster (who comes back to the team from St. Louis). Lowe is 36 years old, Lidster will be 35 in the first month of the season.

Jeff Beukeboom, 30 years old, is also back there along with 25-year-old Alexander Karpovtsev and 23-year-old Mattius Norstrom.

Jay Wells is gone to St. Louis, which wouldn't normally mean much, except that Keenan wanted him. If I were an NHL GM, I'd find out who Keenan wanted and then not trade the guy.

There's very little on the Rangers defence, other than Beukeboom, to make opposing forwards nervous, at least physically, but opposing defensemen might have some sleepless nights trying to stop Leetch and Zubov.

FORWARD: The Rangers had high hopes for Peter Ferraro and Chris Ferraro when they drafted them in 1992. Now, they have a Ferraro who can play for them. That's Ray Ferraro, signed as a free agent from the New York Islanders.

He lines up at center behind the supposedly aging Mark Messier and in front of a supposed hockey player, Petr Nedved.

Messier was up to his same old tricks last season, finishing in the top 10 in scoring, and doing his best to rally the disheartened troops.

Ferraro had an excellent season with the weak Islanders, scoring 22 goals, or five more than any of the Rangers. That projects to a 39 goal season over 84 games, but don't expect more of the same.

Ferraro is up and down, all over the map, when it comes to scoring. Check out his scoring from year to year. Ray Ferraro is like a box of chocolates, you never know what you're gonna get.

Ray Ferraro — NHL stats

	Gm	G	A	Pts
1984-85	44	11	17	28
1985-86	76	30	47	77
1986-87	80	27	32	59
1987-88	68	21	29	50
1988-89	80	41	35	76
1989-90	79	25	29	54
1990-91	76	21	21	42
1991-92	80	40	40	80
1992-93	46	14	13	27
1993-94	82	21	32	53
1994-95	47	22	21	43

After Ferraro is Petr Nedved, and if Ferraro is like a box of chocolates, then Nedved is like a box of fruitcake. Few players have received so much attention for one good season. Rumors had the Rangers trying to trade him all year long but apparently, nobody wants the headaches.

Nathan Lafayette is a center as well, depending on who the Rangers will move back to the wings. Lafayette showed some promise in the playoffs with Vancouver a couple years ago, but was a stranger to the scoresheet in New York last season.

Alexei Kovalev will probably move back to the wing, if he can survive those career-threatening injuries he received on a regular basis last year.

If I were an opposing player, I'd try to get away with as much as possible on Kovalev this year. He's one player NHL referees won't be calling many penalties against after that injury-faking incident in the playoffs that cost Quebec a goal and veteran referee Andy van Hellemond his dignity.

Pat Verbeek and Steve Larmer also patrol the right side, although Larmer was making some noise about retiring over the summer. Last year, he became the 43rd player in NHL history to reach the 1,000 point plateau. Joey Kocur is also a right winger, but he was a free agent and hadn't signed with anyone at press time.

On the other side are Adam Graves, Sergei Nemchinov, Stephane Matteau and Nick Kypreos.

Niklas Sundstrom, the Rangers' first choice, and eighth overall in the 1993 draft, will get a shot at fitting in somewhere.

Joey Mullen, with the Penguins last year, was still a free agent at press time, but he'd like nothing better to finish out his career in his hometown.

And the Rangers managed to sign those Ferraro twins and bring them back to their own farm team in Binghamton from Atlanta. Maybe we could see a full line of Ferraros.

The Rangers had one big line of Graves-Messier-Verbeek towards the end of last season that played very well. After them, it was just a matter of who felt like playing that particular night. More consistency would be nice.

And as long as we're on that topic, if Nedved isn't going to score anyway, it would be to their advantage to get a big centerman who can check. They were looking for that last season, apparently, but didn't find him.

SPECIAL TEAMS: The Rangers have all the components of a great power play. Two quarterbacks on the point in Zubov and Leetch, a sniper in Adam Graves, and a dominant center in Mark Messier. That's about as good as it gets.

Power Play	G	ATT	PCT
Overall	40	200	20.0% (5th NHL)
Home	28	111	25.2% (2nd NHL)
Road	12	89	13.5% (19th NHL)

3 SHORT HANDED GOALS ALLOWED (T-3rd NHL)

Penalty Killing	G	TSH	PCT
Overall	34	211	83.9% (10th NHL)
Home	18	101	82.2% (19th NHL)
Road	16	110	85.5% (5th NHL)

5 SHORT HANDED GOALS SCORED (T-13th NHL)

Penalties	GP	MIN	AVG
RANGERS	48	781	16.3 (7th NHL)

Top Scorers

RANGERS SPECIAL TEAMS SCORING

Power play	G	A	PTS
LEETCH	3	18	21
MESSIER	3	17	20
ZUBOV	6	13	19
GRAVES	9	6	15
VERBEEK	7	4	11
NOONAN	7	3	10
LARMER	3	4	7
KOVALEV	1	5	6

Short handed	G	A	PTS
MESSIER	3	0	3

COACHING AND MANAGEMENT: You have to feel a bit for Colin Campbell. He came in under the worst possible scenario for a new coach. He had nothing to gain and everything to lose. It would be like going on stage after the opening act already brought the house down.

Unfortunately for him, the Rangers are not going to do well again this year, and Campbell will probably pay the price with his job.

Neil Smith has had two very successful seasons since he began his tenure with the Rangers in 1989. Both of them were with outstanding, but controversial coaches — Roger Neilson and Mike Keenan.

That means, unlike some general managers, Smith is more concerned with making the team a winner than with making sure he can control the coach.

He's going to have to do some more work this season because the on-ice Rangers don't appear to have the right chemistry yet to challenge for the championship again.

He needs to get rid of the players who don't want to play and get some who do.

DRAFT

1995 DRAFT SELECTIONS

Round	Sel.	Player	Pos	Amateur Team
2	39	Christian Dube	C	Sherbrooke (QMJHL)
3	65	Mike Martin	D	Windsor (OHL)
4	91	Marc Savard	C	Oshawa (OHL)
5	110	Alexei Vasiljev	D	Russia
5	117	Dale Purinton	D	Tacoma (WHL)
6	143	Peter Salamiar	RW	Slovakia
7	169	Jeff Heil	G	Wis./River Falls (NCAA)
8	195	Ilja Gorohov	n/a	Russia
9	221	Bob Maudie	C	Kamloops (WHL)

The Rangers traded their first round pick to Hartford in the Pat Verbeek deal. Dube was ranked as a late first rounder, but the knock against him is his size (5-11, 170). He had 101 points last year in the Quebec League.

Fourth round pick, Marc Savard, is also small (5-10, 174) but he can score. He led the OHL with 139 points last year.

PROGNOSIS: The Rangers have some talented players, but they just don't seem to have it as a team anymore. Something's missing. Oh, yeah, well we don't want to keep mentioning his name all the time. But, besides that.

The thing is, with as much talent as they have, it won't take too much tinkering to turn them into a winner again.

PREDICTION:
Atlantic Division: 4th
Eastern Conference: 6th
Overall: 13th

STAT SECTION

Team Rankings 1994/95

		Conference Rank	League Rank
Record	22-23-3	8	14
Home	11-10-3	10	17
Away	11-13-0	6	10
Team Plus\Minus	-1	7	11
Goals For	139	5	12
Goals Against	134	7	9
Average Shots For	31.8		
Average Shots Against	26.3		

PLAYERS	1994-95 OVERALL				Projected over 84 games			
	GP	G	A	PTS	G	A	PTS	
M.MESSIER	46	14	39	53	26	71	97	
B.LEETCH	48	9	32	41	16	56	72	
S.ZUBOV	38	10	26	36	22	57	79	
P.VERBEEK	48	17	16	33	30	28	58	
A.GRAVES	47	17	14	31	30	25	55	
S.LARMER	47	14	15	29	25	27	52	
A.KOVALEV	48	13	15	28	23	26	49	
B.NOONAN	45	14	13	27	26	24	50	
P.NEDVED	46	11	12	23	20	22	42	
S.NEMCHINOV	47	7	6	13	13	11	24	
A.KARPOVTSEV	47	4	8	12	7	14	21	
T.LONEY	30	5	4	9	14	11	25	
J.WELLS	43	2	7	9	4	14	18	
N.LAFAYETTE	39	4	4	8	9	9	18	
S.MATTEAU	41	3	5	8	6	10	16	
K.LOWE	44	1	7	8	2	13	15	
M.OSBORNE	37	1	3	4	2	7	9	
N.KYPREOS	40	1	3	4	2	6	8	
J.BEUKEBOOM	44	1	3	4	2	6	8	
J.KOCUR	48	1	2	3	2	3	5	
*M.NORSTROM	9	0	3	3	0	28	28	
*D.LANGDON	18	1	1	2	5	5	10	
J.MESSIER	10	0	2	2	0	17	17	
*J.ROY	3	1	0	1	28	0	28	
*S.MCCOSH	5	1	0	1	17	0	17	
*D.LACROIX	24	1	0	1	3	0	3	
M.HARTMAN	1	0	0	0	0	0	0	

* Projected point totals

MISCELLANEOUS STATS

One Goal Games	9-13
Times outshooting opponent	36
Times outshot	11
Even shots	1
Overtime	0-0-3
Longest Winning streak	3
Longest Undefeated streak	4
Longest Losing streak	7
Longest winless streak	7
Versus Teams Over .500	11-15-0
Versus Teams Under .500	11-8-3
First Half Record	12-9-3
Second Half Record	10-14-0

PLAYOFFS

Results: defeated Quebec 4-2,
lost to Philadelphia 4-0
Record: 4-6
Home: 3-2
Away: 2-4
Goals For: 35 (3.5/gm)
Goals Against 37 (3.7/gm)
Overtime:
Power play: 28.3% (1st)
Penalty Killing: 90.0% (2nd)

PLAYER	GP	G	A	PTS
B. LEETCH	10	6	8	14
M. MESSIER	10	3	10	13
A. KOVALEV	10	4	7	11
S. ZUBOV	10	3	8	11
P. VERBEEK	10	4	6	10
S. NEMCHINOV	10	4	5	9
A. GRAVES	10	4	4	8
P. NEDVED	10	3	2	5
S. LARMER	10	2	2	4
N. KYPREOS	10	0	2	2
M. OSBORNE	7	1	0	1
A. KARPOVTSEV	8	1	0	1
S. MATTEAU	9	0	1	1

K. LOWE	10	0	1	1
T. LONEY	1	0	0	0
M. NORSTROM	3	0	0	0
G. HEALY	5	0	0	0
B.NOONAN	5	0	0	0
M. RICHTER	7	0	0	0
N.LAFAYETTE	8	0	0	0
J. BEUKEBOOM	9	0	0	0
J. KOCUR	10	0	0	0
J WELLS	10	0	0	0

All-Time Rankings — INDIVIDUAL

Goals

Rod Gilbert	406
Jean Ratelle	336
Andy Bathgate	272

Assists

Rod Gilbert	615
Jean Ratelle	481
Andy Bathgate	457

Points

Rod Gilbert	1,021
Jean Ratelle	817
Andy Bathgate	729

Best Individual Seasons

Goals

Adam Graves	1993-94	52
Vic Hadfield	1971-72	50
Mike Gartner	1990-91	49

Assists

Brian Leetch	1991-92	80
Sergei Zubov	1993-94	77
Brian Leetch	1990-91	72

Points

Jean Ratelle	1971-72	109
Mark Messier	1991-92	107
Vic Hadfield	1971-72	106

Ottawa Senators

Things are looking up in Ottawa. Just five or so more years in last place and they have a shot at a winning record.

Okay, so maybe it's not quite that bad. Four years ought to do it.

Nothing has ever gone right for this franchise. Not from day one. Not in year one, year two or year three.

They have the worst record of any expansion team in their first three years.

The first couple years aren't supposed to matter anyway, as long as there's promise for the future. Ottawa has had plenty of promise, if nothing else.

So when do they start to deliver? GM Randy Sexton said before last year that they were going for a .500 record at home and would take a run at a playoff spot.

Hmm...and this year they're going to challenge for the Stanley Cup?

When a GM says that kind of stuff what he's also saying is he's a very poor judge of talent. That means the Senators could be in for a lot more trouble.

It's one thing to be patient and build a team, it's another to build it incorrectly.

So far, this looks like a team that might contend in a European league, but not the NHL. They've loaded up with Europeans and European-type players.

Show any sign of being a character player and it's bye bye. Goodbye to Troy Murray, who along with Chris Dahlquist and Randy Cunneyworth, took it upon themselves to give a long-needed tongue lashing to Alexei Yashin and Alexander Daigle. For trying to make men out of them he's shipped to Pittsburgh for another European. The three players also held a players-only meeting to try to get things on track and put some life into the team. What were they thinking?

Goodbye to Chris Dahlquist, who was offered a termination contract.

Goodbye to Bill Huard, who gave the team some heart and some life with his crashing and banging. No point to a guy like that. Interesting that they had a spot in Quebec for him, though.

Get out of town, guys, got to make room for more "skill" players.

Sexton may not know this, and he's not the only one, but on European teams one of the responsibilites of import Canadians and Americans is to put some life into the dressing room. It's not just the scoring they're after.

Oh, I know we're not supposed to say Europeans are lacking in some areas of the game. We're only supposed to say good things, but let's get with the program. A fact is a fact.

It doesn't apply to all Europeans, but there's no question that a great many of them play with less emotion. One of the most enlightening books on the subject was written by Tod Hartje, an American who played in the Soviet Union for a year. He goes on at length about how little they cared over there about winning or losing, and how lacking they were in emotion and passion for the game.

I'm not trying to be Don Cherry. I think it's good that Europeans play here because it makes the NHL the best league in the world. But, I do believe that pretty skating and fancy stickhandling is nice, but in the right measure and for the right purpose.

The Europeans are considered the "skill" players but it doesn't always translate to winning. Character is just as important a skill, if not more important, when it comes to building winning hockey teams. And the character players can go a long way towards making the skill players more productive - as long as you don't keep getting rid of them.

Speaking of winning hockey teams, just how long is it going to take? It took only to the third season for four true expansion entries to get above .500. The Islanders rise was especially impressive considering how bad they were their first two seasons.

At the other end of the scale is Washington-Colorado-New Jersey. It took them until their fourteenth season.

The Senators can take some solace in the fact that none of the recent expansion entries have had winning seasons, although Florida and San Jose have been close.

Expansion teams - First Winning Season

	Season
Atlanta	3
Buffalo	3
NY Islanders	3
Vancouver	3
Washington	9
Kansas City	14

Still no .500 season

Anaheim	2+
Florida	2+
OTTAWA	3+
Tampa Bay	3+
San Jose	4+

TEAM PREVIEW

GOAL: If not for Don Beaupre, there's no telling how many more games the Senators would have lost last year. The 35-year-old had an outstanding season and earned team MVP honors. He even recorded the first and only shutout in franchise history.

Mind you, Beaupre has a lot of experience. A lot. Not only has he played the most games of any active goaltender, he's in the top 15 of all-time and could move up into the top 10 this season.

All-Time games played by goaltenders

1.	Terry Sawchuck	971
2.	Glenn Hall	906
3.	Tony Esposito	886
4.	Gump Worsley	862
5.	Jacques Plante	837
6.	Harry Lumley	804
7.	Rogatien Vachon	795
8.	Gilles Meloche	788
9.	Billy Smith	680
10.	Mike Liut	663
11.	Dan Bouchard	655
12.	Turk Broda	629
13.	DON BEAUPRE	622 *
14.	Ed Giacomin	610
15.	Bernie Parent	608

Craig Billington is on the goaltending list below, but he was shipped to Boston last season, and became a free agent during the summer.

Darrin Madelay should get into more games as a backup this season, and down on the farm splitting the chores were Mike Bales and J.F. Labbe. Labbe was never drafted but was a Quebec League first all-star in 1990-91 and led that league twice in playoff goals against average. He also played in the Colonial Hockey League. If he plays in the NHL it would make him a rare (maybe only) graduate from that league.

	GP	MIN	GA	AVG	W	L	T	SO
Bales	1	3	0	00	0	0	0	0
Beaupre	38	2161	121	3.36	8	25	3	1
Madeley	5	255	15	3.53	1	3	0	0
Billington	9	472	32	4.07	0	6	2	0

DEFENCE: If they held an expansion draft this year, there would be few veterans on the current Ottawa defence that wouldn't be made available if they were still with other teams.

That means they haven't shown a heck of a lot of improvement.

Certainly, Steve Duchesne was a good pickup from St. Louis, as Mike Keenan continued to dump the players he didn't like. Obtained for a second round draft pick he gives them a proven power play quarterback. He's had seasons of 82 points, 75, two in the 60's and two in the 50's. Something along the lines of what Norm MacIver gave them in their inaugural season when he earned 63 points.

First overall draft pick Bryan Berard could be a prize if he lives up to his press clippings. That's something few players on this team have been able to do, however.

The Senators said they weren't sure top draft pick Bryan Berard would be able to fit in. They had to be joking. If he can fit in his skates he can fit on this team.

Sexton obtained Jason Modry from New Jersey for a fourth round draft pick and immediately called him his second best defenceman

(this was before they obtained Duchesne). Apparently, he wasn't joking about this, but it gives you an idea of how far away they are from being competitive. Modry was a minor-leaguer for New Jersey and would have been lucky to crack the top ten in their depth chart. So, that means Ottawa's second best defenceman (presumably third with Duchesne there now) would be about tenth on New Jersey.

Ottawa's top defenceman last year was Stanislav Neckar, a second round draft pick in 1994. No, of course you've never heard of him. He was a second round pick in 1994.

There are lots of numbers to fit into the remaining slots. Kerry Huffman and Sean Hill are front-runners for jobs and maybe Chris Dahlquist, although he was offered a termination contract which means he's not a big part of their plans. The same is true for Jim Paek and Brad Shaw.

Among the younger players are Daniel Laperriere and Radim Bicanek.

Dennis Vial played 27 games for them last year and was only three penalty minutes away from the team lead, with a measly 65.

Most teams see a need for big, tough defencemen. Apparently, that's not so for the league's worst team. They're the softest, tamest group in the league, which for an expansion team just defies explanation.

But hey, they got Jason Modry, who has 18 PIM in 52 NHL games. What a find.

FORWARD: It's one thing to collect talent, it's another to leave it out there hanging. And it's one thing to collect lots of talent, it's another to make it fit within the team concept.

Finally, it's one thing to have all that talent, it's another when they don't do anything with it.

Yashin is the prize, of course, but what a pain. Even if he thinks he's being treated unfairly, everyone's tired of hearing about how he wants a trade and how he wants his contract renegotiated. Get over it.

The situation got even more bizarre after last season when Yashin and his agent Mark Gandler claimed the Senators didn't pay him his performance bonuses.

Apparently the Senators said they would reopen contract talks this year if he got 46 points. He got 44, but Gandler said Yashin was short-changed three assists in the official NHL stats. He's got to be kidding.

Sheesh, when Yashin was playing with the Las Vegas Thunder in the IHL during the lockout, he even went to management and complained about his ice-time.

When Murray and the other captains took Yashin to task about his puck-hogging and selfish play on the ice, Yashin could have taken it to heart and done something about it. Instead, an angry Gandler stepped in and laid it on the veterans.

After that incident, Bowness sat out Yashin and Daigle for a game. In their next contest, Yashin got a hat-trick and Daigle two assists.

Is Yashin worth all the trouble? Apparently so, because he's one of the few that can score on this team, but that makes him awfully valuable on the open market. Trade him to St. Louis and see how Yashin and Gandler deal with Mike Keenan.

Just like the Ottawa defence, the Ottawa forwards are among the softest in the league.

Daigle fits right into that group although he started to show more scoring potential last year, and they're not counting on his toughness anyway. He had 16 goals and was second on the team with 37 assists.

The next highest goal scorer was Sylvain Turgeon with 11. Turgeon has a unique capability of making himself completely invisible for long stretches at a time.

Maybe that's not so unique on this club.

Martin Straka was obtained from Pittsburgh last year. He had 30 goals two years ago but could only manage four last year on that offensive powerhouse.

Radek Bonk was supposed to supply some offence, but he was a total flop with just three goals. You have to figure he can't get any worse than that.

After Turgeon, the next highest scorer on the team played just 18 games. Steve Larouche was spending his fifth season in the minors lighting up the scoreboard when he got the call to the Ottawa. He had eight goals and 15 assists in those 18 games. He was still an unrestricted free agent at press time.

Free agent Dan Quinn was signed over the summer to help out at center. That could prove very useful because they only have about seven centers already.

Obviously a couple of them will have to move to the wings.

Just fill in the blanks with the rest of the team, figuring if they have low penalty minute totals they'll probably stick; and if they have size, character and toughness, they probably won't.

SPECIAL TEAMS: The power play received a boost over the summer when the Senators obtained Steve Duchesne and drafted Bryan Berard. Those are two guys who should spend a lot of time on the Ottawa points this year.

Duchesne, of course, is a proven performer, while Berard is not. That's good for Berard because he won't have too much offensive responsibility too early.

Throw in Yashin and Daigle and the power play could improve considerably.

Power Play	G	ATT	PCT
Overall	31	215	14.4% (21st NHL)
Home	19	118	16.1% (18th NHL)

Road	12	97	12.4% (22nd NHL)

6 SHORT HANDED GOALS ALLOWED (T-14th NHL)

Penalty Killing	G	TSH	PCT
Overall	39	199	80.4% (20th NHL)
Home	19	94	79.8% (23rd NHL)
Road	20	105	81.0% (15th NHL)

1 SHORT HANDED GOALS SCORED (T-24th NHL)

Penalties	GP	MIN	AVG
SENATORS	48	749	15.6 (4th NHL)

Top Scorers

Power play	G	A	PTS
YASHIN	11	10	21
DAIGLE	4	10	14
LAROUCHE	2	5	7
HILL	0	6	6
PICARD	1	4	5
TURGEON	2	2	4
BONK	1	3	4
STRAKA	0	4	4

Short handed	G	A	PTS
DAIGLE	1	0	1

COACHING AND MANAGEMENT: If the Ottawa Senators are making progress, they're going about it awfully slow. Slower, in fact, than any expansion team in NHL history. So far, GM Randy Sexton and coach Rick Bowness have survived all the firing rumors, but time is just about up.

I'm not impressed with the way Sexton is building the club, or most of the moves he's made. But, you have to figure all those top draft choices are going to pay off sometime, somehow.

It's tough to judge management and coaching on a team that's not supposed to win, but there comes a time when enough is enough.

Bowness is considered an extremely hard worker and you have to give him credit for benching Yashin and Daigle for a game. His problem is no matter how hard he works it's not going to do much good.

DRAFT

1995 DRAFT SELECTIONS

Round	Sel.	Player	Pos	Amateur Team
1	1	Bryan Berard	D	Detroit (OHL)
2	27	Marc Moro	D	Kingston (OHL)
3	53	Brad Larson	LW	Swift Current (WHL)
4	89	Kevin Bolibruck	D	Peterborough (OHL)
4	103	Kevin Boyd	LW	London (OHL)
6	131	David Hruska	RW	Czechoslovakia
7	181	Kaj Linna	D	Boston U. (NCAA)
8	184	Ray Schultz	D	Tri-City (WHL)
9	231	Erik Kasminski	RW	Cleveland (NAJL)

It's difficult to be drafted early in the first round and not be compared to someone. Berard is no different. Leetch, Bourque and Coffey are among those likened to Berard.

Just who were Daigle and Bonk being compared to?

After concentrating on U.S. high school players last year, the Senators turned their attention to the OHL and WHL which they've almost completely ignored in the past. Six of their nine selections came from those two leagues.

PROGNOSIS: This is a terrible team that has very little chance of escaping last place over-all. They have no character, no toughness, few scorers, and little reason for optimism.

Oh, there is a little cause for optimism. If the Senators can somehow convince the NHL to become a non-contact league, Ottawa just might have a shot at a playoff spot.

PREDICTION:

Northeast Divison: Last
Eastern Conference: Last
Overall: Last

STAT SECTION

Team Rankings 1994/95

		Conference Rank	League Rank
Record	9-34-5	14	26
Home	5-16-3	14	26
Away	4-18-2	13	25
Team Plus\Minus	-49	14	26
Goals For	117	14	26
Goals Against	174	14	25

MISCELLANEOUS STATS

One Goal Games	5-13
Times outshooting opponent	12
Times outshot	34
Even shots	2
Average Shots For	25.9
Average Shots Against	32.5
Overtime	1-1-5
Longest Winning streak	3
Longest Undefeated streak	3
Longest Losing streak	9
Longest winless streak	16
Versus Teams Over .500	3-17-4
Versus Teams Under .500	6-17-1

First Half Record	3-17-4
Second Half Record	6-17-1

All-Time Rankings - INDIVIDUAL (3)

Goals

Alexei Yashin	51
Bob Kudelski	47
Sylvain Turgeon	47

Assists

Norm MacIver	73
Alexei Yashin	72
Brad Shaw	53

Points

Alexei Yashin	123
Norm MacIver	97
Sylvain Turgeon	88

Best Individual Seasons

Goals

Alexei Yashin	1993-94	30
Sylvain Turgeon	1992-93	25
Alexei Yashin	1994-95	21
Bob Kudelski	1992-93	21

Assists

Alexei Yashin	1993-94	49
Norm MacIver	1992-93	46
Brad Shaw	1992-93	34

Points

Alexei Yashin	1993-94	79
Norm MacIver	1992-93	63
Alexandre Daigle	1993-94	51

PLAYERS	OVERALL				84 Game Projection		
	GP	G	A	PTS	G	A	PTS
A.YASHIN	47	21	23	44	38	41	79
A.DAIGLE	47	16	21	37	29	38	67
S.TURGEON	33	11	8	19	28	20	48
M.STRAKA	37	5	13	18	11	30	41
*S.LAROUCHE	18	8	7	15	37	33	70
S.HILL	45	1	14	15	2	26	28
R.GAUDREAU	36	5	9	14	12	21	33
M.PICARD	24	5	8	13	17	28	45
S.LEVINS	2	5	6	11	17	21	38
D.MCLLWAIN	43	5	6	11	10	12	22
*R.BONK	42	3	8	11	6	16	22
R.CUNNEYWORTH	48	5	5	10	9	9	18
P.ELYNUIK	41	3	7	10	6	14	20
T.MALLETTE	23	3	5	8	11	18	29
C.DAHLQUIST	46	1	7	8	2	13	15
*P.DEMITRA	16	4	3	7	21	16	37
P.BOURQUE	38	4	3	7	9	7	16
K.HUFFMAN	37	2	4	6	5	9	14
D.ARCHIBALD	14	2	2	4	12	12	24
*S.NECKAR	48	1	3	4	2	5	7
D.VIAL	27	0	4	4	0	12	12
E.DAVYDOV	3	1	2	3	28	56	84
*D.LAPERRIERE	17	1	1	2	5	5	10
J.PAEK	29	0	2	2	0	6	6
C.BOIVIN	3	0	1	1	0	28	28
L.PITLICK	15	0	1	1	0	6	6
B.SHAW	2	0	0	0	0	0	0
*D.GUERARD	2	0	0	0	0	0	0
*R.BICANEK	6	0	0	0	0	0	0

Philadelphia Flyers

The glory days are back. Or at least pretty close.

After a five year hiatus from the playoffs, the Flyers not only finished first in their division but made it to the conference finals.

Now, they're very near to being a legitimate contender for the Stanley Cup. They've been there before, and have two Cups to their credit, but it's been a while. Twenty years to be exact.

When the NHL had their big expansion in 1967-68, Philadelphia finished with the best record of the six new entries. They've been on top ever since. In fact, they're the only one with a winning record. Oakland, which is defunct, is not included in the list below.

All-Time Records
Original Expansion Teams in 1967-68

	W	L	T	Pts	Cups	Finals
Philadelphia	1,084	770	340	2,508	2	6
St. Louis	921	942	331	2,173	0	3
Pittsburgh	877	1,017	300	2,054	2	2
Los Angeles	861	1,012	321	2,043	0	1
Minnesota/Dallas	817	1,022	355	1,989	0	2

The Flyers showed some qualities last season which gave some indication they could be a dominant team. For example, they had the two longest winning streaks. That shows an ability to get on a roll and flatten any and all competition for an extended period. Just what you need to do in the playoffs.

Consecutive Wins - 1994-95

PHILADELPHIA	9
PHILADELPHIA	8
Pittsburgh	7
Quebec	7
Detroit	6

Another strong contender quality is the ability to turn it on when it really counts. A good area of judgement for that is how well teams play in the third period.

Best Records when tied after two periods 1994-95

	W	L	T
Detroit	5	1	1
PHILADELPHIA	13	4	0
Pittsburgh	6	3	0
Edmonton	6	3	0
Quebec	6	3	3
Florida	8	4	5
Boston	8	5	3
Buffalo	8	5	4
St. Louis	7	5	3

Let's see now, what else might indicate an ability to be a dominant team. Oh yeah, how about the best player in the game.

There's only been three dominant superstars in this era. Gretzky, of course, is one, Mario Lemieux is another, and now Eric Lindros.

Gretzky and Lemieux have their Stanley Cup victories and so will Lindros. Both Gretzky and Lemieux proved they couldn't do it on their own, but their presence means not as much is needed from the supporting cast, and that makes going all the way considerably easier.

Lindros had a point in almost half of the Flyers goals scored last year. Consider the following list:

Player	Team	Pts	Team Goals	Percentage
Lindros	Phi.	70	150	46.7%
Recchi	Mtl.	43	100	43.0% **
Zhamnov	Wpg.	65	157	41.4%
Jagr	Pit.	70	181	38.7%
Messier	NYR	53	139	38.1%
Renberg	Phi.	57	150	38.0%
Yashin	Ott.	44	117	37.6%
Mogilny	Buf.	47	130	36.2%
LeClair	Phi.	54	150	36.0%
Fleury	Cgy	58	163	35.6%

**Recchi's points and Montreal's goals are only from the time he joined the Canadiens.

Lindros was clearly most valuable to his team in terms of percentage of points scored which also carried his linemates into the top ten. The most interesting name on the list, however, is Mark Recchi, who had a point in 43% of the Montreal goals while he was with the club. Recchi, of course, was traded from the Flyers last year in the LeClair deal.

Recchi got off to a slow start in Philadelphia, but would have come on eventually, as he did with Montreal, and would have probably at least matched LeClair's output.

Gretzky, incidentally ranked 15th last year with a point in 33.8% of his team's goals. In his glory years he was usually around the 50% mark. Mario Lemieux got up as high as 57%.

TEAM PREVIEW

GOAL: For awhile during last year's playoffs, Ron Hextall thought it was 1987. That was the year he carried the Flyers to the finals and won the Conn Smythe Trophy as the playoff team, despite losing to the Edmonton Oilers in seven games.

Heading into the playoffs it was said the Flyers couldn't win with Hextall in net. He proved them wrong and proved them right. He was nothing short of spectacular for part of the post-season and nothing short of lousy for another part.

Even when Hextall is hot, however, there's always that nagging suspicion in the back of your head that he can't keep it up. The 31-year-old doesn't exactly inspire a lot of confidence, and when you're a team ready to go to the next level that just won't do.

At press time, Edmonton still had goalies Curtis Joseph and Bill Ranford. They weren't going to keep them both, so it could be that the Flyers would make a deal for one of them.

If the situation remains the same, other Philadelphia goalies in line for work are Domenic Roussel and Garth Snow, acquired from Colorado during the summer.

	GP	MIN	GA	AVG	W	L	T	SO
Roussel	19	1075	42	2.34	11	7	0	1
Hextall	31	1824	88	2.89	17	9	4	1

DEFENCE: Eric Desjardins might have gotten a little stale in Montreal, but he came alive in Philadelphia, earning a second team Hockey News all-star berth.

He established himself as the leader on a young, big, mobile defense.

Chris Therien (6-4, 230) and Karl Dykhuis (6-3, 195) were two of the biggest defencemen and two of the biggest surprises. Therien earned his way up after playing well in the minors with Hershey and Dykhuis was plucked from the Chicago Blackhawks farm system. Therien earned a spot on the NHL's all-rookie team.

Kevin Haller, Petr Svoboda and Dimitri Yushkevich are mobile types which, along with the size gives the Flyers a good mix. The only problem with Svoboda is he's one of the most injury-prone players in the league.

The Flyers added even more size during the summer when they signed free agent Kjell Samulesson away from Pittsburgh.

Throw in Jason Bowen, another big guy with some scrappiness, and you've got a pretty good top eight.

The only thing they might be able to use is a quarterback for the power play. The people they have can do the job, but Desjardins isn't really the quarterback type.

If it becomes apparent that they're lacking in that area, it won't remain a problem for long because Bobby Clarke will go out and get someone.

FORWARD: Okay, they've got the best first line in hockey and they're pretty strong down the middle.

Then what? Then there's a problem.

Who else is going to score?

People keep saying you can't win with just one line although that's exactly what the Flyers did last season. Maybe it helps when a member of the line is the best player in the league and all three finish in the top 11 in scoring. Perhaps that's how you win with one line.

The Legion of Doom, featuring Lindros between LeClair and Renberg, had 80 goals, while the rest of the team scored 70.

Maybe, it's that you can't win with one line on the road, or in the playoffs. Teams can match up against that one unit when the Flyers visit, and just have to worry about shutting them down.

On the road last year, the Flyers were 12-9-3, first in the Eastern Conference and fourth in the league. After getting LeClair they were 12-5-2. That doesn't appear to be much of a problem. As well, they scored 150 goals in total, and 73 of them were on the road, almost half.

We're arguing the merits of one scoring line, but ideally you want at least two. That would make the first one even more effective.

They have a center for that second line in Rod Brind'Amour and defensive centers Craig MacTavish and free agent signee Joel Otto for the third and fourth lines.

But some scoring wingers are needed. Brent Fedyk (still an unrestricted free agent at press time) and Kevin Dineen were the two second line wingers last season, but they're not ideal for those spots. Fedyk can score, as long as he's playing with Lindros, and Dineen used to be a big scorer, but he's going to be 32 years old this season and no longer has the touch.

Other winger regulars last season were low scoring Shjon Podein, Patrik Juhlin, Rob DiMaio, and Shawn Antoski who fill fills the enforcer role.

Fighting for playing time will be Anatoli Semenov, who has played for five teams in the last four years; disappointing Gilbert Dionne, who has had a couple 20 goals seasons, but had none with Philly last year; Yanick Dupre, Rob Brown and Clayton Norris

But, don't expect the above lineup to remain intact. Clarke knows they need more scoring from the second line and he'll find it somewhere.

SPECIAL TEAMS: The power play could be even better with an all-star quarterback on the point, but whose wouldn't. As it is they stick out Renberg, LeClair, Lindros, Brind'Amour and Desjardins. Lindros will play the point in order to keep him out for the full two minutes.

The danger with putting a forward on the point, however, is that it can cost the team short-handed goals. Only the Canucks and the Islanders allowed more than the nine Philadelphia gave up.

Before LeClair joined the team, the Flyers were 20th in the league. They improved all the way up to eighth.

The penalty killing percentage was in the lower echelon of the league but I can't think of a good reason why it would be. That should improve this year with Joel Otto and Kjell Samuelsson helping out in that area.

Power Play	G	ATT	PCT
Overall	40	204	19.6% (8th NHL)
Home	24	100	24.0% (3rd NHL)
Road	16	104	15.4% (15th NHL)

9 SHORT HANDED GOALS ALLOWED (24th NHL)

Penalty Killing	G	TSH	PCT
Overall	37	193	80.8% (18th NHL)
Home	13	84	84.5% (T-9th NHL)
Road	24	109	78.0% (22nd NHL)

2 SHORT HANDED GOALS SCORED (23rd NHL)

Penalties	GP	MIN	AVG
FLYERS	48	741	15.4 (2nd NHL)

Top Scorers
FLYERS SPECIAL TEAMS SCORING

Power play	G	A	PTS
LINDROS	7	17	24
LECLAIR	6	11	17
BRIND'AMOUR	4	12	16
RENBERG	8	4	12
DESJARDINS	1	11	12

Short handed	G	A	PTS
BRIND'AMOUR	1	1	2
YUSHKEVICH	1	0	1
SEMENOV	0	1	1
PODEIN	0	1	1
DINEEN	0	1	1

COACHING AND MANAGEMENT: Terry Murray finished third in the Jack Adams Award voting for coach of the year, behind Quebec's Marc Crawford and Scotty Bowman of Detroit.

If the voting took place after the playoffs, Murray would have at least been second and maybe first. He did a good job with this team, bringing them in one year from a non-playoff team to a Stanley Cup contender. Mind you, Clarke got him the horses, but Murray still had to make them run.

In the playoffs, they were the only team to give New Jersey a scare, and with a break or two they might have beat them. Instead of whining about the neutral zone trap, Murray tried to do something about it and certainly his plan was more effective than Detroit's.

Bob Clarke has a golden touch when it comes to trades. It worked with Florida and it worked with Philadelphia in his first season back. He performed almost a complete makeover on this team. Only eight players who were regulars at the end of the 1993-94 season were regulars last year.

Clarke doesn't have a great reputation when it comes to the draft table, but he has an ability to recognize undervalued talent in the NHL or minor pro league. And if he spent all his time scouting junior players he'd probably be one of the best at that as well.

Clarke will make more trades during the season, because the Flyers aren't quite there yet. Chances are they'll be excellent deals.

DRAFT

1995 DRAFT SELECTIONS

Round	Sel.	Player	Pos	Amateur Team
1	22	Brian Boucher	G	Tri-City (WHL)
2	48	Shane Kenny	D	Owen Sound (OHL)
4	100	Radovan Somik	RW	Slovakia
6	132	Dimitri Tertshny	D	Russia
6	135	Jamie Sokolsky	D	Belleville (OHL)
6	152	Martin Spanhel	LW	Czechoslovakia
7	178	Martin Streit	LW	Czechoslovakia
8	204	Rusian Shafikov	C	Russia
9	230	Jeff Lank	D	Prince Albert (WHL)

Brian Boucher was the third goaltender chosen in the first round and the second from Woonsocket, Rhode Island. Bryan Berard was the first, and the two are former teammates. At Mount Saint Charles High School, just two years ago, he sported a 0.57 goals against average.

PROGNOSIS: A New Jersey - Philadelphia Eastern Conference final repeat is very easy to envision. A Philadelphia win this time is more a possibility. They've already improved from last year and will improve even more. Improvement for New Jersey is less likely.

A front-line goaltender would help gain them a Stanley Cup final and a scorer or two for the second line would just about ensure it. Otherwise they have everything they need and then some. What they don't have, they'll get.

Look for the Flyers in the Stanley Cup finals.

PREDICTION:
Atlantic Division: 1st
Eastern Conference: 1st
Overall: 4th

STAT SECTION

Team Rankings 1994/95

		Conference Rank	League Rank
Record	28-16-4	3	5
Home	16-7-1	5	7
Away	12-9-3	1	4
Team Plus\Minus	+15	4	8
Goals For	150	3	9
Goals Against	132	6	8

MISCELLANEOUS STATS

One Goal Games	14-5
Times outshooting opponent	27
Times outshot	21
Even shots	0
Average Shots For	27.3
Average Shots Against	26.8
Overtime	3-1-4
Longest Winning streak	9
Longest Undefeated streak	9
Longest Losing streak	3
Longest winless streak	3
Versus Teams Over .500	11-8-2
Versus Teams Under .500	15-8-2
First Half Record	12-9-3
Second Half Record	16-5-1

PLAYERS	OVERALL				84 Game Projection		
	GP	G	A	PTS	G	A	PTS
E.LINDROS	46	29	41	70	53	75	128
M.RENBERG	47	26	31	57	46	55	101
J.LECLAIR	46	26	28	54	47	51	98
R.BRIND'AMOUR	48	12	27	39	21	47	68
E.DESJARDINS	43	5	24	29	10	47	57
D.YUSHKEVICH	40	5	9	14	11	19	30
K.DINEEN	40	8	5	13	17	11	28
C.THERIEN	48	3	10	13	5	17	22
B.FEDYK	30	8	4	12	22	11	33
C.MACTAVISH	45	3	9	12	6	17	23
A.SEMENOV	41	4	6	10	8	12	20
S.PODEIN	44	3	7	10	6	13	19
K.HALLER	36	2	7	9	5	16	21
G.DIONNE	26	0	9	9	0	29	29
K.DYKHUIS	33	2	6	8	5	15	20
P.SVOBODA	37	0	8	8	0	18	18
P.JUHLIN	42	4	3	7	8	6	14
R.DIMAIO	36	3	1	4	7	2	9
D.BROWN	28	1	2	3	3	6	9
J.MONTGOMERY	13	1	1	2	6	6	12
R.ZETTLER	32	0	1	1	0	3	3
S.ANDERSON	1	0	0	0	0	0	0
S.MALGUNAS	4	0	0	0	0	0	0
J.BOWEN	4	0	0	0	0	0	0
Y.DUPRE	22	0	0	0	0	0	0
S.ANTOSKI	32	0	0	0	0	0	0

PLAYOFFS

Results: defeated Buffalo 4-1
defeated NY Rangers 4-0
lost to New Jersey 4-2
Record: 10-5
Home: 5-3
Away: 5-2
Goals For: 50 (3.3/gm)
Goals Against 43 (2.9/gm)
Overtime: 4-0
Power play: 12.9% (12th)
Penalty Killing: 77.3% (10th)

Playoff Scoring

	GP	G	A	PTS
ROD BRIND'AMOUR	15	6	9	15
ERIC LINDROS	12	4	11	15
MIKAEL RENBERG	15	6	7	13
JOHN LECLAIR	15	5	7	12
KEVIN DINEEN	15	6	4	10
ERIC DESJARDINS	15	4	4	8
KEVIN HALLER	15	4	4	8
KARL DYKHUIS	15	4	4	8
ROB DIMAIO	15	2	4	6
ANATOLI SEMENOV	15	2	4	6
DIMITRI YUSHKEVICH	15	1	5	6
CRAIG MACTAVISH	15	1	4	5
BRENT FEDYK	9	2	2	4
SHJON PODEIN	15	1	3	4
PETR SVOBODA	14	0	4	4
JIM MONTGOMERY	7	1	0	1
PATRIK JUHLIN	13	1	0	1
SHAWN ANTOSKI	13	0	1	1
RON HEXTALL	15	0	1	1
ROB ZETTLER	1	0	0	0
DOMINIC ROUSSEL	1	0	0	0
DAVE BROWN	3	0	0	0
GILBERT DIONNE	3	0	0	0
CHRIS THERIEN	15	0	0	0

All-Time Rankings - INDIVIDUAL

Goals

Bill Barber	420
Brian Propp	369
Tim Kerr	363

Assists

Bobby Clarke	852
Brian Propp	480
Bill Barber	463

Points

Bobby Clarke	1,210
Bill Barber	883
Brian Propp	849

Best Seasons (3)

Goals

Reg Leach	1975-76	61
Tim Kerr	1986-87	58
Tim Kerr	1985-86	58

Assists

Bobby Clarke	1975-76	89
Bobby Clarke	1974-75	89
Mark Recchi	1992-93	70

Points

Mark Recchi	1992-93	123
Bobby Clarke	1975-76	119
Bobby Clarke	1974-75	116

Pittsburgh Penguins

Last player to leave Pittsburgh turn out the lights.

The Penguins not only cleaned house, they tore it right down.

Gone: Larry Murphy (34), traded to Toronto for underacheiving and inconsistent defenceman Dimitri Mironov (29).

Gone: Kevin Stevens (30), traded to Boston with Shawn McEachern for good young prospect Bryan Smolinski (23) and disappointment Glen Murray (22).

Gone: Shawn McEachern (26), see trade above.

Gone: Joe Mullen (38), not offered contract.

Gone: John Cullen (31), not offered contract.

Gone: Troy Murray (33), signed as free agent by Colorado.

Gone: Kjell Samuelsson (36), signed as free agent by Philadelphia

Gone: Mike Hudson (28) not offered contract.

Gone: Jim McKenzie (26) signed as free agent by NY Islanders.

Gone: Peter Taglianetti (32) and goalie Wendel Young (32).

Most of those gone are oldsters and the Penguins can't afford old any more - in terms of salary and in terms of competitiveness. An outstanding array of talent was put together, at a high cost, and when they failed to do any damage in the playoffs the last two years the writing was on the wall.

In today's NHL, a player has to give value for the money he's paid, and there was no guarantee that would happen anymore.

There's still some decent talent left, with Mario Lemieux returning part-time; Jaromir Jagr, the scoring champ; Thomas Sandstrom and Luc Robiaille, both of whom had great seasons; and goaltenders Ken Wregget and Tom Barrasso.

It's been a great run for the Penguins. Over the last five years, they've won two Stanley Cups and finished first in their division three times.

Last year, they started off the season unbeaten in 13 regular season games, only two away from the NHL record, set by Edmonton in 1984-84

Plus, over that span, they have more regular season wins than anybody else.

NHL Records - Last five years

		W	L	T	Pts	%
1.	PITTSBURGH	209	129	38	456	.606
2.	Detroit	203	132	41	447	.594
3.	Boston	200	129	47	447	.594
4.	Chicago	195	132	49	439	.584
5.	NY Rangers	194	142	40	428	.569
6.	St. Louis	188	139	49	425	.565
7.	Montreal	187	140	49	423	.563
8.	Calgary	186	139	51	423	.563
9.	Washington	186	150	40	412	.548
10.	New Jersey	179	144	53	411	.547

11. Vancouver	175	156	45	395	.525
12. Buffalo	165	154	57	387	.515
13. Los Angeles	163	158	55	381	.507
14. Philadelphia	164	166	46	374	.497
15. Toronto	161	166	49	371	.493
16. Florida	53	56	23	129	.489
17. Dallas	154	171	51	359	.477
18. NY Islanders	150	181	45	345	.459
19. Colorado	147	180	49	343	.456
20. Winnipeg	139	188	49	327	.435
21. Edmonton	141	193	42	324	.432
22. Anaheim	49	73	10	108	.409
23. Hartford	129	203	44	302	.402
24. Tampa Bay	70	125	21	161	.373
25. San Jose	80	189	27	187	.316
26. Ottawa	33	165	18	84	.194

Now, it's time to rebuild. Rebuilding is easier when you still have some great talent on board. Not much depth anymore, so finding the talent to rebuild won't be easy.

At any rate, it's a whole new Pittsburgh Penguins at economical price.

TEAM PREVIEW

GOAL: The Penguins found out last season how fortunate they were to have two number one goalies. Even though Barrasso was considered the number one man, Wregget also had the credentials, and proved it when Barrasso had to miss almost the entire season with a wrist injury.

Wregget was outstanding for most of the year before slowing down some at the end. Or it could have just been that the team slowed down.

With the Penguins being so offensive-minded, Wregget was bombarded with shots night after night. In fact, the Penguins only outshot their opponents 16 times in the 48 games, extremely unusual for a team with such a good record. When an offensive team

gets outshot night after night, you know they're giving up lots of good scoring opportunities. Even during the 13 game season-opening unbeaten streak, Pittsburgh only had the most shots in three games.

Wregget was in net for those 13 games and stayed there for all but one of the team's first 31 games. At that point his win-loss record was 21-5-2.

Barrasso came back late in the season and got into some playoff action, but was ineffective. Wregget handled most of the playoff duties and played very well for the most part.

You'd expect to see the two goalies back again this year, but you never know with what is going on in Pittsburgh. Maybe they can't afford two number one goalies. Mind you, last year they couldn't afford not to have them.

	GP	MIN	GA	AVG	W	L	T	SO
De Rouville	1	60	3	3.00	1	0	0	0
Wregget	38	2208	118	3.21	25	9	2	0
Young	10	497	27	3.26	3	6	0	0
Barrasso	2	125	8	3.84	0	1	1	0

DEFENCE: You can still find some people left over from last year's defence if you look hard enough. You won't find second team all-star Larry Murphy and you won't find Kjell Samuelsson, and a bunch of others.

Ulf Samuelsson was still with the club at press time but it's unlikely he will be by the time you read this. He was a restricted free agent, giving Pittsburgh the right to match, something they probably won't want to do, considering their salary reduction campaign.

Chris Joseph is still there along with Norm MacIver, Francois Leroux, Chris Tamer, Drake Berhowsky and newcomer Dimitri Mironov.

Mironov came over from Toronto in the deal for Murphy, which is like trading a thoroughbred for one of those broom handles with a horse head on top.

Sure, Murphy was old and expensive, but Mironov isn't that young either and he doesn't understand the game of hockey. Mironov has some skills and will show them off, sometimes for two games in a row. He takes the rest of the games off, or looks like it. But, he might be a fun guy to have around for the fans. If the game is boring they can play "Where's Dimitri." Some nights the only time you'll see him is when opposing forwards or defencemen go around him and shoot the puck in the net. Pat Burns in Toronto didn't even want to play him anymore, so getting a second team all-star for nothing would certainly make him happy.

A well-known funny media type in Toronto brought his son to a game one night a couple seasons back. For some reason, the son liked Mironov and was excited about the chance to see him.

In the press room, long before the game, he called out to his father, "Hey Dad, I'm going to go look for Mironov, okay?"

"Sure son," replied the father. "But, don't bother looking in the corners."

The Penguins are left without a quarterback for the powerplay, and if they think it's going to be Mironov then they also think Terry Bradshaw is going to quarterback the Steelers to the Super Bowl this year.

Norm MacIver is an okay offensive defenceman, he had a good year in Ottawa a couple seasons back, but he has injury problems.

How important is it, anyway, with Lemieux up front? All you have to do is stand there, wait until the puck goes on your stick and then pass it to Lemieux. Hey, maybe Mironov can do the job.

The Penguins also obtained Drake Berehowsky from Toronto last year for Grant Jennings. Whoever Pittsburgh has scouting the Toronto team ought to be fired. Berehowsky isn't even as good as Mironov.

Few players in Toronto have been given as much of an opportunity to earn full-time employment, meaning few have blown it as many times. He didn't play much with Pittsburgh after they acquired him. Just four games, which may be four more than he'll play this year.

Chris Joseph was obtained on waivers from Tampa Bay before the start of the season, but he did a decent job and could be their best defenceman this year.

Francois Leroux was obtained in the same waiver draft from Ottawa of all teams. The 6-6, 225 pounder was apparently a fan favorite, so they'll keep him around. You might wonder how good can he be if the worst team in the league lets him go. Don't use that to judge, however, because they (Ottawa) don't know how to judge talent anyway.

Chris Tamer got into 36 games last season with the Pens, which makes him a veteran this year.

We don't really know who else might get to play. Ian Moran got called up from Cleveland and played eight games in the playoffs. Paul Dyck also got called up for the playoffs but didn't play in any games. Corey Foster, who has spent most of his career in the minors after being a first round draft pick in 1988, was signed as free agent. Greg Andrusak is still around as well.

Two Russians, Alexei Krivchenkov and Sergei Voronov will also be in training camp and could earn a spot.

FORWARD: The Pittsburgh forwards had better score a lot of goals this year, because there's going to be a lot scored against them.

Lemieux is expected to play the home games and perhaps short road trips that won't aggravate his back. As he says, he's not coming back to be mediocre. He'll be a big-time scorer in the games he plays.

The Penguins can put together a great first line with Robitaille on the left side of Lemieux and Jagr on the right.

They can put together two-thirds of a good second line as well, with Ron Francis at center and Tomas Sandstrom on the right side. Francis is coming of another outstanding year as winner of the Frank Selke Award as the best defensive forward, and the Lady Byng Trophy.

And they have at least one-third of a good third line with newcomer Bryan Smolinski at center.

After that they'll be holding open auditions. Those should include underachievers Markus Naslund and Glen Murray. Naslund was a first round choice of the Penguins in 1991 and expected to be a star. Even something close to acceptable would have been nice, but he only has six goals in the last two seasons, and last year divided his time between Cleveland, the press box and Pittsburgh.

Murray has been considerably better but still a disappointment. After scoring 18 goals in his first full season with Boston, he slumped to just five goals last year.

Murray seems a more likely pick to get back on track, but you never know, Naslund could still come around.

Jagr had an outstanding season for the Penguins, winning the scoring title and being classy enough to admit he wouldn't have won if Lindros had been healthy for the last couple games of the season.

Jagr actually tied in points with Lindros but won on the strength of more goals. He is the first European to win a scoring championship and the first player not named Gretzky or Lemieux to lead the league in scoring for 14 years.

The following chart shows all the Europeans who have made the top 10 in scoring and which place they finished. Jagr becomes only the fourth European to make a repeat showing in the top 10 and the first in six years.

Peter Stastny and Jari Kurri have easily been the best and most consistent Europeans, with five top 10 finishes. Kent Nilsson had two, and now Jagr has two.

Europeans in the Top 10 in Scoring

Season	No. in top 10	Players and Top 10 Standing
1994-95	3	Jagr(1), Zhamnov(3), Renberg(8)
1993-94	3	Fedorov(2), Bure(5), Jagr(10)
1992-93	2	Selanne(5), Mogilny(7)
1991-92	0	
1990-91	0	
1989-90	0	
1988-89	1	Kurri(8)
1987-88	2	Stastny,P(6), Loob(9)
1986-87	1	Kurri(2)
1985-86	3	Kurri(4), Stastny(6), Naslund(8)
1984-85	1	Kurri(2)
1983-84	2	Stastny(4), Kurri(7)
1982-83	2	Stastny(2), Nilsson(10)
1981-82	1	Stastny
1980-81	2	Nilsson(3), Stastny(6)

While we're on the subject of non-Canadians, and since there's not much more to say about the Pittsburgh forward situation, we can note that last year Joe Mullen became the first American to earn 1,000 points.

Top American Scorers of All-Time

Joe Mullen	1,026
Phil Housley	882
Neal Broten	880
Pat LaFontaine	852

Dave Christian	773
Mark Howe	742

The situation isn't really all that bleak. They will have plenty of scoring, and filling in the blanks with the kind of nucleus they have won't be all that difficult. The blanks will have to include some defensive forwards and some toughness.

Others with an opportunity to play include Richard Park, Jeff Christian, Joe Dziedzic, Ed Patterson, Dave Roche (114 points for Windsor in the OHL), Oleg Belov and Chris Wells (108 points for Seattle in the WHL).

SPECIAL TEAMS: The power play is where this team should excel. Mario Lemieux makes everybody else better and automatically makes the power play one of the best in the league.

They don't have Larry Murphy back there to quarterback anymore, but they might be able to get away with it.

Unfortunately, the situation while short-handed doesn't look to be in line for much improvement, but you can never tell.

Power Play	G	ATT	PCT
Overall	42	221	19.0% (10th NHL)
Home	25	110	22.7% (T-4th NHL)
Road	17	111	15.3% (T-16th NHL)

4 SHORT HANDED GOALS ALLOWED (T-9th NHL)

Penalty Killing	G	TSH	PCT
Overall	46	229	79.9% (23rd NHL)
Home	15	98	84.7% (7th NHL)
Road	31	131	76.3% (25th NHL)

8 SHORT HANDED GOALS SCORED (T-4th NHL)

Penalties	GP	MIN	AVG
PENGUINS	48	1036	21.6 (17th NHL)

Top Scorers
PENGUINS SPECIAL TEAMS SCORING

Power play	G	A	PTS
JAGR	8	14	22
FRANCIS	3	18	21
MURPHY	4	7	11
STEVENS	6	4	10
MULLEN	5	4	9
SANDSTROM	4	5	9
CULLEN	2	7	9
ROBITAILLE	5	3	8
MACIVER	2	5	7
JOSEPH	3	2	5

Short handed	G	A	PTS
JAGR	3	0	3
MULLEN	2	1	3
SANDSTROM	1	2	3
MURPHY	0	3	3
MCEACHERN	2	0	2

COACHING AND MANAGEMENT: Give Chairman of the Board, Howard Baldwin credit. When the team decided to rid themselves of salaries and half their team, he didn't leave GM Craig Patrick hanging on his own. Baldwin came out in the media and explained the situation, and told how they needed to exercise some fiscal restraint.

This season, Patrick and coach Ed Johnston will have to work harder to earn their money.

Patrick has put together two Stanley Cup winning teams, but Johnston hasn't been very successful. He's coached in six playoffs with three different teams and only has one playoff series win.

DRAFT

1995 DRAFT SELECTIONS

Round	Sel.	Player	Pos	Amateur Team
1	24	Alexei Morozov	LW	Russia
3	76	J. Aubin	G	Sherbrooke (QMJHL)
4	102	Oleg Belov	C	Russia
5	128	Jan Hrdina	C	Seattle (WHL)
6	154	Alexei Kolkunov	C	Russia
7	180	Derrick Pyke	RW	Halifax (QMJHL)
8	206	Sergei Voronov	D	Russia
9	232	Frank Ivankovic	G	Oshawa (OHL)

This is the fifth time in six years that GM Craig Patrick has selected a European in the first round. Morozov is considered a risk because of some inconsistencies, but he also has a chance to be an offensive star.

PROGNOSIS: If nothing else, it should be an interesting season in Pittsburgh. Who knows what's going to happen? They haven't been completely decimated, after all, and they do have Lemieux coming back.

They could have a good season or a rotten one. Pretty unpredictable, in other words.

Fortunately for them, the conference is going to be weaker this year, especially in their division.

PREDICTION:
Northeast Division: 2nd (or 5th)
Eastern Conference: 4th (or 9th)
Overall: 8th (or 16th)

STAT SECTION

Team Rankings 1994/95

		Conference Rank	League Rank
Record	29-16-3	2	3
Home	18-5-1	2	2
Away	11-11-2	4	7
Team Plus\Minus	+27	2	4
Goals For	181	2	2
Goals Against	158	12	19

MISCELLANEOUS STATS

One Goal Games	11-6
Times outshooting opponent	16
Times outshot	30
Even shots	2
Average Shots For	29.1
Average Shots Against	32.8
Overtime	1-1-3
Longest Winning streak	7
Longest Undefeated streak	13
Longest Losing streak	3
Longest winless streak	3
Versus Teams Over .500	11-8-3
Versus Teams Under .500	18-8-0
First Half Record	16-6-2
Second Half Record	13-10-1

PLAYERS	1995-95 OVERALL				PROJECTED OVER 84 GAMES		
	GP	G	A	PTS	G	A	PTS
J.JAGR	48	32	38	70	56	66	122
R.FRANCIS	44	11	48	59	21	92	113
T.SANDSTROM	47	21	23	44	38	41	79
L.ROBITAILLE	46	23	19	42	42	35	77
L.MURPHY	48	13	25	38	23	44	77
J.MULLEN	45	16	21	37	30	39	79
J.CULLEN	46	13	24	37	24	44	68
K.STEVENS	27	15	12	27	47	37	84
S.MCEACHERN	44	13	13	26	25	25	50
N.MACIVER	41	4	16	20	8	33	41
T.MURRAY	46	4	12	16	7	22	29
U.SAMUELSSON	44	1	15	16	2	29	31
C.JOSEPH	33	5	10	15	13	25	38
L.BARRIE	48	3	11	14	5	19	24
M.HUDSON	40	2	9	11	4	19	23
K.SAMUELSSON	41	1	6	7	2	12	14
G.HAWGOOD	21	1	4	5	4	16	20
M.NASLUND	14	2	2	4	12	12	24
G.ANDRUSAK	7	0	4	4	0	48	48
J.MCKENZIE	39	2	1	3	4	2	6
C.TAMER	36	2	0	2	5	0	5
D.BEREHOWSKY	29	0	2	2	0	6	6
F.LEROUX	40	0	2	2	0	4	4
R.FITZGERALD	4	1	0	1	21	0	21
R.PARK	1	0	1	1	0	84	84
P.TAGLIANETTI	13	0	1	1	0	6	6
J.CHRISTIAN	1	0	0	0	0	0	0

PLAYOFFS
Results: defeated Washington 4-3
lost to New Jersey 4-1
Record: 5-7
Home: 4-3
Away: 1-4
Goals For: 37 (3.1/gm)
Goals Against: 43 (3.6/gm)
Overtime: 1-1
Power play: 19.0 (7th)
Penalty Killing: 83.6% (7th)

Playoff Scoring

PLAYER	GP	G	A	PTS
RON FRANCIS	12	6	13	19
JAROMIR JAGR	12	10	5	15
LARRY MURPHY	12	2	13	15
LUC ROBITAILLE	12	7	4	11
KEVIN STEVENS	12	4	7	11
TOMAS SANDSTROM	12	3	3	6
NORM MACIVER	12	1	4	5
TROY MURRAY	12	2	1	3
JOE MULLEN	12	0	3	3
CHRIS JOSEPH	10	1	1	2
ULF SAMUELSSON	7	0	2	2
JOHN CULLEN	9	0	2	2
SHAWN MCEACHERN	11	0	2	2
FRANCOIS LEROUX	12	0	2	2
LEN BARRIE	4	1	0	1
KJELL SAMUELSSON	11	0	1	1
DRAKE BEREHOWSKY	1	0	0	0
TOM BARRASSO	2	0	0	0
RICHARD PARK	3	0	0	0
PETER TAGLIANETTI	4	0	0	0
CHRIS TAMER	4	0	0	0
JIM MCKENZIE	5	0	0	0
RUSTY FITZGERALD	5	0	0	0
IAN MORAN	8	0	0	0
MIKE HUDSON	11	0	0	0
KEN WREGGET	11	0	0	0

All-Time Rankings - INDIVIDUAL

Goals
Mario Lemieux	494
Jean Pronovost	316
Rick Kehoe	312

Assists
Mario Lemieux	703
Syl Apps	349
Paul Coffey	332

Points
Mario Lemieux	1,211
Rick Kehoe	636
Jean Pronovost	603

Best Individual Seasons

Goals
Mario Lemieux	1988-89	85
Mario Lemieux	1987-88	70
Mario Lemieux	1992-93	69

Assists
Mario Lemieux	1988-89	114
Mario Lemieux	1987-88	98
Mario Lemieux	1985-86	93

Points
Mario Lemieux	1988-89	199
Mario Lemieux	1987-88	168
Mario Lemieux	1992-93	160

Tampa Bay Lightning

The Tampa Bay Lightning are probably the quietest team in the league. You never hear about them - no major controversies, no major trades. They're not too good, they're not too bad. They don't have a major star. No major basket case (maybe Klima, but we never even hear about him anymore). Not even any coach firings to get things stirred up.

All this on a team run by Phil Esposito is hard to imagine.

Dubbed Trader Phil for his heavy trading action early in his career, he seems to have settled back in a big rocking chair, content to make minor adjustments until the young talent starts to pay dividends.

Maybe he'll be back to his old self once the team gets in position to be a contender. The patient attitude is just what an expansion team needs. And Esposito does just enough to keep them competitive, unlike Ottawa. It's slow and it's painful, but like the tortoise, they'll get there.

In the meantime, despite the shortened season the Lightning set a number of team records. Not all that hard to do in just their third season, but what the heck.

One of the more impressive ones had nothing to do with scoring goals. Enrico Ciccone, in only 41 games, set a new team record with 225 penalty minutes. Those penalty minutes over 84 games would have given him 461 minutes, close to the all-time

record of 472 set by Dave Schultz in his days with the Broad Street Bullies in Philadelphia.

Most PIM - 1994-95

ENRICO CICCONE	T.B.	225
Shane Churla	Dal.	186
Bryan Marchment	Edm.	184
Craig Berube	Wsh.	173
Rob Ray	Buf.	173
Mike Peluso	N.J.	167
Ronnie Stern	Cgy.	163
Tie Domi	Tor.	159
Jim Cummins	Chi.	158
Lyle Odelein	Mtl.	152
Keith Tkachuk	Wpg.	152

Rob Zamuner set a team mark for most shorthanded goals in a season with three. It may not sound like much, but it placed him up among the league leaders, and matched the most any individual had scored in total for Tampa in their first two full seasons.

Chris Gratton set a team mark for most consecutive games played with 116, and was set to challenge Cal Ripken before injuring his shoulder missing two games. Only Roman Hamrlik and Marc Bureau played in all of Tampa's games last season. Gratton was the only one to play all 84 the previous year.

Hamrlik also set a team record in the short-season with 12 goals, the most by a defenceman. That's actually a little more exciting than it sounds because it represents much more. The first draft choice overall in 1993 was finally starting to justify his high selection.

Those 12 goals placed Hamrlik up with some elite company in the NHL last year. In his previous two seasons he had only scored nine in total.

Most goals by a defenceman - 1994-95

Paul Coffey	Det.	14
Larry Murphy	Pit.	13
ROMAN HAMRLIK	T.B.	12
Ray Bourque	Bos.	12
Steve Duchesne	St.L.	12
Gary Suter	Chi.	10
Kevin Hatcher	Dal.	10
Nicklas Lidstrom	Det.	10
Sergei Zubov	NYR	10

TEAM PREVIEW

GOAL: Darren Puppa was the team MVP last season for the second straight time. He's come a long way since being an unwanted commodity in the expansion draft.

His goals against average of 2.68 was the lowest in his career, but even so it placed him in the middle of the pack among NHL goalies. In other words, his average was average, but on a poor team that makes it good. Got it?

It was a tough year to judge goals against averages. They don't mean the same as they did a couple years ago with overall scoring down.

Last year, the average number of goals scored in a game throughout the league was 5.97. You have to go all the way back to 1969-70 to get that low.

We can compare what a goals against average today would mean in previous years. We just assume that if it's a higher scoring league, all goaltenders would have more goals

scored against them. We keep the goalies in the same order as they were last year, using 6.0 as the base, and then increase everyone's GAA at the same rate as overall scoring.

Sounds a little complicated but in the chart below, using Puppa's GAA, we can see what his GAA of 2.68 would mean in different seasons.

Puppa 94-95 League Goals Average

	GAA	Total	Revised GAA
1994-95	2.68	6.0	-
1993-94	2.68	6.5	2.90
1992-93	2.68	7.2	3.22
1991-92	2.68	6.9	3.02
1990-91	2.68	6.9	3.02
1989-90	2.68	7.3	3.26
1988-89	2.68	7.5	3.35
1983-84	2.68	7.9	3.53
1981-82	2.68	8.3	3.70

J.C. Bergeron handled the backup chores behind Puppa last season, and the prospect is Tyler Moss. He was named goaltender of the year in the OHL with Kingston last year.

	GP	MIN	GA	AVG	W	L	T	SO
Puppa	36	2013	90	2.68	14	19	2	1
C. Bergeron	17	883	49	3.33	3	9	1	1

DEFENCE: The defence isn't great, by any means, but it's okay, which is pretty good.

The key was the emergence of Hamrlik into an offensive force and one who is starting to live up to his star billing.

With the signing of Bill Houlder, formerly of St. Louis, now there is somebody to help him out with the offensive load.

Last year, after Hamrlik's 23 points, the next highest scoring defenceman had six.

Corey Cross (6-5), Adrien Plavsic (6-1), Marc Bergevin (6-1), Enrico Ciccone (6-4),

Eric Charron (6-3) and Hamrlik (6-2) give them one of the biggest groups of rearguards in the league.

That's a nice thing to have on an expansion team that isn't ready yet to intimidate with offensive talent.

Cross and Charron were both rookies last season and, while making rookie mistakes, also showed they can play in the NHL.

Cross is one of those rare breed who has made the NHL after playing in the Canadian University system. Mike Ridley of Vancouver and Anaheim's Steve Rucchin are a couple others.

It's a young defence that also includes Adrien Plavsic, who was squeezed out of Vancouver. Marc Bergevin, 30, is one of the few veterans in the picture. Drew Bannister, a second round choice in 1992, played his first pro season, all of it in Atlanta, and could get an opportunity to play if there are a lot of injuries.

FORWARD: A good sign that an expansion team is improving is when there starts to be more competition for the first line. And the second and third and fourth.

Near the end of last season, Paul Ysebeart, Brian Bradley and John Tucker was the team's top line. Maybe now, newcomer Brian Bellows takes the left wing spot instead of Ysebeart. Maybe some of the young centers will start to challenge Bradley for the center position. Maybe Selivanov will take a run at the first line right wing position.

All healthy scenarios for an emerging team.

At center, Tampa Bay lines up with Bradley, Gratton, Semak and probably Langkow. Selivanov is also a center but there's more room for him on the right side.

Bradley has done everything asked of him in Tampa Bay. He's led the team in scoring all three years. He's a guy who might have been

drummed right out of the league had he not gone to Tampa Bay. In the 1990-91 season, he was traded from Vancouver to Toronto and played 26 games without getting a single goal. The next year, he didn't do much better and was left open in the expansion draft.

This could be Gratton's breakout season. Young players often take three or four years before they emerge as top scorers. This will be Gratton's third. A couple mediocre point scoring years and then BOOM. That's how it happens.

Consider how the scoring of some of the other top power forward types evolved in their first couple years.

	Year 1		Year 2		Year 3		Year 4	
	Gms	Pts	Gms	Pts	Gms	Pts	Gms	Pts
B. Shanahan	65	26	68	50	73	72		
K. Tkachuk	17	8	83	51	84	81		
G. Roberts	32	15	74	28	71	38	78	72
C. Neely	56	31	72	39	73	34	75	72

Put Jason Wiemer in the same boat as Gratton, but not necessarily Daymond Langkow. He could just bust loose right from the start. He was such a prolific scorer in junior, and he's so feisty that needing to gain confidence may not be a factor with him.

Alexander Semak will probably be the other center. He came over from New Jersey with Ben Hankinson for Shawn Chambers and Danton Cole, a couple guys who picked up Stanley Cup rings. Semak went from a 37 goal, 79 point performance for the Devils in 1992-93 to falling right off the face of the earth, and right out of the Devils lineup.

Ysebeart, who patrols the left side, performed a similar disappearing act as Semak. He had 35 and 34 goal seasons in Detroit before dropping to 14 the next year in Winnipeg and Chicago, and finally dropping out of the picture. He appeared revitalized in Tampa Bay.

Bellows, obtained from Montreal for Marc Bureau, is hoping to get his career back on track as well. No longer part of the picture, or the scoring summaries, in Montreal, he'll be given an opportunity for plenty more responsibility. He's had nine 30 plus goal seasons, with his last one coming just two years ago.

Second year high draft pick Wiemer only scored one goal last season. During the lockout he went back and played with Portland in the WHL, but broke his ankle there. He was ready to go by the time the NHL season opened, but didn't manage a point until his 12th game and didn't get his first NHL goal until his 31st game.

Look for Rob Zamuner on the left side as well. He's coming off a much-improved season. Gratton may play there also. He had a four point game when he was moved from center to left, but not long after he was moved back to center.

On right wing is John Tucker, Alexander Selivanov, Petr Klima, Mikael Andersson, Ben Hankinson, and Brantt Myhres, who is the designated enforcer.

Tucker, like so many Lightning players, was brought back from the dead after a failing NHL career and a season in Europe. Klima, is often considered a member of the living dead in terms of his hockey production. He's had some good NHL seasons, but more often than not he doesn't live up to his promise. He finished off the season with zero goals in his last 17 games. Klima's real value is as trade bait but Esposito has to wait until he gets some attention after one of his hot spells. Then he has to move fast to get something of value for him before it all falls apart.

SPECIAL TEAMS: The penalty killing was decent, the power play was not. But Houlder helping out Hamrlik on the points should improve that situation. Brian Bellows, who

has been a power play sniper in the past, could help the unit improve as well.

Power Play	G	ATT	PCT
Overall	25	177	14.1% (22nd NHL)
Home	11	94	11.7% (26th NHL)
Road	14	83	16.9% (T-10th NHL)

5 SHORT HANDED GOALS ALLOWED (T-11th NHL)

Penalty Killing	G	TSH	PCT
Overall	32	205	84.4% (T-7th NHL)
Home	14	109	87.2% (3rd NHL)
Road	18	96	81.3% (14th NHL)

6 SHORT HANDED GOALS SCORED (T-11th NHL)

Penalties	GP	MIN	AVG
LIGHTNING	48	1040	21.7 (18th NHL)

LIGHTNING SPECIAL TEAMS TOP SCORERS

Powerplay	G	A	PTS
BRADLEY	3	7	10
HAMRLIK	7	2	9
KLIMA	4	4	8
TUCKER	2	6	8
GRATTON	2	6	8

Shorthanded	G	A	PTS
ZAMUNER	3	2	5
HAMRLIK	1	1	2
BUREAU	1	1	2

COACHING AND MANAGEMENT: Coach Terry Crisp has come a long way since coaching the Calgary Flames to the Stanley Cup in 1989.

What's that? He's a better coach now?

Sure. That Flames team pretty much coached themselves, and according to some of the stories, at times did it literally.

But, Crisp has something going in Tampa Bay. He's shown he won't tolerate a lack of effort, and has been able to convince the players of the importance of team defence, which has kept them competitive before their time.

It may be a little more difficult now, however, with Esposito attempting to increase the skill level on the team by adding more Europeans. The tradeoff is reduced defense for improved offence. Often, that doesn't translate into more wins, however, so we'll see what Crisp can do with them this year.

And, of course, his job would be a lot easier if the young players started to bloom.

Esposito has shown remarkable patience building this team, making minor trades here and there. He hasn't been dormant by any means, but all of the deals involve retreads or underachievers. There's no way anybody is touching the future stars.

But it's their fourth year now and he may be getting a little antsy. If there's not marked improvement this season, look for Trader Phil to start making major moves.

DRAFT

1995 DRAFT SELECTIONS

Round	Sel.	Player	Pos	Amateur Team
1	5	D. Langkow	C	Tri-City (WHL)
2	30	Mike McBain	D	Red Deer (WHL)
3	56	Shane Willis	RW	Prince Albert (WHL)
5	108	K.Golokhvastov	RW	Russia
6	134	Eduard Pershin	C	Russia
7	160	Cory Murphy	D	S.S. Marie (OHL)
8	186	Joe Cardarelli	LW	Spokane (WHL)
9	212	Zac Bierk	G	Peterborough (OHL)

Daymond Langkow led the WHL in scoring last year with 67 goals and 73 assists for 140 points. He's considered small at 5-10, 170, but makes up for it with his toughness.

The Lightning can use everything he has to offer, probably this year. It's not as if he has anything left to do or prove in junior hockey. Plus, the Lightning's previus three high first round draft selections - Roman Hamrlik, Chris Gratton and Jason Wiemer all stepped directly into the NHL.

PROGNOSIS: The Lightning haven't shown anything yet that would cause you to think they're ready to move up to the next level of competition. When it happens, it will be sudden. One day the young rookie prospects are going to explode.

The fuse has already been lit on Hamrlik and this could be the year for Gratton and/or Wiemer. Daymond Langkow, the Lightning first round draft choice this year, is an explosive player and might not take as long as the others. Gratton and Wiemer are big guys, and they're often slower to come around.

So, let's say all four of these young guns do it this year. All of a sudden this becomes an exciting young team, and more importantly, a serious playoff contender.

They're already solid in goal and the defence is okay. Once the forwards get moving they're no longer an also-ran.

Is it going to happen this year? Maybe, but not likely.

Soon, though. Soon.

PREDICTION
Atlantic Division: 6th
Eastern Conference: 12th
Overall: 21st

STAT SECTION

PLAYERS	OVERALL				Projected over 84 games		
	GP	G	A	PTS	G	A	Pts
B.BRADLEY	46	13	27	40	24	49	73
P.YSEBAERT	44	12	16	28	23	31	54
C.GRATTON	46	7	20	27	13	37	50
P.KLIMA	47	13	13	26	23	23	46
J.TUCKER	46	12	13	25	22	24	46
R.HAMRLIK	48	12	11	23	21	19	40
A.SEMAK	41	7	11	18	14	23	37
A.SELIVANOV	43	10	6	16	20	12	32
R.ZAMUNER	43	9	6	15	18	12	30
M.BUREAU	48	2	12	14	3	21	24
M.ANDERSSON	36	4	7	11	9	16	25
E.CICCONE	41	2	4	6	4	8	12
M.BERGEVIN	44	2	4	6	4	8	12
C.CROSS	43	1	5	6	2	10	12
B.HALKIDIS	31	1	4	5	3	11	14
J.WIEMER	36	1	4	5	2	9	11
E.CHARRON	45	1	4	5	2	7	9
A.PLAVSIC	18	2	2	4	9	9	18
B.MYHRES	15	2	0	2	11	0	11
R.POESCHEK	25	1	1	2	3	3	6
B.HANKINSON	26	0	2	2	0	6	6
B.GRETZKY	3	0	1	1	0	27	27
G.GALLANT	1	0	0	0	0	0	0
C.LIPUMA	1	0	0	0	0	0	0

Team Rankings 1994/95

		Conference Rank	League Rank
Record	17-28-3	12	23
Home	10-14-0	13	24
Away	7-14-3	11	20
Team Plus\Minus	-17	13	20
Goals For	120	12	24
Goals Against	144	10	15

MISCELLANEOUS STATS

One Goal Games	6-10
Times outshooting opponent	19
Times outshot	24
Even shots	5
Average Shots For	26.6
Average Shots Against	27.6
Overtime	2-2-3
Longest Winning streak	2
Longest Undefeated streak	3
Longest Losing streak	6
Longest winless streak	6
Versus Teams Over .500	6-17-2
Versus Teams Under .500	10-10-1
First Half Record	9-13-2
Second Half Record	7-14-1

All-Time Rankings - INDIVIDUAL

Goals

Brian Bradley	79
John Tucker	46
Petr Klima	41

Assists

Brian Bradley	111
John Tucker	75
Shawn Chambers	64

Points

Brian Bradley	190
John Tucker	121
Shawn Chambers	85

Best Individual Seasons

Goals

Brian Bradley	1992-93	43
Petr Klima	1993-94	28
Chris Kontos	1992-93	27

Assists

Brian Bradley	1992-93	44
Brian Bradley	1993-94	40
John Tucker	1992-93	39

Points

Brian Bradley	1992-93	86
Brian Bradley	1993-94	64
John Tucker	1992-93	56

Washington Capitals

The date was March 1, 1995 and it was a memorable one. On that day the Capitals had a record of 3-10-5. They were last in the Atlantic Division, second last in the Eastern Conference, and second last in the NHL. Their biggest concern at that point was holding off the Ottawa Senators for last place. Their scouts were starting to look more carefully at the top three picks in the upcoming draft.

But, then it happened.

Jim Carey was called up from the AHL affiliate in Portland.

March 2, 1995 - Carey makes his NHL debut on the road against the New York Islanders in front of a small crowd of 9,138. They win 4-3, with the third goal going in with one second left after the Islanders pulled their goalie. It ended the Caps five-game losing streak and was their first victory on the road in 11 tries.

March 4, 1995 - Carey makes his home debut, a 5-1 win over Montreal, giving the Caps two straight victories, their longest winning streak of the season.

March 13, 1995 - Since March 4, Carey and the Caps have defeated the Rangers 4-2, beat Boston (in Boston) 3-1, tied Ottawa 2-2, and defeated Tampa Bay 3-1. Carey's record is 5-0-1, same as the team's since his callup, and his GAA is 1.64. The day after being named the NHL player of the week, he records his first shutout, a 3-0 win in Tampa.

March 16, 1995 - The Caps lose their first game since Carey's callup. Carey is pulled after allowing three goals on 14 shots in 28 minutes, and relieved by Olaf Kolzig.

March 20, 1995 - Carey's second NHL shutout.

March 21, 1995 - Carey's third NHL shutout.

March 25, 1995 - Carey ties Philadelphia 2-2. His GAA of 1.38 and save percentage of .941 is the highest in the league. His record is 9-1-2.

April 4, 1995 - After a 4-3 loss in overtime on March 26, Carey records his fourth straight win. He is named the NHL Player of the Month for March, and the NHL Rookie of the Month. He becomes the first player to ever win both awards in the same month.

April 14, 1995 - After losing three straight games, in which the Capitals didn't score more than one goal, and didn't allow more than three, Carey records his fourth shutout, a 3-0 win over Florida.

April 16, 1995 - And then he rested. After 21 straight starts, Carey gets a day off. Kolzig gets the call and the Caps lose 4-2.

April 24, 1995 - Two nights after a 2-1 win in Pittsburgh, Carey allows three goals in just six minutes against the New York Rangers, and gets the rest of the night off. Including his time in the AHL, he has played 79 games so far.

May 2, 1995 - The season ends. Carey's record is 18-6-3, the team's is 19-8-3.

May 18, 1995 - So, the news isn't all good. The Caps are eliminated from the playoffs. Carey plays poorly.

The point is this: the insertion of a single rookie goaltender turned around a faltering franchise. Carey has a bright future.

Washington will sport a new logo and uniform this year. The logo features a swooping eagle. If a team were being named today, the Capitals wouldn't cut it according to the marketing experts. Hence the eagle, to make the logo more attractive and marketable.

More than 20 years ago, when the team had a name-the-team contest, the most popular submission was the Comets. Some of the other submissions: Watergate Bugs, Buggers, Apes, Largo Lizards, Mosquitoes, Catfish, Turtles, Otters, Pandas, Cheetahs, Snowflakes, Ice Caps, Pink Violins, Cold Cuts, and Chimney Sweeps.

It ain't over until it's over for teams facing the Capitals in the playoffs, especially if it's Pittsburgh. It's rare for teams to lose after earning 3-1 leads in the playoffs, but the Caps did it for the third time last year. They were up 3-1, and then lost game five in overtime, before losing the final two. They also blew 3-1 to Pittsburgh in 1992, and to the Islanders in 1987.

TEAM PREVIEW

GOAL: The curious thing about Carey's rise to prominence was that there was a goaltending glut on the Caps before the start of last season, and Carey wasn't included. Don Beaupre, Olaf Kolzig, Rick Tabaracci and Byron Dafoe were all supposed to fight it out for number one status.

One of the amazing things about Carey is that despite his prominence in the NHL last season, he also won the AHL Rookie of the Year award and the league's Most Outstanding Goaltender. He had a 30-14-11 mark with Portland, a 2.76 GAA, had six shutouts, and had set an AHL record with a 16 game unbeaten streak to open the season.

Counting the playoffs, and the Washington and Portland regular seasons, Carey played 90 games last season.

Despite all the success in the nets, the Capitals acquired yet another goalie in the off-season when they got Mike Torchia from Dallas. Dafoe was traded to Los Angeles, and Tabaracci went to Calgary during the season, where oddly enough, his combined GAA was 2.11, tying him with Dominik Hasek for best in the league. He did, however, only play in 13 games.

	GP	MIN	GA	AVG	W	L	T	SO
Carey	28	1604	57	2.13	18	6	3	4
Tabaracci	8	394	16	2.44	1	3	2	0
Kolzig	14	724	30	2.49	2	8	2	0
Dafoe	4	187	11	3.53	1	1	1	0

DEFENCE: The saga of Brendan Witt finally ended on the eve of the draft after a bizarre two-year standoff. If the Caps hadn't signed him, he would have gone back into the draft, and Washington would have received a second round pick as compensation.

Witt, whose salary demands were considered unreasonable by Washington, and just about everyone else, would have been subject to the rookie salary cap had he not signed.

It might be understandable had he returned to his junior team, just as Todd Bertuzzi did, who was in a similar situation. But, Witt took the year off. Didn't play at all.

Ironically, one of Witt's attractions is that he's considered a character player. Hmmm...

At any rate, Witt is still projected as an outstanding prospect. His on-ice strength is his defensive play and his bodychecking. He isn't projected as much of a scorer.

The Capitals have another outstanding prospect in Nolan Baumgartner, the 10th player chosen in the 1994 draft. He played in Kamloops last season in the WHL and was chosen that league's playoff MVP.

Calle Johansson will handle the point on the power play. Last year, Joe Juneau spent a lot of time on the other one. Sylvain Cote is the only other offensive threat of note.

Mark Tinordi is a valuable character player on the blue-line along with Joe Reekie. Jim Johnson, Igor Ulanov, Sergei Gonchar and Ken Klee will battle it out for the remaining ice time.

The trend, not too long ago, was for mobile-type defences. Some still go that route. But, size, toughness, and defensive play have taken on more importance in recent years.

If the rookies on this team come through, this could very well be the best defensive unit in the league. At least in terms of strictly defensive play.

FORWARD: The Caps would have been in big trouble if not for Peter Bondra last year. After his 34 goals, tops in the league, the next highest goal scorer was Keith Jones, with only 14.

Bondra's goals accounted for an amazing 25 percent of Washington's production. That was highest in the league, by a wide margin.

Player	Tm.	Goals	% of Team Goals
Peter Bondra	Wsh.	34	25.0%
Eric Lindros	Phi.	29	19.3%
Alexei Yashin	Wpg.	30	19.1%
Donald Audette	Buf.	24	18.5%
Cam Neely	Bos.	27	18.0%
Alexei Yashin	Ott.	21	17.9%
Theoren Fleury	Cgy.	29	17.8%
Jaromir Jagr	Pit.	32	17.7%
Ray Ferraro	NYI	22	17.5%

Obviously, the Capitals need somebody else scoring, especially with Bondra's checkered past of good-year bad-year. He was streaky last season, as well, scoring 23 of the 34 in the second half.

So, who's going to score the goals? The problem is there's not a lot of potential in that area.

Steve Konawalchuk scored 10 goals of his 11 goals in the team's last 22, and that included an 11 game scoring drought. He might come on an be more consistent.

Keith Jones had 14 last year, Khristich 12, Kelly Miller and Pivonka each 10.

Of that group, Khristich was traded to Los Angeles in a ridiculously good deal for Washington. They get the Kings' number one draft pick next season, which could turn out to be first overall.

The Capitals will either have to look at the trade route, or ensure that some of their prospects to come through. Maybe Pat Peake, who had a nightmare season that included a bout with mononucleosis; maybe Jason Allison, a big time junior scorer, who got off to a poor start last year with the Caps; maybe Rob Pearson, who was projected as a goal scorer, but got one more in the playoffs than he did during the regular season, which was zero; maybe Martin Gendron, who led Portland with 36 goals and had two 70-goal seasons in junior; maybe Alexander Kharlamov, son of the legendary Valeri Kharlamov, who was a first round pick in 1994 and has been signed.

Or maybe none of the above.

The Caps have their share of good, strong, tough guys. Craig Berube (free agent at press time) had 173 penalty minutes, and doesn't hurt the team with his hockey playing ability.

Kevin Kaminski adds a big spark when he's on the ice. At only 5-9, 170 pounds he's afraid of no one. He even took on big Mike Peluso in a fight, and won.

Kaminski has some unbelievable minor league penalty totals. Twice he's led minor pro league in penalty minutes, once with 455 minutes (499 minutes in total) and another time with 345 minutes. But, even more impressively, he once had 169 minutes during a playoff season, in just 19 games. Another time he had 91 PIM in just 16 games.

Speaking of high penalty minute totals, Dale Hunter moved up to second place last season in the all-time rankings.

All-Time Career Penalty Minutes

Dave (Tiger) Williams	3,966
Dale Hunter	3,106 *
Chris Nilan	3,043
Tim Hunter	2,889 *
Marty McSorley	2,723 *
Willi Plett	2,572
Basil McRae	2,405 *
Garth Butcher	2,302 *
Dave Schultz	2,294
Jay Wells	2,279 *

* active in the NHL last year

SPECIAL TEAMS: These were special teams that were, well, special. Not only did they finish sixth in both power play and penalty killing, but they finished first in most short-handed goals scored, and first in fewest short-handed goals allowed.

Bondra scored the most shorthanded goals in the league. He was joined by Konowalchuk and Pivonka in the top 10 shorthanded points.

Bondra was also fourth with 12 power play goals. Johansson and Juneau finished in the top 10 in power play points.

Power Play	G	ATT	PCT
Overall	45	226	19.9% (6th NHL)
Home	23	117	19.7% (11th NHL)
Road	22	109	20.2% (6th NHL)

2 SHORT HANDED GOALS ALLOWED (T-1st NHL)

Penalty Killing	G	TSH	PCT
Overall	34	220	84.5% (6th NHL)
Home	12	98	87.8% (1st NHL)
Road	22	122	82.0% (12th NHL)

13 SHORT HANDED GOALS SCORED (T-1st NHL)

Penalties	GP	MIN	AVG
CAPITALS	48	1144	23.8 (T-23rd NHL)

CAPITALS SPECIAL TEAMS TOP SCORERS

Power play	G	A	PTS
JUNEAU	3	22	25
JOHANSSON	4	20	24
BONDRA	12	6	18
PIVONKA	4	9	13
KHRISTICH	8	4	12
HUNTER	3	4	7
COTE	1	6	7
MILLER	2	3	5

Short handed	G	A	PTS
BONDRA	6	0	6
KONOWALCHUK	3	2	5
PIVONKA	2	2	4
COTE	0	3	3
POULIN	2	0	2
REEKIE	0	2	2

TINORDI	0	1	1	
MILLER	0	1	1	

COACHING AND MANAGEMENT: David Poile has to be considered one of the best general managers in the game. Maybe the best. Although they've had some tough luck in the playoffs, his teams are always among the best during the regular season. And it only takes one season to change the playoff reputation.

The deal he made sending a disappointing Dmitri Khristich to Los Angeles for a first round draft pick is one of the big steals of the year, especially if that pick ends up being first overall.

Jim Schoenfeld, considered an emotional motivator type, begins his third season as Washington coach. Being behind the Washington bench can be a dangerous place. Their coaching staff led the league last year in injuries. Schoenfeld was cut for eight stiches when a puck hit him in the mouth, and assistant Keith Allain took 13 when a puck hit him in the back of the head.

DRAFT

1995 DRAFT SELECTIONS

Round	Sel.	Player	Pos	Amateur Team
1	17	Brad Church	LW	Prince Albert (WHL)
1	23	Milkka Elomo	LW	Finland
2	43	Duane Hay	LW	Guelph (OHL)
4	93	S. Charpentier	G	Laval (QMJHL)
4	95	Joel Theriault	D	Beauport (QMJHL)
5	105	Benoit Gratton	C	Laval (QMJHL)
5	124	Joel Cort	D	Guelph (OHL)
6	147	Frederic Jobin	D	Laval (QMJHL)
8	199	Vasili Turkovsky	D	Russia
9	225	Scott Swanson	D	Omaha (USHL)

The Caps took left-wingers with their first three picks.

Brad Church is a big, tough winger who hasn't shown a lot yet in the scoring department yet, but might when he moves up Prince Albert's depth chart. Finn Milkka Elomo went next and then Duane Hay, another who might move up the depth chart in Guelph, considering the talent that was ahead of him on that team.

PROGNOSIS: You might be worried with this team about their scoring ability but goals sometimes come from unexpected places. Defence is less of an unexpected. Either you have it or you don't. The Caps do.

Besides, if the other team doesn't score, they don't have to score so much themselves.

Either way, the Caps are building a winner, and it's only a matter of time.

Could it be this year? Maybe, but there's still too many ifs.

PREDICTION
Atlantic Division: 3rd
Eastern Conference: 5th
Overall: 10th

STAT SECTION

Team Rankings 1994/95

		Conference Rank	League Rank
Record	22-18-8	6	10
Home	15-6-3	6	8
Away	7-12-5	8	16
Team Plus\Minus	+5	5	9
Goals For	136	6	13
Goals Against	120	2	4

PLAYERS	1994-95 OVERALL				Projected over 84 games		
	GP	G	A	PTS	G	A	Pts
P.BONDRA	47	34	9	43	61	16	77
J.JUNEAU	44	5	38	43	10	73	83
M.PIVONKA	46	10	23	33	18	42	60
C.JOHANSSON	46	5	26	31	9	47	56
D.KHRISTICH	48	12	14	26	21	24	45
S.KONOWALCHUK	46	11	14	25	20	26	46
K.MILLER	48	10	13	23	17	23	40
D.HUNTER	45	8	15	23	15	28	43
K.JONES	40	14	6	20	29	13	42
S.COTE	47	5	14	19	9	25	34
J.JOHNSON	47	0	13	13	0	23	23
M.TINORDI	42	3	9	12	6	18	24
D.POULIN	29	4	5	9	12	14	26
M.EAGLES	40	3	4	7	6	8	14
*S.GONCHAR	31	2	5	7	5	14	19
J.REEKIE	48	1	6	7	2	11	13
C.BERUBE	43	2	4	6	4	8	12
R.PEARSON	32	0	6	6	0	16	16
I.ULANOV	22	1	4	5	4	15	19
*K.KLEE	23	3	1	4	11	4	15
P.PEAKE	18	0	4	4	0	19	19
*M.GENDRON	8	2	1	3	21	11	32
*J.ALLISON	12	2	1	3	14	7	21
J.SLANEY	16	0	3	3	0	16	16
*K.KAMINSKI	27	1	1	2	3	3	6
*J.NELSON	10	1	0	1	8	0	8

MISCELLANEOUS STATS

One Goal Games	7-6
Times outshooting opponent	31
Times outshot	16
Even shots	1
Overtime	0-1-8
Average Shots For	28.8
Average Shots Against	24.8
Longest Winning streak	4
Longest Undefeated streak	7
Longest Losing streak	3
Longest winless streak	5
Versus Teams Over .500	7-12-4
Versus Teams Under .500	15-6-4
First Half Record	8-10-6
Second Half Record	14-8-2

PLAYOFFS

Results: lost to Pittsburgh in conference quarter-finals 4-3.
Record: 3-4 Home: 2-1 Away: 1-2
Goals For: 26 (3.7/gm)
Goals Against: 29 (4.1/gm)
Overtime: 0-1
Power play: 13.6% (9th)
Penalty Killing: 76.2% (11th)

PLAYER	GP	G	A	PTS
P.BONDRA	7	5	3	8
D. HUNTER	7	4	4	8
K. JONES	7	4	4	8
J. JUNEAU	7	2	6	8
S. KONOWALCHUK	7	2	5	7
D. KHRISTICH	7	1	4	5
M. PIVONKA	7	1	4	5
C. JOHANSSON	7	3	1	4
S. GONCHAR	7	2	2	4
S. COTE	7	1	3	4
K.MILLER	7	0	3	3
M. EAGLES	7	0	2	2
J.JOHNSON	7	0	2	2
R. PEARSON	3	1	0	1

M.TINORDI	1	0	0	0
B. DAFOE	1	0	0	0
O.KOLZIG	2	0	0	0
D.POULIN	2	0	0	0
I.ULANOV	2	0	0	0
K.KAMINSKI	5	0	0	0
C.BERUBE	7	0	0	0
J.REEKIE	7	0	0	0
K.KLEE	7	0	0	0
J.CAREY	7	0	0	0

All-Time Rankings - INDIVIDUAL

Goals

Mike Gartner	397
Mike Ridley	218
Bengt Gustafsson	196

Assists

Mike Gartner	392
Bengt Gustafsson	359
Michal Pivonka	333

Points

Mike Gartner	789
Bengt Gustafsson	555
Mike Ridley	547

Best Individual Seasons

Goals

Dennis Maruk	1981-82	60
Bob Carpenter	1984-85	53
Mike Gartner	1984-85	50
Dennis Maruk	1980-81	50

Assists

Dennis Maruk	1981-82	76
Scott Stevens	1988-89	61
Scott Stevens	1987-88	60

Points

Dennis Maruk	1981-82	136
Mike Gartner	1984-85	102
Dennis Maruk	1980-81	97

TOWNSEND'S ULTIMATE POOL PICKS

Let's go through the categories, and rest assured we wouldn't be bothering if there wasn't a measure of success.

The player's list ranks them in order of expected performance. The categories are self-explanatory in most cases, but here is a guide to their relevance:

POWER PLAY POINTS

There would be no such thing as a 100 point scorer in the NHL if it weren't for the power play. Two years ago, for example, Sergei Fedorov led all scorers at even strength with 81 points. Jaromir Jagr was second at 70, and in rounding out the top ten you get down to players in the fifties.

Those numbers are even more pronounced for defensemen. Most of the top scoring rearguards earned more than half their points with the man advantage. The leader, two seasons ago, Brian Leetch, had 67 percent of his points on the power play.

Just getting on the power play makes all the difference.

The same goes for forwards. You want your players inhabiting the number one unit. Sometimes that's more difficult to do on strong teams because there are others in line for that time. So, oddly enough, if two players are of equal ability, often you want the one playing for the weaker team.

Another thing to consider when using the player rankings is that if there are two players who have around the same number of points, it's better to take the one with fewer from the power play. Players get moved on and off power play units, so one who we know will still score at even strength is a more valuable commodity.

As well, some power plays don't work as well from one year to the next. Too many players get moved around. If a team's power play unit stays the same for too long, it's opponents know what to expect and are better prepared.

AGE

The peak age for NHL players is between 24 and 28. That's an average. Plenty of good scoring before and after for many, but the younger ones can be inconsistent and when a player hits the not-so-magic age of 30, you start rolling the dice.

When a player appears to be losing it, he can be gone quickly. Patience wears thinnier in relation to birth certificates. The thinking changes. When he goes into a slump, people start whispering that his career could be winding down. The oldster doesn't have the same time frame to work out slumps as does the younger guy.

Poor teams with older players start thinking about next year. They're quicker to dump the older guy and bring in the youth.

The ages listed in the player rankings are as of October 1, the starting date of the NHL season.

INJURY STATUS

"A" players miss very few games. They're the ironmen of the league or at least have been for a number of years. Steve Larmer and Mark Recchi are examples.

"B" players are average or haven't been around long enough to be classified. They're injury status is not a consideration when picking them.

"C" guys are injury prone or have established injuries that make them risky picks. Mario Lemieux, Wendel Clark and Pat Flatley are a few of those.

INDICATOR

The indicators show the liklihood of a player increasing his point production considerably (U), staying around the same (E), decreasing considerably (D), increasing gradually (GU) or decreasing gradually (GD).

The indicator is based on a player's projected points over 84 games as opposed to actual totals. In some cases, however, injuries have to be considered. If Mario Lemieux were to play 84 games, he would be the leading scorer, no contest.

Most of a player's ranking is based on where he fits on the team depth chart - first line, second line, third line, fourth line, fighting for a job, top power play unit, etc.

That means his abilities are often a reflection of his teammates abilities, or the style of play the coach prefers.

Something to keep in mind is that players with "U" or "D" beside their name are the most speculative in nature. Other pool players aren't likely to judge them the same way so you can adjust your selection process accordingly. "U" players can be selected later than listed, while "D" players may still be worth picking higher if they're available.

Many of the indicators also reflect general principles about scoring that have been studied over the years. A couple examples: rookies with big point totals often suffer the sophomore jinx the following season (it's not just a myth); a player who is going to be a top point getter often has his breakout season in his third or fourth year; someone who all of a sudden has a high point total, after eight or nine years in the league, often reverts to form the following season; someone who had a poor season after a number of good ones, especially if he's younger, also often reverts to form.

A number of other things were done to help determine the rankings. A depth chart was constructed to determine where an individual fits on the team; the history, and consistency of each player was checked over his career; playoff performances for younger players from last year, which could be telling us a bigger role is planned for them; and first and second half points were checked for each player. That helps determine if a young player is coming on, an older player is starting to fade, or if his role changed in the latter part of the season.

Good luck. But, hey, be careful out there. There's lots of pool sharks around.

THE TOP 300

	Team	93/94 GP	93/94 Pts	Proj. Pts (84 games)	PP Pts	Age	Inj Status	Ind Status
Lindros	Phi	46	70	128	24	22	B	U
Bure	Van	44	43	82	13	24	B	U
Jagr	Pit	48	70	122	22	23	B	GD
Roenick	Chi	33	34	86	18	25	B	U
Renberg	Phi	47	57	102	12	23	B	E
Zhamnov	Wpg	48	65	114	25	25	B	GD
Recchi	Mtl	49	48	82	16	27	A	U
Oates	Bos	48	53	93	23	33	B	E
Shanahan	StL	45	41	77	11	26	B	U
Sakic	Col	47	62	111	22	26	B	E
Fleury	Cgy	47	58	104	20	27	A	E
Turgeon	Mtl	49	47	81	17	26	A	U
Mogilny	Buf	44	47	90	26	26	C	D
Fedorov	Det	42	50	100	16	25	B	E
Tkachuk	Wpg	48	51	89	17	23	A	E
Sundin	Tor	47	47	84	19	24	A	U
Nieuwendyk	Cgy	46	50	91	15	29	B	E
LeClair	Phi	46	54	99	17	26	B	E
Forsberg	Col	47	50	89	15	22	B	E
Stevens	Bos	27	27	84	10	30	B	GU
20								
Selanne	Wpg	45	48	90	18	25	B	E
Yzerman	Det	47	38	68	19	30	C	U
Juneau	Wsh	44	43	82	25	27	B	GU
LaFontaine	Buf	22	27	103	16	30	C	E
Linden	Van	48	40	70	23	25	A	U
Gilmour	Tor	44	33	63	15	32	B	U
Reichel	Cgy	48	35	62	13	24	A	U
Housley	Cgy	43	43	84	20	30	B	E
Robitaille	Pit	46	42	77	8	29	A	GU
Hull	StL	48	50	87	16	31	B	E
MacInnis	StL	32	28	74	12	32	B	GU
Coffey	Det	45	58	108	31	34	B	D
Nolan	Col	46	49	89	17	23	C	E
Modano	Dal	30	29	81	11	25	B	GU
Damphousse	Mtl	48	40	70	14	27	A	U
Sanderson	Hfd	46	32	58	9	23	B	U
Gretzky	LA	48	48	84	22	34	A	E
Roberts	Cgy	8	4	42	3	29	C	U
Sheppard	Det	43	40	78	13	29	B	E
Murphy	Chi	40	41	86	15	27	B	E
40								
Leetch	NYR	48	41	72	21	27	B	E
Hawerchuk	StL	23	16	58	10	32	B	U

	Team	93/94 GP	93/94 Pts	Proj. Pts (84 games)	PP Pts	Age	Inj Status	Ind Status
Francis	Pit	44	59	113	21	32	B	D
Lemieux	Pit	-	-	-	-	29	C	-
Neely	Bos	42	41	82	19	30	C	E
Harvey	Dal	40	20	42	8	20	B	U
Arnott	Edm	42	37	74	18	20	B	E
Brind'Amour	Phi	48	39	68	16	25	A	U
Brown	Van	33	31	79	21	29	B	E
Friesen	SJ	48	25	44	7	19	B	U
O'Neill	Hfd	-	-	-	-	19	-	-
Sandstrom	Pit	47	44	79	9	31	C	E
Kariya	Ana	47	39	70	15	21	A	U
Kozlov	Det	46	33	60	12	23	B	U
Richer	NJ	45	39	73	3	29	B	E
Tocchet	LA	36	35	82	12	31	C	E
Yashin	Ott	47	44	79	21	22	B	E
Muller	NYI	45	27	50	7	29	A	U
Janney	SJ	35	27	65	12	28	B	GU
Ridley	Van	48	37	65	9	32	A	GU
60								
Bourque	Bos	46	43	79	29	34	B	GD
Messier	NYR	46	53	97	20	34	B	D
Primeau	Det	45	42	78	9	23	B	E
MacLean	NJ	46	29	53	8	30	B	U
Audette	Buf	46	37	68	23	26	B	E
Zubov	NYR	38	36	80	19	25	B	GD
Graves	NYR	47	31	55	15	27	A	U
Bradley	TB	46	40	73	10	30	B	E
Blake	LA	24	11	38	6	25	B	U
Andreychuk	Tor	48	38	66	14	32	A	E
Malakhov	Mtl	40	21	44	11	27	B	U
King	NYI	43	26	51	11	28	B	U
Courtnall,G	STL	45	34	63	16	33	B	E
Ferraro	NYR	47	43	77	7	31	B	D
Granato	LA	33	24	61	4	31	C	E
Ricci	Col	48	36	63	16	23	B	E
Weight	Edm	48	40	70	21	24	B	E
Gratton	TB	46	27	49	8	20	B	U
Thomas	NYI	47	26	46	9	32	B	U
Daigle	Ott	47	37	66	14	20	B	E
80								
Verbeek	NYR	48	33	58	11	31	A	GU
Zelepukin	NJ	4	3	63	0	27	B	U
Barnes	Fla	41	29	59	6	24	B	GU
Gagner	Dal	48	42	74	19	30	B	GD

	Team	93/94 GP	93/94 Pts	Proj. Pts (84 games)	PP Pts	Age	Inj Status	Ind Status
Clark	Col	37	30	68	8	28	C	E
Young	Col	48	39	68	12	28	B	E
Emerson	Wpg	48	37	65	14	28	A	E
Chelios	Chi	48	38	67	23	33	B	E
Poulin	Chi	45	30	56	6	22	B	GU
Cassels	Hfd	46	37	68	9	26	B	GD
Niedermayer	Fla	48	10	17	3	20	B	U
Zhitnik	Buf	32	14	37	8	22	B	U
Smolinski	StL	44	31	59	9	23	B	E
Bondra	Wsh	47	43	77	18	27	B	D
Dahlen	SJ	46	34	62	13	28	B	E
Bertuzzi	NYI	-	-	-	-	20	B	-
Sillinger	Ana	28	15	45	4	24	B	U
Duchesne	Ott	47	26	46	13	30	B	U
Amonte	Chi	48	35	61	13	25	A	E
Belanger	Fla	47	29	52	14	26	B	GU
100								
Kamensky	Col	40	30	63	12	29	B	E
Murphy	Tor	48	38	66	11	34	A	D
Khristich	LA	48	26	45	12	26	B	U
Mellanby	Fla	48	25	44	10	29	B	GU
Oliver	Edm	44	30	57	16	24	B	E
Rolston	NJ	40	18	38	3	22	B	U
Straka	Ott	37	18	41	4	23	B	U
Turcotte	Hfd	47	35	63	10	27	B	E
Nylander	Cgy	6	1	14	0	22	C	U
Mironov	Pit	33	17	43	10	29	B	U
Mullen	F/A	45	37	69	9	38	B	GD
Suter	Chi	48	37	64	24	30	B	E
McEachern	Bos	44	26	50	2	26	B	GU
Sydor	LA	48	23	40	4	23	A	U
Ozolinsh	SJ	48	25	44	5	23	B	GU
Kovalev	NYR	48	28	49	6	22	B	GU
Drake	Wpg	43	26	51	3	26	B	U
Zalapski	Cgy	48	28	49	7	27	B	GU
Koivu	Mtl	-	-	-	-	20	B	-
Dawe	Buf	42	11	22	2	22	B	U
120								
Pivonka	Wsh	46	33	60	13	29	B	E
Quinn	Ott	44	31	59	6	30	B	E
Corson	StL	48	36	63	11	29	B	GD
Falloon	SJ	46	19	35	1	23	B	U
Niedermayer	NJ	48	19	33	8	22	B	U
Guerin	NJ	48	25	44	6	24	B	E
Wiemer	TB	36	5	12	0	19	B	U
Courtnall,R	Van	45	35	65	12	30	B	GD
Kennedy	Cgy	30	15	42	1	26	B	U

	Team	93/94 GP	93/94 Pts	Proj. Pts (84 games)	PP Pts	Age	Inj Status	Ind Status
Lidstrom	Det	43	26	51	11	25	A	E
Hogue	Tor	45	16	30	3	28	B	U
Smyth	Edm	3	0	0	0	19	B	-
Savage	Mtl	37	19	43	0	24	B	U
Iafrate	Bos	-	-	-	-	29	C	-
May	Buf	33	6	15	1	23	B	U
Stillman	Cgy	10	2	17	1	21	B	U
Larouche	Ott	18	15	70	7	24	B	D
Nedved	NYR	46	23	42	4	23	C	GU
Ciccarelli	Det	42	43	86	17	35	C	D
Nikolishin	Hfd	39	18	39	4	22	B	U
140								
Schneider	NYI	43	29	57	13	26	B	E
Selivanov	TB	43	16	31	5	24	B	U
Konowalchuk	Wsh	46	25	46	3	23	B	U
Marchant	Edm	45	27	50	7	22	B	E
Lemieux	NJ	45	19	35	1	30	B	U
Stevens	NJ	48	22	38	6	31	B	U
Quint	Wpg	-	-	-	-	19	B	-
Hamrlik	TB	48	23	40	9	21	B	U
Bellows	TB	41	16	33	5	31	B	U
Shannon,Darrin	Wpg	19	8	35	4	25	B	U
Kovalenko	Col	45	24	45	4	25	B	GU
Nemchinov	NYR	47	13	23	0	30	B	U
Ronning	Van	41	25	51	12	30	B	E
Whitney	SJ	39	25	54	8	25	B	E
Nicholls	Chi	48	51	89	28	34	B	D
Kurri	LA	38	29	64	15	35	B	D
Berenek	Van	51	31	51	9	25	B	E
Van Allen	Ana	45	29	54	8	28	B	SD
Wesley	Hfd	48	16	28	11	27	B	U
Galley	Buf	47	32	57	17	32	B	GD
160								
Desjardins	Phi	43	29	57	12	26	B	GD
Brylin	NJ	26	14	45	4	21	B	E
Flatley	NYI	45	27	50	2	31	C	E
Jovanovski	Fla	-	-	-	-	19	B	-
Krivokrasov	Chi	41	19	39	6	21	B	GU
Lumme	Van	36	17	40	6	29	B	GU
Murray	StL	35	7	17	0	23	B	U
Holzinger	Buf	4	3	63	0	22	B	-
Titov	Cgy	40	24	50	5	29	B	E
Craven	Chi	16	7	36	1	31	B	U
Eastwood	Wpg	49	19	33	1	28	B	U
Kozlov	SJ	16	2	11	0	20	B	U
Lindsay	Fla	48	19	33	1	24	A	U
Hatcher,K	Dal	47	29	52	13	29	B	E

	Team	93/94 GP	93/94 Pts	Proj. Pts (84 games)	PP Pts	Age	Inj Status	Ind Status
Langenbrunner	Dal	2	0 0	0	20		B	-
Ysebeart	TB	44	28	53	2	29	B	GD
Laperriere	StL	37	27	61	3	21	B	D
Palffy	NYI	33	17	43	3	23	B	E
Adams	Dal	43	21	41	7	32	C	E
Larmer	NYR	47	29	52	7	34	A	E
180								
Burr	Det	42	14	28	0	29	B	U
Tverdovsky	Ana	36	12	28	3	19	B	U
Donnelly,M	Dal	44	27	52	7	31	B	GD
Peca	Buf	33	12	31	4	21	B	U
Pronger	StL	43	14	27	5	20	B	U
Johansson	Wsh	46	31	57	24	28	B	D
Leach	Bos	35	11	26	3	29	C	U
MacIver	Pit	41	20	41	7	31	C	E
Holan	Ana	30	11	34	4	24	B	SU
Numminen	Wpg	42	21	42	8	27	B	E
Donato	Bos	47	20	36	3	26	A	GU
Tikkanen	StL	43	23	45	13	30	B	E
Semak	TB	41	18	37	2	29	B	GU
Larionov	SJ	33	24	61	2	34	C	D
Haller	Phi	36	9	21	0	25	B	U
Dowd	NJ	10	5	42	3	26	B	E
Ciger	Edm	5	4	67	2	25	B	-
Savard	Chi	43	25	49	8	33	B	E
Tucker	TB	46	25	46	8	31	C	E
Czercawski	Bos	47	26	46	8	23	B	E
200								
Brown,K	LA	23	5	18	0	21	B	U
McInnis	NYI	41	16	33	2	25	B	GU
Craig	Tor	37	10	23	1	24	B	U
Heinze	Bos	36	16	37	0	25	B	GU
Bure	Mtl	24	4	14	0	24	B	U
Brunet	Mtl	45	25	47	2	27	B	E
Chiasson	Cgy	45	25	47	12	28	B	E
Rucinsky	Col	20	9	38	0	24	C	E
Momesso	Tor	48	25	44	6	30	B	E
Bassen	StL	47	27	48	0	30	B	D
Stumpel	Bos	44	18	35	3	23	B	GU
Boucher	LA	15	6	34	2	22	B	GU
Perreault	LA	26	7	23	1	24	B	U
Klima	TB	47	26	46	8	30	C	E
Bonk	Ott	42	11	22	4	29	B	U
Hunter	Wsh	45	23	43	7	35	B	E
McCarty	Det	31	13	35	2	23	B	GU
Kron	Hfd	37	18	41	6	28	C	E
Millen	Dal	45	23	43	4	31	B	E

	Team	93/94 GP	93/94 Pts	Proj. Pts (84 games)	PP Pts	Age	Inj Status	Ind Status
Rice	Hfd	40	21	44	8	23	B	E
220								
Berard	Ott	-	-	-	-	18	B	-
Elynuik	Ott	41	10	20	3	27	B	U
Daze	Chi	4	2	42	0	20	B	-
Kisio	F/A	12	11	77	5	36	C	D
Klatt	Dal	47	22	39	8	24	B	E
Kennedy	Dal	44	18	34	2	23	B	GU
Korolev	Wpg	45	30	56	5	25	B	D
Allison	Wsh	12	3	21	3	20	B	U
Miller,Kev	SJ	36	20	47	2	32	B	GD
Gartner	Tor	38	20	44	3	35	B	E
Driver	FA	41	16	33	9	33	B	GU
Noonan	StL	45	27	50	10	30	B	GD
Creighton	StL	48	34	59	7	30	B	D
Pearson	Wsh	32	6	16	1	24	B	U
Ranheim	Hfd	47	20	36	1	29	A	E
Jones,K	Wsh	40	20	24	3	26	B	U
Draper	Det	36	8	19	0	24	B	U
Picard	Ott	24	13	45	5	25	B	E
Gelinas	Van	46	23	42	1	25	B	E
Deadmarsh	Col	48	17	30	0	20	B	U
240								
Makarov	SJ	43	24	47	3	37	B	D
Errey	Det	43	21	41	3	31	B	E
Lachance	NYI	26	13	42	6	22	B	E
Lindros	NYI	33	4	10	0	19	B	U
Wood	Tor	48	24	42	3	31	A	E
Jonsson	Tor	39	9	19	5	20	B	U
Langkow	TB	-	-	- -	19		B	-
Ledyard	Dal	38	18	40	6	33	C	E
Brisebois	Mtl	35	12	29	3	24	B	U
Lang	LA	36	12	28	1	24	B	GU
Elik	Bos	35	23	55	7	29	B	D
Kravchuk	Edm	36	18	42	8	29	A	GD
Lapointe	Det	39	10	22	0	22	B	U
Malik	Hfd	1	1	84	0	20	B	-
Druce	LA	43	20	39	4	29	B	E
Bodger	Buf	44	20	38	12	29	B	E
Lilley	Ana	9	4	47	1	23	B	E
Darby	NYI	13	2	13	0	23	B	-
Miller,Kelly	Wsh	48	23	40	5	32	A	E
Olczyk	Wpg	33	13	33	4	29	B	E
260								
Holik	NJ	48	20	35	1	24	B	E
King	Ana	-	-	-	-	26	C	-
Walz	F/A	39	18	39	5	25	B	E

	Team	93/94 GP	93/94 Pts	Proj. Pts (84 games)	PP Pts	Age	Inj Status	Ind Status
LaFayette	NYR	39	8	17	0	22	B	U
Broten	NJ	47	32	57	7	35	B	D
Fedyk	F/A	30	12	34	5	28	B	E
Joseph	Pit	33	15	38	5	26	B	E
Shantz	Chi	45	18	33	2	21	B	E
Krupp	Col	44	23	44	12	30	B	GD
Gill	Tor	47	32	57	12	29	B	D
Gaudreau	Ott	36	14	33	2	25	B	E
Green	NYI	42	13	26	1	24	B	GU
Beers	F/A	22	9	34	2	28	B	E
Lacroix	LA	45	16	30	3	24	B	E
Corbet	Col	8	3	32	0	22	B	E
Tancill	SJ	26	14	45	0	27	B	D
Norton	StL	48	30	53	6	30	B	D
Roberts	StL	19	11	49	5	25	B	D
Sacco,J	Ana	41	18	36	4	26	B	E
Racine	Mtl	47	11	20	4	26	B	U
280								
Brown	Det	45	21	39	1	30	B	E
Slegr	Edm	31	12	33	3	24	B	E
Primeau,W	Buf	1	1	84	0	19	B	-
Murphy	Fla	46	22	40	11	28	B	GD
Svensson	Fla	19	7	31	3	31	B	E
Hull	Fla	46	19	35	1	26	B	E
Plante	Buf	47	22	39	10	24	B	E
Carnback	Ana	41	21	43	2	27	B	SD
Samuelsson,U	Pit	44	16	31	4	31	B	E
Naslund	Pit	14	4	24	1	22	B	GU
Houlder	TB	41	18	37	4	28	B	E
Yushkevich	Phi	40	14	29	4	23	B	E
Hatcher,D	Dal	43	16	31	6	23	B	E
Zezel	F/A	30	11	31	1	30	C	E
Peake	Wsh	18	4	19	2	22	B	U
Oksuita	Van	38	20	44	6	25	B	D
Wooley	Fla	34	13	32	7	26	B	E
Karpov	Ana	30	11	31	0	24	B	U
Manson	Wpg	44	18	34	8	28	B	E
Sweeney	Bos	47	22	39	7	29	B	E
300								

1995-96 NHL SCHEDULE

Fri Oct 06, 1995
DETROIT AT COLORADO

Sat Oct 07, 1995
NY ISLANDERS AT BOSTON
NY RANGERS AT HARTFORD
TORONTO AT PITTSBURGH
BUFFALO AT OTTAWA
PHILADELPHIA AT MONTREAL
FLORIDA AT NEW JERSEY
ST. LOUIS AT WASHINGTON
CALGARY AT TAMPA BAY
DALLAS AT WINNIPEG
CHICAGO AT SAN JOSE
COLORADO AT LOS ANGELES

Sun Oct 08, 1995
CALGARY AT FLORIDA
DETROIT AT EDMONTON

Mon Oct 09, 1995
BUFFALO AT BOSTON
ANAHEIM AT WINNIPEG
PITTSBURGH AT COLORADO
DETROIT AT VANCOUVER

Tue Oct 10, 1995
NY ISLANDERS AT TORONTO
EDMONTON AT ST. LOUIS
CALGARY AT DALLAS
CHICAGO AT LOS ANGELES

Wed Oct 11, 1995
ANAHEIM AT HARTFORD
WINNIPEG AT NY RANGERS
WASHINGTON AT PHILADELPHIA
MONTREAL AT FLORIDA
BOSTON AT COLORADO

Thu Oct 12, 1995
WINNIPEG AT NEW JERSEY
MONTREAL AT TAMPA BAY
PITTSBURGH AT CHICAGO
ST. LOUIS AT DALLAS
BOSTON AT SAN JOSE
VANCOUVER AT LOS ANGELES

Fri Oct 13, 1995
ANAHEIM AT BUFFALO
COLORADO AT WASHINGTON
OTTAWA AT FLORIDA
EDMONTON AT DETROIT

Sat Oct 14, 1995
CHICAGO AT HARTFORD
ANAHEIM AT PITTSBURGH
NEW JERSEY AT MONTREAL
PHILADELPHIA AT NY ISLANDERS
TAMPA BAY AT WASHINGTON
NY RANGERS AT TORONTO
COLORADO AT ST. LOUIS
BOSTON AT DALLAS
VANCOUVER AT SAN JOSE

Sun Oct 15, 1995
NEW JERSEY AT BUFFALO
EDMONTON AT PHILADELPHIA
OTTAWA AT TAMPA BAY
NY ISLANDERS AT FLORIDA
CALGARY AT CHICAGO
DETROIT AT WINNIPEG
LOS ANGELES AT VANCOUVER

Mon Oct 16, 1995
HARTFORD AT NY RANGERS

Tue Oct 17, 1995
NY RANGERS AT NY ISLANDERS
EDMONTON AT NEW JERSEY
CHICAGO AT FLORIDA
SAN JOSE AT TORONTO
CALGARY AT DETROIT
BOSTON AT ST. LOUIS
WASHINGTON AT DALLAS
TAMPA BAY AT WINNIPEG

Wed Oct 18, 1995
EDMONTON AT BUFFALO
WASHINGTON AT COLORADO
PHILADELPHIA AT LOS ANGELES
VANCOUVER AT ANAHEIM

Thu Oct 19, 1995
CALGARY AT OTTAWA
DETROIT AT NEW JERSEY
TAMPA BAY AT CHICAGO
DALLAS AT ST. LOUIS
SAN JOSE AT WINNIPEG

Fri Oct 20, 1995
PITTSBURGH AT HARTFORD
NY RANGERS AT BUFFALO
MONTREAL AT NY ISLANDERS
LOS ANGELES AT WASHINGTON
CALGARY AT TORONTO
PHILADELPHIA AT ANAHEIM

Sat Oct 21, 1995
LOS ANGELES AT PITTSBURGH
TORONTO AT MONTREAL
OTTAWA AT NEW JERSEY
HARTFORD AT FLORIDA
BOSTON AT DETROIT
CHICAGO AT ST. LOUIS

TAMPA BAY AT DALLAS
VANCOUVER AT EDMONTON

Sun Oct 22, 1995
ST. LOUIS AT BUFFALO
OTTAWA AT NY RANGERS
PHILADELPHIA AT CHICAGO
SAN JOSE AT EDMONTON
WINNIPEG AT ANAHEIM

Mon Oct 23, 1995
LOS ANGELES AT MONTREAL
ANAHEIM AT COLORADO

Tue Oct 24, 1995
VANCOUVER AT NY RANGERS
FLORIDA AT TORONTO
OTTAWA AT DETROIT
BUFFALO AT DALLAS

Wed Oct 25, 1995
ST. LOUIS AT HARTFORD
FLORIDA AT MONTREAL
VANCOUVER AT NEW JERSEY
NY ISLANDERS AT PHILADELPHIA
COLORADO AT CALGARY
WINNIPEG AT SAN JOSE

Thu Oct 26, 1995
WASHINGTON AT BOSTON
LOS ANGELES AT OTTAWA
PITTSBURGH AT NY ISLANDERS
NY RANGERS AT TAMPA BAY
TORONTO AT CHICAGO
ANAHEIM AT DALLAS

Fri Oct 27, 1995
MONTREAL AT HARTFORD
ANAHEIM AT ST. LOUIS
BUFFALO AT COLORADO
DETROIT AT CALGARY
WINNIPEG AT EDMONTON

Sat Oct 28, 1995
HARTFORD AT BOSTON
FLORIDA AT OTTAWA
CHICAGO AT MONTREAL
PHILADELPHIA AT NY ISLANDERS
PITTSBURGH AT NEW JERSEY
WASHINGTON AT TAMPA BAY
LOS ANGELES AT TORONTO

WINNIPEG AT VANCOUVER
DALLAS AT SAN JOSE

Sun Oct 29, 1995
TORONTO AT NY RANGERS
OTTAWA AT PHILADELPHIA
BUFFALO AT CHICAGO
WASHINGTON AT ST. LOUIS
CALGARY AT ANAHEIM
Mon Oct 30, 1995
COLORADO AT DALLAS
DETROIT AT WINNIPEG
SAN JOSE AT VANCOUVER

Tue Oct 31, 1995
MONTREAL AT BOSTON
TAMPA BAY AT PHILADELPHIA
NY ISLANDERS AT FLORIDA
NEW JERSEY AT EDMONTON
NY RANGERS AT SAN JOSE
CALGARY AT LOS ANGELES

Wed Nov 01, 1995
TAMPA BAY AT PITTSBURGH
DETROIT AT BUFFALO
MONTREAL AT WASHINGTON
CHICAGO AT DALLAS
TORONTO AT WINNIPEG
CALGARY AT COLORADO
EDMONTON AT VANCOUVER
ST. LOUIS AT ANAHEIM

Thu Nov 02, 1995
DETROIT AT BOSTON
OTTAWA AT HARTFORD
FLORIDA AT PHILADELPHIA
NEW JERSEY AT SAN JOSE
NY RANGERS AT LOS ANGELES

Fri Nov 03, 1995
PITTSBURGH AT BUFFALO
FLORIDA AT WASHINGTON
NY ISLANDERS AT TAMPA BAY
COLORADO AT WINNIPEG
TORONTO AT VANCOUVER
NY RANGERS AT ANAHEIM

Sat Nov 04, 1995
PHILADELPHIA AT PITTSBURGH
HARTFORD AT OTTAWA
BOSTON AT MONTREAL

WASHINGTON AT NY ISLANDERS
DALLAS AT DETROIT
VANCOUVER AT CALGARY
TORONTO AT EDMONTON
ST. LOUIS AT SAN JOSE
NEW JERSEY AT LOS ANGELES

Sun Nov 05, 1995
WINNIPEG AT BUFFALO
HARTFORD AT PHILADELPHIA
TAMPA BAY AT FLORIDA
COLORADO AT CHICAGO
NEW JERSEY AT ANAHEIM
Mon Nov 06, 1995
CALGARY AT NY RANGERS

Tue Nov 07, 1995
SAN JOSE AT HARTFORD
VANCOUVER AT NY ISLANDERS
BOSTON AT WASHINGTON
PHILADELPHIA AT FLORIDA
ANAHEIM AT TORONTO
EDMONTON AT DETROIT
LOS ANGELES AT ST. LOUIS

Wed Nov 08, 1995
SAN JOSE AT BUFFALO
PITTSBURGH AT OTTAWA
ANAHEIM AT MONTREAL
TAMPA BAY AT NY RANGERS
CALGARY AT NEW JERSEY
LOS ANGELES AT DALLAS

Thu Nov 09, 1995
OTTAWA AT BOSTON
CALGARY AT PHILADELPHIA
EDMONTON AT FLORIDA
VANCOUVER AT CHICAGO
DALLAS AT COLORADO

Fri Nov 10, 1995
NY ISLANDERS AT NY RANGERS
EDMONTON AT TAMPA BAY
WASHINGTON AT TORONTO
WINNIPEG AT ST. LOUIS

Fri Nov 10, 1995
PITTSBURGH AT SAN JOSE

Sat Nov 11, 1995
TORONTO AT BOSTON

NY RANGERS AT HARTFORD
ANAHEIM AT OTTAWA
ST. LOUIS AT NY ISLANDERS
PHILADELPHIA AT NEW JERSEY
CHICAGO AT WASHINGTON
BUFFALO AT FLORIDA
MONTREAL AT CALGARY
COLORADO AT VANCOUVER
DETROIT AT SAN JOSE
PITTSBURGH AT LOS ANGELES

Sun Nov 12, 1995
NEW JERSEY AT PHILADELPHIA
BUFFALO AT TAMPA BAY
EDMONTON AT CHICAGO
MONTREAL AT VANCOUVER

Mon Nov 13, 1995
LOS ANGELES AT ANAHEIM

Tue Nov 14, 1995
DALLAS AT PITTSBURGH
HARTFORD AT NEW JERSEY
PHILADELPHIA AT WASHINGTON
BOSTON AT TAMPA BAY
TORONTO AT FLORIDA
NY RANGERS AT ST. LOUIS
CHICAGO AT WINNIPEG
EDMONTON AT CALGARY
NY ISLANDERS AT SAN JOSE
DETROIT AT LOS ANGELES

Wed Nov 15, 1995
OTTAWA AT HARTFORD
DALLAS AT BUFFALO
MONTREAL AT EDMONTON
COLORADO AT ANAHEIM

Thu Nov 16, 1995
NEW JERSEY AT BOSTON
OTTAWA AT PHILADELPHIA
TORONTO AT TAMPA BAY
VANCOUVER AT FLORIDA
NY RANGERS AT CHICAGO
SAN JOSE AT ST. LOUIS
NY ISLANDERS AT LOS ANGELES

Fri Nov 17, 1995
PITTSBURGH AT WASHINGTON

SAN JOSE AT DALLAS
NY RANGERS AT WINNIPEG
COLORADO AT CALGARY
DETROIT AT EDMONTON
NY ISLANDERS AT ANAHEIM

Sat Nov 18, 1995
ST. LOUIS AT BOSTON
PHILADELPHIA AT HARTFORD
WASHINGTON AT PITTSBURGH
OTTAWA AT MONTREAL

Sat Nov 18, 1995
BUFFALO AT NEW JERSEY
VANCOUVER AT TAMPA BAY
WINNIPEG AT TORONTO
CALGARY AT COLORADO
FLORIDA AT LOS ANGELES

Sun Nov 19, 1995
OTTAWA AT BUFFALO
VANCOUVER AT PHILADELPHIA
SAN JOSE AT CHICAGO
FLORIDA AT ANAHEIM

Mon Nov 20, 1995
HARTFORD AT MONTREAL
COLORADO AT EDMONTON

Tue Nov 21, 1995
WINNIPEG AT BOSTON
PITTSBURGH AT NY RANGERS
LOS ANGELES AT PHILADELPHIA
SAN JOSE AT WASHINGTON
NEW JERSEY AT FLORIDA
ST. LOUIS AT TORONTO
ANAHEIM AT CALGARY

Wed Nov 22, 1995
MONTREAL AT HARTFORD
NY RANGERS AT PITTSBURGH
WINNIPEG AT OTTAWA
LOS ANGELES AT NY ISLANDERS
NEW JERSEY AT TAMPA BAY
SAN JOSE AT DETROIT
VANCOUVER AT DALLAS
CHICAGO AT COLORADO
ANAHEIM AT EDMONTON

Thu Nov 23, 1995
VANCOUVER AT ST. LOUIS

Fri Nov 24, 1995
LOS ANGELES AT BOSTON
NY ISLANDERS AT BUFFALO
DETROIT AT PHILADELPHIA
TAMPA BAY AT WASHINGTON
HARTFORD AT TORONTO
EDMONTON AT CALGARY
CHICAGO AT ANAHEIM

Sat Nov 25, 1995
WASHINGTON AT HARTFORD
BUFFALO AT PITTSBURGH
BOSTON AT OTTAWA
COLORADO AT MONTREAL
TAMPA BAY AT NY ISLANDERS
NY RANGERS AT DETROIT
TORONTO AT ST. LOUIS
NEW JERSEY AT DALLAS
VANCOUVER AT SAN JOSE

Sun Nov 26, 1995
LOS ANGELES AT FLORIDA
EDMONTON AT WINNIPEG
CHICAGO AT CALGARY

Mon Nov 27, 1995
NEW JERSEY AT NY RANGERS
LOS ANGELES AT TAMPA BAY
BUFFALO AT ST. LOUIS
Tue Nov 28, 1995
OTTAWA AT PITTSBURGH
COLORADO AT NY ISLANDERS
MONTREAL AT DETROIT
TORONTO AT WINNIPEG
CHICAGO AT EDMONTON

Wed Nov 29, 1995
BUFFALO AT NY RANGERS
COLORADO AT NEW JERSEY
HARTFORD AT TAMPA BAY
PHILADELPHIA AT FLORIDA
MONTREAL AT ST.LOUIS
CHICAGO AT VANCOUVER
CALGARY AT SAN JOSE
WASHINGTON AT ANAHEIM

Thu Nov 30, 1995
PITTSBURGH AT BOSTON
NY ISLANDERS AT OTTAWA
TORONTO AT PHILADELPHIA
ST. LOUIS AT WINNIPEG
WASHINGTON AT LOS ANGELES

Fri Dec 01, 1995
FLORIDA AT PITTSBURGH
HARTFORD AT BUFFALO
COLORADO AT NY RANGERS
TAMPA BAY AT NEW JERSEY
ANAHEIM AT DETROIT
CALGARY AT EDMONTON
SAN JOSE AT VANCOUVER

Sat Dec 02, 1995
BUFFALO AT BOSTON
FLORIDA AT HARTFORD
NY RANGERS AT OTTAWA
DETROIT AT MONTREAL
NEW JERSEY AT NY ISLANDERS
ANAHEIM AT TORONTO
CHICAGO AT WINNIPEG
ST. LOUIS AT EDMONTON
WASHINGTON AT SAN JOSE
DALLAS AT LOS ANGELES

Sun Dec 03, 1995
BOSTON AT PHILADELPHIA
PITTSBURGH AT TAMPA BAY
CALGARY AT WINNIPEG
DALLAS AT COLORADO

Mon Dec 04, 1995
ANAHEIM AT NY RANGERS

Tue Dec 05, 1995
DALLAS AT BOSTON
PITTSBURGH AT NY ISLANDERS
FLORIDA AT WASHINGTON
OTTAWA AT TORONTO
PHILADELPHIA AT DETROIT
SAN JOSE AT COLORADO

Tue Dec 05, 1995
ST. LOUIS AT CALGARY
EDMONTON AT VANCOUVER

Wed Dec 06, 1995
NY ISLANDERS AT HARTFORD
NEW JERSEY AT MONTREAL
CHICAGO AT NY RANGERS
ANAHEIM AT TAMPA BAY
WINNIPEG AT LOS ANGELES

Thu Dec 07, 1995
MONTREAL AT PITTSBURGH
TORONTO AT NEW JERSEY
BUFFALO AT PHILADELPHIA
ANAHEIM AT FLORIDA
DALLAS AT DETROIT
OTTAWA AT CHICAGO
EDMONTON AT COLORADO
WINNIPEG AT SAN JOSE

Fri Dec 08, 1995
WASHINGTON AT BUFFALO
DETROIT AT NY RANGERS
BOSTON AT TAMPA BAY
ST. LOUIS AT VANCOUVER

Sat Dec 09, 1995
HARTFORD AT PITTSBURGH
COLORADO AT OTTAWA
NY RANGERS AT MONTREAL
NY ISLANDERS AT NEW JERSEY
BOSTON AT FLORIDA
DALLAS AT TORONTO
VANCOUVER AT CALGARY
EDMONTON AT SAN JOSE
ST. LOUIS AT LOS ANGELES

Sun Dec 10, 1995
TAMPA BAY AT BUFFALO
NY ISLANDERS AT PHILADEL-
PHIA
HARTFORD AT CHICAGO
WASHINGTON AT WINNIPEG
EDMONTON AT ANAHEIM

Mon Dec 11, 1995
DALLAS AT NY RANGERS
FLORIDA AT NEW JERSEY
COLORADO AT TORONTO
LOS ANGELES AT CALGARY

Tue Dec 12, 1995
FLORIDA AT NY ISLANDERS
DETROIT AT ST. LOUIS
MONTREAL AT WINNIPEG
OTTAWA AT SAN JOSE

Wed Dec 13, 1995
TAMPA BAY AT HARTFORD
COLORADO AT BUFFALO
BOSTON AT NY RANGERS
CHICAGO AT DETROIT
CALGARY AT DALLAS
VANCOUVER AT EDMONTON
OTTAWA AT LOS ANGELES
PITTSBURGH AT ANAHEIM

Thu Dec 14, 1995
FLORIDA AT BOSTON
TAMPA BAY AT PHILADELPHIA
NY ISLANDERS AT WASHINGTON
CALGARY AT ST. LOUIS
TORONTO AT SAN JOSE

Fri Dec 15, 1995
COLORADO AT HARTFORD
NY RANGERS AT BUFFALO
NEW JERSEY AT DETROIT
MONTREAL AT CHICAGO
PITTSBURGH AT DALLAS
EDMONTON AT WINNIPEG
OTTAWA AT ANAHEIM

Sat Dec 16, 1995
CALGARY AT BOSTON
PHILADELPHIA AT MONTREAL
HARTFORD AT NY ISLANDERS
BUFFALO AT NEW JERSEY
NY RANGERS AT WASHINGTON
FLORIDA AT TAMPA BAY
SAN JOSE AT ST. LOUIS
TORONTO AT LOS ANGELES

Sun Dec 17, 1995
PITTSBURGH AT PHILADELPHIA
WINNIPEG AT CHICAGO
SAN JOSE AT DALLAS
OTTAWA AT VANCOUVER
TORONTO AT ANAHEIM

Mon Dec 18, 1995
HARTFORD AT MONTREAL
WASHINGTON AT NY RANGERS
VANCOUVER AT COLORADO
OTTAWA AT EDMONTON

Tue Dec 19, 1995
CALGARY AT PITTSBURGH
PHILADELPHIA AT NEW JERSEY
WINNIPEG AT TAMPA BAY
NY ISLANDERS AT ST. LOUIS
SAN JOSE AT ANAHEIM

Wed Dec 20, 1995
CALGARY AT HARTFORD
MONTREAL AT BUFFALO
CHICAGO AT TORONTO
COLORADO AT EDMONTON
VANCOUVER AT LOS ANGELES
DETROIT AT ANAHEIM

Thu Dec 21, 1995
NY RANGERS AT PHILADELPHIA
NEW JERSEY AT TAMPA BAY
WINNIPEG AT FLORIDA
TORONTO AT CHICAGO
NY ISLANDERS AT DALLAS

Fri Dec 22, 1995
MONTREAL AT PITTSBURGH
BOSTON AT BUFFALO
HARTFORD AT NY RANGERS
EDMONTON AT WASHINGTON
ST. LOUIS AT COLORADO
DETROIT AT CALGARY
LOS ANGELES AT SAN JOSE
VANCOUVER AT ANAHEIM

Sat Dec 23, 1995
TAMPA BAY AT BOSTON
PHILADELPHIA AT HARTFORD
BUFFALO AT OTTAWA
PITTSBURGH AT MONTREAL
WASHINGTON AT NY ISLANDERS
NEW JERSEY AT FLORIDA
EDMONTON AT TORONTO
CHICAGO AT DALLAS
ST. LOUIS AT WINNIPEG
DETROIT AT VANCOUVER
COLORADO AT LOS ANGELES

Tue Dec 26, 1995
BUFFALO AT PITTSBURGH
BOSTON AT NY ISLANDERS
OTTAWA AT NY RANGERS
MONTREAL AT WASHINGTON
ST. LOUIS AT DETROIT
DALLAS AT CHICAGO
CALGARY AT VANCOUVER
COLORADO AT SAN JOSE

Wed Dec 27, 1995
OTTAWA AT BUFFALO
NY ISLANDERS AT NEW JERSEY
TORONTO AT CALGARY
PHILADELPHIA AT EDMONTON
ANAHEIM AT LOS ANGELES

Thu Dec 28, 1995
HARTFORD AT PITTSBURGH
MONTREAL AT TAMPA BAY
WASHINGTON AT FLORIDA
WINNIPEG AT CHICAGO
DALLAS AT ST. LOUIS
NY RANGERS AT VANCOUVER

Fri Dec 29, 1995
CHICAGO AT BUFFALO
DETROIT AT DALLAS
NEW JERSEY AT WINNIPEG
TORONTO AT COLORADO
PHILADELPHIA AT CALGARY
LOS ANGELES AT EDMONTON
SAN JOSE AT ANAHEIM

Sat Dec 30, 1995
FLORIDA AT PITTSBURGH
MONTREAL AT OTTAWA
HARTFORD AT WASHINGTON
TORONTO AT ST. LOUIS
NY RANGERS AT EDMONTON

Sun Dec 31, 1995
NY ISLANDERS AT BUFFALO
TAMPA BAY AT OTTAWA
HARTFORD AT DETROIT
NEW JERSEY AT CHICAGO
BOSTON AT WINNIPEG
NY RANGERS AT CALGARY
PHILADELPHIA AT VANCOUVER
LOS ANGELES AT ANAHEIM

Mon Jan 01, 1996
PITTSBURGH AT WASHINGTON
NY ISLANDERS AT FLORIDA
TORONTO AT DALLAS

Tue Jan 02, 1996
CHICAGO AT BOSTON
TAMPA BAY AT CALGARY

Wed Jan 03, 1996
WASHINGTON AT HARTFORD
OTTAWA AT PITTSBURGH
MONTREAL AT NY RANGERS
BOSTON AT TORONTO
DALLAS AT DETROIT
NEW JERSEY AT COLORADO
TAMPA BAY AT EDMONTON
FLORIDA AT VANCOUVER
PHILADELPHIA AT SAN JOSE
WINNIPEG AT LOS ANGELES

Thu Jan 04, 1996
MONTREAL AT NY ISLANDERS
ST. LOUIS AT CHICAGO
PHILADELPHIA AT COLORADO

Fri Jan 05, 1996
OTTAWA AT HARTFORD
DETROIT AT PITTSBURGH
TORONTO AT BUFFALO
NY RANGERS AT WASHINGTON
WINNIPEG AT DALLAS
ANAHEIM AT CALGARY
FLORIDA AT EDMONTON
LOS ANGELES AT SAN JOSE

Sat Jan 06, 1996
HARTFORD AT BOSTON
BUFFALO AT MONTREAL
OTTAWA AT NY ISLANDERS
WASHINGTON AT NEW JERSEY
COLORADO AT TORONTO
CHICAGO AT DETROIT
PITTSBURGH AT ST. LOUIS
FLORIDA AT CALGARY
TAMPA BAY AT VANCOUVER
SAN JOSE AT LOS ANGELES

Sun Jan 07, 1996
DALLAS AT CHICAGO
ANAHEIM AT EDMONTON

Mon Jan 08, 1996
COLORADO AT BOSTON
VANCOUVER AT PITTSBURGH
TAMPA BAY AT MONTREAL
WASHINGTON AT NY RANGERS
WINNIPEG AT DETROIT
LOS ANGELES AT DALLAS
FLORIDA AT SAN JOSE

Tue Jan 09, 1996
CHICAGO AT NY ISLANDERS
ST. LOUIS AT NEW JERSEY
ANAHEIM AT PHILADELPHIA
HARTFORD AT EDMONTON

Wed Jan 10, 1996
VANCOUVER AT MONTREAL
SAN JOSE AT NY RANGERS
LOS ANGELES AT TORONTO
DETROIT AT DALLAS
BUFFALO AT WINNIPEG
FLORIDA AT COLORADO
HARTFORD AT CALGARY

Thu Jan 11, 1996
ANAHEIM AT BOSTON
TORONTO AT NY ISLANDERS
SAN JOSE AT NEW JERSEY
ST. LOUIS AT PHILADELPHIA
OTTAWA AT WASHINGTON

Fri Jan 12, 1996
MONTREAL AT PITTSBURGH
LOS ANGELES AT DETROIT
ANAHEIM AT CHICAGO
FLORIDA AT DALLAS
HARTFORD AT WINNIPEG
BUFFALO AT CALGARY

Sat Jan 13, 1996
NEW JERSEY AT BOSTON
SAN JOSE AT PITTSBURGH
ST. LOUIS AT MONTREAL
NY RANGERS AT PHILADELPHIA
DETROIT AT WASHINGTON

OTTAWA AT TAMPA BAY
VANCOUVER AT TORONTO
BUFFALO AT EDMONTON

Sun Jan 14, 1996
ST. LOUIS AT NY RANGERS
DALLAS AT NEW JERSEY
LOS ANGELES AT CHICAGO
ANAHEIM AT WINNIPEG
CALGARY AT COLORADO

Mon Jan 15, 1996
VANCOUVER AT BOSTON
TAMPA BAY AT NY ISLANDERS
DALLAS AT PHILADELPHIA

Tue Jan 16, 1996
VANCOUVER AT HARTFORD
COLORADO AT PITTSBURGH
WINNIPEG AT WASHINGTON
SAN JOSE AT FLORIDA
EDMONTON AT ST. LOUIS
CALGARY AT LOS ANGELES

Wed Jan 17, 1996
PITTSBURGH AT BUFFALO
MONTREAL AT OTTAWA
HARTFORD AT NY ISLANDERS
BOSTON AT NEW JERSEY
SAN JOSE AT TAMPA BAY
WINNIPEG AT TORONTO
COLORADO AT DETROIT
WASHINGTON AT CHICAGO
EDMONTON AT DALLAS
CALGARY AT ANAHEIM

Mon Jan 22, 1996
BOSTON AT PITTSBURGH
CHICAGO AT OTTAWA
TAMPA BAY AT MONTREAL
LOS ANGELES AT NY RANGERS
FLORIDA AT PHILADELPHIA
NY ISLANDERS AT COLORADO
DALLAS AT VANCOUVER

Tue Jan 23, 1996
LOS ANGELES AT NEW JERSEY
FLORIDA AT WASHINGTON

Wed Jan 24, 1996
HARTFORD AT BUFFALO
PITTSBURGH AT OTTAWA
PHILADELPHIA AT NY RANGERS
CHICAGO AT TORONTO
SAN JOSE AT DETROIT
ST. LOUIS AT WINNIPEG
NY ISLANDERS AT CALGARY
DALLAS AT EDMONTON
ANAHEIM AT VANCOUVER

Thu Jan 25, 1996
TAMPA BAY AT BOSTON
LOS ANGELES AT HARTFORD
DETROIT AT OTTAWA
WASHINGTON AT NEW JERSEY
MONTREAL AT FLORIDA
SAN JOSE AT CHICAGO
VANCOUVER AT COLORADO

Fri Jan 26, 1996
BUFFALO AT WASHINGTON
DALLAS AT CALGARY
NY ISLANDERS AT EDMONTON

Sat Jan 27, 1996
NY RANGERS AT BOSTON
NEW JERSEY AT HARTFORD
PHILADELPHIA AT PITTSBURGH
TORONTO AT OTTAWA
WINNIPEG AT MONTREAL
BUFFALO AT FLORIDA
DETROIT AT CHICAGO
TAMPA BAY AT ST. LOUIS
NY ISLANDERS AT VANCOUVER
COLORADO AT SAN JOSE
ANAHEIM AT LOS ANGELES

Sun Jan 28, 1996
BOSTON AT MONTREAL
PHILADELPHIA AT WASHINGTON

Mon Jan 29, 1996
ST. LOUIS AT OTTAWA
PITTSBURGH AT FLORIDA
WINNIPEG AT DALLAS

Tue Jan 30, 1996
BUFFALO AT NY ISLANDERS
TORONTO AT DETROIT

EDMONTON AT CALGARY
NEW JERSEY AT VANCOUVER
HARTFORD AT SAN JOSE

Wed Jan 31, 1996
FLORIDA AT BUFFALO
BOSTON AT OTTAWA
WASHINGTON AT MONTREAL
PITTSBURGH AT TAMPA BAY
ST. LOUIS AT TORONTO
NY RANGERS AT DALLAS
CHICAGO AT EDMONTON
HARTFORD AT LOS ANGELES
COLORADO AT ANAHEIM

Thu Feb 01, 1996
FLORIDA AT BOSTON
WASHINGTON AT OTTAWA
MONTREAL AT PHILADELPHIA
VANCOUVER AT ST. LOUIS
WINNIPEG AT COLORADO
NEW JERSEY AT CALGARY
LOS ANGELES AT SAN JOSE

Fri Feb 02, 1996
VANCOUVER AT DALLAS
HARTFORD AT ANAHEIM

Sat Feb 03, 1996
BUFFALO AT BOSTON
NEW JERSEY AT OTTAWA
NY ISLANDERS AT WASHINGTON
FLORIDA AT TAMPA BAY
MONTREAL AT TORONTO
PITTSBURGH AT DETROIT
PHILADELPHIA AT ST. LOUIS
NY RANGERS AT COLORADO
LOS ANGELES AT CALGARY
CHICAGO AT SAN JOSE

Sun Feb 04, 1996
TAMPA BAY AT BUFFALO
DALLAS AT NY ISLANDERS
VANCOUVER AT WINNIPEG
CHICAGO AT ANAHEIM

Mon Feb 05, 1996
MONTREAL AT COLORADO
TORONTO AT SAN JOSE

Tue Feb 06, 1996
BOSTON AT PITTSBURGH
NY RANGERS AT NY ISLANDERS

Tue Feb 06, 1996
FLORIDA AT DETROIT
DALLAS AT ST. LOUIS
OTTAWA AT CALGARY
CHICAGO AT LOS ANGELES

Wed Feb 07, 1996
BOSTON AT BUFFALO
PITTSBURGH AT NEW JERSEY
MONTREAL AT DALLAS
TAMPA BAY AT COLORADO
WASHINGTON AT EDMONTON
HARTFORD AT VANCOUVER
TORONTO AT ANAHEIM

Thu Feb 08, 1996
NY ISLANDERS AT NY RANGERS
BUFFALO AT PHILADELPHIA
DETROIT AT FLORIDA
CHICAGO AT ST. LOUIS
OTTAWA AT WINNIPEG
WASHINGTON AT CALGARY
TORONTO AT LOS ANGELES

Fri Feb 09, 1996
HARTFORD AT COLORADO
VANCOUVER AT EDMONTON

Sat Feb 10, 1996
PHILADELPHIA AT BOSTON
CHICAGO AT PITTSBURGH
OTTAWA AT MONTREAL
ANAHEIM AT NY ISLANDERS
NY RANGERS AT NEW JERSEY
DETROIT AT TAMPA BAY
BUFFALO AT TORONTO
ST. LOUIS AT DALLAS
WINNIPEG AT CALGARY
WASHINGTON AT VANCOUVER
SAN JOSE AT LOS ANGELES

Sun Feb 11, 1996
ANAHEIM AT NEW JERSEY
COLORADO AT PHILADELPHIA
NY RANGERS AT TAMPA BAY

ST. LOUIS AT FLORIDA
HARTFORD AT DALLAS
CALGARY AT EDMONTON

Mon Feb 12, 1996
SAN JOSE AT MONTREAL
OTTAWA AT NY ISLANDERS
PITTSBURGH AT TORONTO

Tue Feb 13, 1996
CALGARY AT WASHINGTON
ST. LOUIS AT TAMPA BAY
LOS ANGELES AT DETROIT
WINNIPEG AT VANCOUVER

Wed Feb 14, 1996
BOSTON AT HARTFORD
LOS ANGELES AT BUFFALO
PHILADELPHIA AT FLORIDA
SAN JOSE AT TORONTO
ANAHEIM AT EDMONTON

Thu Feb 15, 1996
SAN JOSE AT OTTAWA
CALGARY AT NY ISLANDERS
MONTREAL AT NY RANGERS
COLORADO AT TAMPA BAY
WASHINGTON AT DETROIT
BOSTON AT CHICAGO
ANAHEIM AT VANCOUVER

Fri Feb 16, 1996
NEW JERSEY AT BUFFALO
TORONTO AT WASHINGTON
COLORADO AT FLORIDA
DETROIT AT ST. LOUIS
EDMONTON AT DALLAS
PITTSBURGH AT WINNIPEG

Sat Feb 17, 1996
BUFFALO AT HARTFORD
NY RANGERS AT OTTAWA
CALGARY AT MONTREAL
SAN JOSE AT NY ISLANDERS
PHILADELPHIA AT TAMPA BAY
BOSTON AT VANCOUVER
ANAHEIM AT LOS ANGELES

Sun Feb 18, 1996
NY RANGERS AT PITTSBURGH
WASHINGTON AT NEW JERSEY
DALLAS AT FLORIDA
DETROIT AT TORONTO
EDMONTON AT CHICAGO
WINNIPEG AT ST. LOUIS

Mon Feb 19, 1996
NEW JERSEY AT PHILADELPHIA
DALLAS AT TAMPA BAY
VANCOUVER AT DETROIT
EDMONTON AT COLORADO
BOSTON AT LOS ANGELES

Tue Feb 20, 1996
OTTAWA AT ST. LOUIS
SAN JOSE AT CALGARY

Wed Feb 21, 1996
MONTREAL AT HARTFORD
PITTSBURGH AT BUFFALO
FLORIDA AT NEW JERSEY
TAMPA BAY AT TORONTO
VANCOUVER AT WINNIPEG
LOS ANGELES AT EDMONTON
BOSTON AT ANAHEIM

Thu Feb 22, 1996
NY ISLANDERS AT NY RANGERS
WASHINGTON AT PHILADELPHIA
TORONTO AT DETROIT
ST. LOUIS AT CHICAGO
OTTAWA AT DALLAS

Fri Feb 23, 1996
HARTFORD AT PITTSBURGH
PHILADELPHIA AT BUFFALO
TAMPA BAY AT NY ISLANDERS
MONTREAL AT NEW JERSEY
CHICAGO AT WINNIPEG
LOS ANGELES AT COLORADO
ANAHEIM AT CALGARY
BOSTON AT EDMONTON
SAN JOSE AT VANCOUVER

Sat Feb 24, 1996
PITTSBURGH AT MONTREAL
NEW JERSEY AT WASHINGTON
NY RANGERS AT FLORIDA
DALLAS AT TORONTO

TAMPA BAY AT DETROIT
LOS ANGELES AT ST. LOUIS
BOSTON AT CALGARY

Sun Feb 25, 1996
DALLAS AT HARTFORD
FLORIDA AT BUFFALO
EDMONTON AT NY ISLANDERS
CHICAGO AT PHILADELPHIA
OTTAWA AT COLORADO
SAN JOSE AT ANAHEIM

Mon Feb 26, 1996
LOS ANGELES AT WINNIPEG
ANAHEIM AT COLORADO
MONTREAL AT SAN JOSE

Tue Feb 27, 1996
EDMONTON AT BOSTON
DETROIT AT NY ISLANDERS
PITTSBURGH AT VANCOUVER

Wed Feb 28, 1996
EDMONTON AT HARTFORD
BUFFALO AT OTTAWA
BOSTON AT NY RANGERS
PHILADELPHIA AT DALLAS
TORONTO AT WINNIPEG
TAMPA BAY AT LOS ANGELES
MONTREAL AT ANAHEIM

Thu Feb 29, 1996
WASHINGTON AT FLORIDA
NY ISLANDERS AT DETROIT
COLORADO AT CHICAGO
PITTSBURGH AT CALGARY
ST. LOUIS AT VANCOUVER

Fri Mar 01, 1996
WINNIPEG AT HARTFORD
PHILADELPHIA AT OTTAWA
BUFFALO AT NY RANGERS
NY ISLANDERS AT NEW JERSEY
CHICAGO AT COLORADO
PITTSBURGH AT EDMONTON
TAMPA BAY AT SAN JOSE

Sat Mar 02, 1996
WASHINGTON AT BOSTON
FLORIDA AT HARTFORD
NEW JERSEY AT OTTAWA

Sat Mar 02, 1996
VANCOUVER AT DETROIT
TORONTO AT DALLAS
MONTREAL AT LOS ANGELES

Sun Mar 03, 1996
VANCOUVER AT BUFFALO
WINNIPEG AT NY ISLANDERS
PHILADELPHIA AT WASHINGTON
DETROIT AT CHICAGO
TORONTO AT COLORADO
ST. LOUIS AT EDMONTON
CALGARY AT SAN JOSE
TAMPA BAY AT ANAHEIM

Mon Mar 04, 1996
NEW JERSEY AT NY RANGERS

Tue Mar 05, 1996
WINNIPEG AT PITTSBURGH
BOSTON AT NY ISLANDERS
CHICAGO AT TAMPA BAY
FLORIDA AT ST. LOUIS
SAN JOSE AT COLORADO
DALLAS AT ANAHEIM

Wed Mar 06, 1996
DETROIT AT HARTFORD
NEW JERSEY AT TORONTO
BUFFALO AT VANCOUVER
DALLAS AT SAN JOSE
EDMONTON AT LOS ANGELES

Thu Mar 07, 1996
NY ISLANDERS AT BOSTON
OTTAWA AT PITTSBURGH
NY RANGERS AT TAMPA BAY
CALGARY AT ST. LOUIS
FLORIDA AT WINNIPEG

Fri Mar 08, 1996
TORONTO AT HARTFORD
L.OS ANGELES AT CHICAGO
DETROIT AT COLORADO
SAN JOSE AT EDMONTON
BUFFALO AT ANAHEIM

Sat Mar 09, 1996
PHILADELPHIA AT BOSTON
NEW JERSEY AT PITTSBURGH
OTTAWA AT MONTREAL

NY RANGERS AT WASHINGTON
CALGARY AT TORONTO
HARTFORD AT ST. LOUIS
NY ISLANDERS AT WINNIPEG
COLORADO AT VANCOUVER

Sun Mar 10, 1996
NEW JERSEY AT PHILADELPHIA
WASHINGTON AT TAMPA BAY
BOSTON AT FLORIDA
DETROIT AT WINNIPEG
BUFFALO AT SAN JOSE
LOS ANGELES AT ANAHEIM

Mon Mar 11, 1996
DALLAS AT MONTREAL
FLORIDA AT CHICAGO

Tue Mar 12, 1996
VANCOUVER AT WASHINGTON
WINNIPEG AT DETROIT
ST. LOUIS AT CALGARY

Wed Mar 13, 1996
PITTSBURGH AT HARTFORD
DALLAS AT OTTAWA
FLORIDA AT NY RANGERS
MONTREAL AT NEW JERSEY
TAMPA BAY AT PHILADELPHIA
WINNIPEG AT TORONTO
EDMONTON AT SAN JOSE
BUFFALO AT LOS ANGELES
COLORADO AT ANAHEIM

Thu Mar 14, 1996
PITTSBURGH AT BOSTON
VANCOUVER AT CHICAGO

Fri Mar 15, 1996
CALGARY AT BUFFALO
VANCOUVER AT OTTAWA
TAMPA BAY AT NEW JERSEY
BOSTON AT WASHINGTON
DALLAS AT TORONTO
ST. LOUIS AT SAN JOSE

Sat Mar 16, 1996
BUFFALO AT HARTFORD
NY ISLANDERS AT PITTSBURGH

NY RANGERS AT MONTREAL
WINNIPEG AT PHILADELPHIA
EDMONTON AT LOS ANGELES

Sun Mar 17, 1996
TAMPA BAY AT OTTAWA
SAN JOSE AT PHILADELPHIA
DALLAS AT WASHINGTON
NEW JERSEY AT FLORIDA
VANCOUVER AT TORONTO
CALGARY AT DETROIT
NY ISLANDERS AT CHICAGO
EDMONTON AT COLORADO
ST. LOUIS AT ANAHEIM

Mon Mar 18, 1996
SAN JOSE AT BOSTON
TAMPA BAY AT HARTFORD
BUFFALO AT MONTREAL
ST. LOUIS AT LOS ANGELES

Tue Mar 19, 1996
EDMONTON AT NY RANGERS
NY ISLANDERS AT PHILADELPHIA
ANAHEIM AT WASHINGTON
OTTAWA AT FLORIDA
TORONTO AT DETROIT
COLORADO AT VANCOUVER

Wed Mar 20, 1996
HARTFORD AT MONTREAL
BOSTON AT NEW JERSEY
DETROIT AT TORONTO

Wed Mar 20, 1996
CALGARY AT CHICAGO
ST. LOUIS AT DALLAS
SAN JOSE AT WINNIPEG
COLORADO AT LOS ANGELES

Thu Mar 21, 1996
OTTAWA AT BOSTON
EDMONTON AT PITTSBURGH
WASHINGTON AT TAMPA BAY

Fri Mar 22, 1996
MONTREAL AT BUFFALO
HARTFORD AT OTTAWA
CHICAGO AT NEW JERSEY

COLORADO AT DETROIT
ANAHEIM AT ST. LOUIS
PHILADELPHIA AT WINNIPEG
SAN JOSE AT CALGARY
DALLAS AT VANCOUVER

Sat Mar 23, 1996
NY RANGERS AT BOSTON
BUFFALO AT PITTSBURGH
EDMONTON AT MONTREAL
NEW JERSEY AT NY ISLANDERS
HARTFORD AT WASHINGTON
FLORIDA AT TAMPA BAY
PHILADELPHIA AT TORONTO
CALGARY AT VANCOUVER
DALLAS AT LOS ANGELES

Sun Mar 24, 1996
EDMONTON AT OTTAWA
PITTSBURGH AT NY RANGERS
ANAHEIM AT CHICAGO
DETROIT AT ST. LOUIS
COLORADO AT WINNIPEG

Mon Mar 25, 1996
NY ISLANDERS AT MONTREAL
HARTFORD AT PHILADELPHIA
ANAHEIM AT DETROIT
TORONTO AT CALGARY
LOS ANGELES AT VANCOUVER

Tue Mar 26, 1996
ST. LOUIS AT PITTSBURGH
WASHINGTON AT NY ISLANDERS
NEW JERSEY AT TAMPA BAY
WINNIPEG AT DALLAS

Wed Mar 27, 1996
BOSTON AT HARTFORD
PHILADELPHIA AT OTTAWA
WASHINGTON AT MONTREAL
FLORIDA AT NY RANGERS
BUFFALO AT DETROIT
WINNIPEG AT COLORADO
CHICAGO AT CALGARY
LOS ANGELES AT EDMONTON
TORONTO AT VANCOUVER

Thu Mar 28, 1996
MONTREAL AT BOSTON
PITTSBURGH AT FLORIDA
NEW JERSEY AT ST. LOUIS
ANAHEIM AT DALLAS
COLORADO AT SAN JOSE

Fri Mar 29, 1996
PHILADELPHIA AT BUFFALO
OTTAWA AT WASHINGTON
LOS ANGELES AT CALGARY
WINNIPEG AT EDMONTON
CHICAGO AT VANCOUVER

Sat Mar 30, 1996
NY ISLANDERS AT HARTFORD
NEW JERSEY AT PITTSBURGH
MONTREAL AT OTTAWA
TAMPA BAY AT FLORIDA
TORONTO AT EDMONTON

Sun Mar 31, 1996
BOSTON AT BUFFALO
NY RANGERS AT NY ISLANDERS
PITTSBURGH AT PHILADELPHIA
TAMPA BAY AT WASHINGTON
ST. LOUIS AT DETROIT
DALLAS AT CHICAGO
WINNIPEG AT CALGARY
ANAHEIM AT SAN JOSE

Mon Apr 01, 1996
BOSTON AT OTTAWA
BUFFALO AT MONTREAL
HARTFORD AT FLORIDA
EDMONTON AT VANCOUVER

Tue Apr 02, 1996
PHILADELPHIA AT NY ISLANDERS
NEW JERSEY AT NY RANGERS
DETROIT AT SAN JOSE

Wed Apr 03, 1996
WASHINGTON AT BUFFALO
FLORIDA AT OTTAWA
BOSTON AT MONTREAL
HARTFORD AT TAMPA BAY
CHICAGO AT TORONTO
DALLAS AT WINNIPEG

ST. LOUIS AT COLORADO
VANCOUVER AT CALGARY
DETROIT AT LOS ANGELES
EDMONTON AT ANA HEIM

Thu Apr 04, 1996
MONTREAL AT BOSTON
WASHINGTON AT PITTSBURGH
HARTFORD AT NEW JERSEY
NY RANGERS AT PHILADELPHIA
TORONTO AT ST. LOUIS
EDMONTON AT SAN JOSE

Fri Apr 05, 1996
NY ISLANDERS AT OTTAWA
PHILADELPHIA AT NY RANGERS
BUFFALO AT TAMPA BAY

Fri Apr 05, 1996
CHICAGO AT DALLAS
DETROIT AT ANAHEIM

Sat Apr 06, 1996
NEW JERSEY AT HARTFORD
TAMPA BAY AT PITTSBURGH
WASHINGTON AT OTTAWA
FLORIDA AT MONTREAL
BUFFALO AT NY ISLANDERS
ST. LOUIS AT TORONTO
CALGARY AT WINNIPEG
SAN JOSE AT COLORADO
VANCOUVER AT LOS ANGELES

Sun Apr 07, 1996
NY RANGERS AT NEW JERSEY
BOSTON AT PHILADELPHIA
DETROIT AT CHICAGO
COLORADO AT DALLAS
ANAHEIM AT SAN JOSE

Mon Apr 08, 1996
PITTSBURGH AT HARTFORD
FLORIDA AT NY RANGERS
NY ISLANDERS AT TAMPA BAY
WINNIPEG AT ST. LOUIS
CALGARY AT EDMONTON
VANCOUVER AT ANAHEIM

Tue Apr 09, 1996
DALLAS AT CALGARY

Wed Apr 10, 1996
NY ISLANDERS AT PITTSBURGH
OTTAWA AT BUFFALO
WASHINGTON AT NY RANGERS
PHILADELPHIA AT NEW JERSEY
TAMPA BAY AT FLORIDA
WINNIPEG AT DETROIT
ANAHEIM AT COLORADO
DALLAS AT EDMONTON
SAN JOSE AT LOS ANGELES

Thu Apr 11, 1996
HARTFORD AT BOSTON
PITTSBURGH AT OTTAWA
MONTREAL AT PHILADELPHIA
NEW JERSEY AT WASHINGTON
TORONTO AT CHICAGO
COLORADO AT ST. LOUIS

Fri Apr 12, 1996
FLORIDA AT NY ISLANDERS
TAMPA BAY AT NY RANGERS
CHICAGO AT DETROIT
LOS ANGELES AT WINNIPEG
CALGARY AT SAN JOSE
DALLAS AT ANAHEIM

Sat Apr 13, 1996
BOSTON AT HARTFORD
NY ISLANDERS AT MONTREAL
OTTAWA AT NEW JERSEY
BUFFALO AT WASHINGTON

Sat Apr 13, 1996
EDMONTON AT TORONTO
CALGARY AT VANCOUVER

Sun Apr 14, 1996
PITTSBURGH AT BOSTON
HARTFORD AT BUFFALO
PHILADELPHIA AT TAMPA BAY
NY RANGERS AT FLORIDA
ST. LOUIS AT CHICAGO
DETROIT AT DALLAS
LOS ANGELES AT COLORADO
WINNIPEG AT ANAHEIM

PRINTED IN CANADA